THE TRANSSEXUAL EMPIRE

THE

TRANSSEXUAL

The Making of the She-Male

EMPIRE

JANICE G. RAYMOND

Beacon Press : Boston

Beacon Press books are published under the auspices
of the Unitarian Universalist Association
Published simultaneously in Canada by
Fitzhenry & Whiteside Limited, Toronto

(hardcover) 9 8 7 6 5 4 3 2 1

Grateful acknowledgment is made to the following for
permission to reprint material in this volume: from
Sexual Signatures: On Being a Man or a Woman by John
Money and Patricia Tucker, copyright © 1975 by John
Money and Patricia Tucker, by permission of Little,
Brown and Company; from *Man and Woman, Boy and
Girl* by John Money and Anke Ehrhardt, copyright ©
1972 by The Johns Hopkins University Press, by per-
mission of The Johns Hopkins University Press; and
from *Transsexualism and Sex Reassignment*, edited by
Richard Green and John Money, copyright © 1969 by
The Johns Hopkins University Press, by permission of
The Johns Hopkins University Press.

Library of Congress Cataloging in Publication Data

Raymond, Janice G.
   The transsexual empire.

   Includes bibliographical references and index.
   1. Change of sex. 2. Lesbians. 3. Sex roles.
4. Medicine—Philosophy. I. Title.
RC560.C4R38   301.41'5   78-53783
ISBN 0-8070-2164-4

For Mary Daly

    Who has moved me
        to the Moors of the Mind . . .
    Who has taught me
        to feel with all my intellect
        and think with all my heart . . .

With Gratitude, Awe, and Love

CONTENTS

ACKNOWLEDGMENTS

This book has been long in process. It began as a conference paper delivered at the New England Regional American Academy of Religion Meeting in 1972. Much of it had
another life as my doctoral dissertation, which was fin-
ished at Boston College in 1977. Finally, it metamor-
phosed into a book. There are many people to thank for
all of this.

My parents' love, trust, and support have been an important source of encouragement. Many of my students
offered creative insights and critical commentary as the
work was in progress. I would like to thank Jan Stiefel
who, in proofreading with me, read the entire manuscript
aloud. Amy Hines and Judy Gold were valuable search
assistants who found material for me often at short notice.
Chris Decker applied her creative and prestidigitatory talents to the index of this book, as well as to the proofreading of the galleys. Anne Dellenbaugh snooped out
many difficult-to-find sources, read over many of these
herself, offered original comments, and taught me how to
sail.

Some people read selected parts of my work, either in chapter or in article form, and made helpful suggestions. Among these are Jackie Pritzen, Fern Johnson, and Lisa Buck. Eileen van Tassell was particularly helpful in reading over Chapter II. Julia Stanley assisted in clarifying several of my linguistic applications. Andrea Dworkin commented on Chapter IV.

Mary Howell and Max Stackhouse served on my dissertation committee and read this manuscript in another one of its lives. Mary Howell helped me to explain the medical aspects of the issue and to integrate certain ethical aspects with issues current in the women's health movement. Max Stackhouse assisted me in organizing the methodological aspects of my work. Michael Gross has been both a supportive colleague and critic. In reading the manuscript early on, he gave me invaluable suggestions on the sex difference literature, Chapter II, and the history of medicine and science.

For their friendship and support, I would like to thank Kate Lehmann, Linda Scaparotti, Karin Krut, Kath Wetzel, and Marcia Liebermann. For many years, Wilma Miley has been a very special friend and supporter. Michelle Cliff gave me many insights into the publishing world and encouraged, in many ways, the publication of this book. I have known Emily Culpepper since I first began work on this topic. She has provided me with many resources and insights, and she invented the key phrase that I use throughout this book (male-to-*constructed*-female). Conversations with Linda Barufaldi were always fun, and her friendship and creativity have been important in the process of this book. Nelle Morton's work, example, and friendship have profoundly affected my life and work. Robin Morgan has encouraged my work in this area for many years. Her writing, insight, and counsel have been vital to me.

Nancy Sunflower gave an intelligent and careful typing of the manuscript. MaryAnn Lash made editorial suggestions which helped to clarify the content and structure of my book.

Adrienne Rich has been a very special friend and critic.

She has read the manuscript through all of its stages and provided resources, creative criticism, and constant encouragement. Her work, and her recognition of my work, have meant a great deal to me in the process of this writing.

I hope the dedication of this book adequately expresses the gratitude I owe to Mary Daly. Her friendship, wisdom, and creativity are enspiriting and, more than anyone, she has sparked my creativity. It is difficult for me to separate my words and ideas from her own.

Pat Hynes has been with this book in the deepest way. She has read the manuscript and made detailed, discerning, and perceptive observations throughout. To her, I say that "Friendship is a divine affection." Be-ing with her, in all ways, is a life-giving experience.

PREFACE

Transsexualism has taken only twenty-five years to become a household word. It is likely that most of us were initially made aware of the topic with the publication of the famed Christine Jorgensen case in 1953. A little over a decade later, Johns Hopkins Hospital announced that it would become the first American medical institution to devote itself to the performance of transsexual surgery on a select but serious scale. In 1974 the subject again received notice with the publication of Jan Morris's *Conundrum*. The latest transsexual notable has been Renee Richards who has succeeded in hitting the benefits of sex discrimination back into the male half of the court. The public recognition and success that it took Billie Jean King and women's tennis years to get, Renee Richards has achieved in one set. The new bumper stickers might well read: "It takes castrated balls to play women's tennis."

Adding to the publicity that transsexualism has received are the news magazines, such as *Time* and *Newsweek*, which almost yearly publish an article or two that could comprise the basic educational requirements for a crash course entitled Transsexualism 101. Women's magazines with wide circulation such as *Redbook* and *Good House-keeping* have run autobiographical or biographical accounts of transsexualism in the true confessional genre. In October of 1976, even the *National Observer* saw fit to garnish its front page with the lead article: "What Makes a Person Want to Switch Sexes?" Television and the movies (e.g., "Medical Center" and *Dog Day Afternoon*), as well as the TV talk shows, have media-ized transsexualism. Covert transsexual appeals have also entered the world of advertising in the guise of what Wilson Bryan Key has called "subliminal seduction."[1]

This book is not only a book about transsexualism. It goes further and considers the *context* that makes trans-sexualism possible. While various individuals have looked at the issue of transsexualism very few have ever really seen it. Transsexuals see themselves as women (men) "trapped in male (female) bodies." Doctors fixate on hormonal techniques and constructed genitalia—artificial vaginas, breast implants, and the like. Therapists view transsexualism as a humane solution to the agony of "gender dysphoria." The public sees the media's image of the talk-show transsexual, which beeps out a benevolent picture of the transsexual experience. Many women see the transsexual who claims to be a lesbian-feminist as the man who has paid the ultimate price of manhood in a patriarchal society—giving up his balls.

All these perspectives are fragmented and ultimately blur the issue. They are like the vision of a deer at night who, facing an oncoming car, is hypnotized by the headlights and fails to see the approaching automobile. They focus on the *foreground* of the transsexual phenomenon rather than on its multidimensional *background*.[2] My purpose is to depict the wider environment in which trans-sexualism is created and to do a truly ecological analysis.

What, then, is the context of the transsexual issue? The title of this book conveys a partial answer to that question. *The Transsexual Empire* is basically the medical conglom-erate that has created the treatment and technology that

makes anatomical sex conversion possible. I have chosen to
call this an empire for several reasons. Primarily, *empire*
means a political unit having a territory of great extent,
or a number of territories under a single sovereign authority. What we witness in the transsexual context is a number of medical specialties combining to create transsexuals—urologists, gynecologists, endocrinologists, plastic
surgeons, and the like. The proliferation of treatments that
has been generated to take care of the "problem" is aston-
ishing. These range from the initial and basic operative procedures undergone by all transsexuals to highly specialized
forms of cosmetic surgery—such as eye, nose, and chin
operations—to electrolysis and speech therapy. Drug com-
panies and hospitals—what have been called medical collusion complexes—also benefit from transsexualism. Hormone therapy and surgery are not cheap.

Medicine also coalesces with other professions to make
transsexualism a reality. Psychiatrists and psychologists
work in concert with medical specialists by referring candidates for treatment and surgery. They also camouflage the
sovereignty of the medical empire and its role in creating
transsexualism by highlighting the "need" of the transsexual. Thus transsexual surgery becomes a therapeutic
"necessity" to alleviate "gender dysphoria."[3] Therapy becomes a way of life.

Physicians also join with lawyers and legislators to validate transsexuals as legal women (or men). Ultimately,
however, it is medicine that dominates. Without its sovereign intervention, transsexualism would not be a reality.
Historically, individuals may have wished to change sex,
but until medical science developed the specialties, which
in turn created the demand for surgery, sex conversion did
not exist. It is instructive that Johns Hopkins from the out-
set defined transsexualism as a *medical problem* and got
the law to affirm its judgment. Thus, if sex-conversion surgery were challenged in the future, it could be defended as
legitimate medical territory.[4]

The subtitle of this book, *The Making of the She-Male*,
signifies that most transsexuals are *male-to-constructed-*

females. [5] There are many reasons for this preponderance. Most significant is the male recognition of the power that women have, by virtue of female biology. This power, which is evident in giving birth, cannot be reduced to procreation. Rather birthing is only representative of the many levels of creativity that women have exercised in the history of civilization. Transsexualism may be one way by which men attempt to possess females' creative energies, by possessing artifactual female organs. The male-to-constructed-female transsexual not only wants female biological capacities but wants to *become* the biological female.

In its attempt to wrest from women the power inherent in female biology, transsexualism is not an isolated or aberrant biomedical procedure. It can be placed along a continuum of other male interventionist technologies such as cloning, test-tube fertilization, and sex selection. Seen in this context, the transsexual not only represents the "she-male" but also the "he-mother," who rejects his mothered birth and gives birth to "herself" (with the aid, of course, of the medical "father-mothers").

Transsexualism, however, is artifactual femaleness. The "she-male" is made—i.e., constructed, fashioned, and fabricated. *The Making of the She-Male* is only one manifestation of the tradition of men making female artifacts. Also in this tradition are male fashion designers who prescribe female apparel; men who train women in beauty techniques, finishing school manners, and charm; men who portray the female "form" in pornography and "great art." Instead of using fabric, cosmetics, or paint, the "makers" of the "she-male" primarily use flesh. Long before the advent of transsexualism, patriarchy—and later patriarchal medicine—molded and mutilated female flesh. The history of foot-binding, clitoridectomy and infibulation, corset mutilation, and, most recently, cosmetic surgery, unnecessary hysterectomies, and radical mastectomies, testify to this. Now, patriarchy is molding and mutilating *male* flesh, but for the purpose of *constructing women.*

As female energy, spirit, and vitality have not proved

conquerable, in spite of all the attempts of men to harness them, so too has female flesh been difficult to mold and manipulate according to patriarchal standards. Witness the number and intensity of attempts. Perhaps male flesh will prove much more malleable. Given the historical difficulties in molding both female flesh and energy to patriarchal standards, an alternative is to make the biological woman obsolete by the creation of man-made "she-males." One transsexual confirms this perspective:

Free from the chains of menstruation and child-bearing, transsexual women are obviously far superior to Gennys in many ways. . . .

Genetic women are becoming quite obsolete, which is obvious, and the future belongs to transsexual women. We know this, and perhaps some of you suspect it. All you have left is your "ability" to bear children, and in a world which will groan to feed 6 billion by the year 2000, that's a negative asset.[6]

Transsexualism also offers a unique perspective on sex-role stereotyping in a patriarchal society. Put simply, here we have the stereotypes of masculinity and femininity on stage, so to speak, for all to see in an alien body. Medicalized transsexualism creates male-to-constructed-females who are more feminine (in actions, speech, and self-definition) than most biological women.

The gender identity clinics—where would-be transsexuals are counseled and evaluated—along with the medical establishment foster and reinforce stereotypical behavior. It is a primary requirement of these centers, in counseling persons who desire to be transsexed, that they "pass" as "true women" in order to qualify for treatment and eventually surgery. "Passing" requirements evaluate everything from feminine dress and feminine body language to feminine positions in intercourse. Candidates for surgery are required to live out opposite-sex roles for certain periods of time. Thus the influence of these clinics and clinicians in reinforcing sex-role stereotypes is significant. It has consequences that reach far beyond the issue of transsexualism.

What we are witnessing here is a "benevolent" form

of behavior control and modification under the guise of therapy. It is not inconceivable that gender identity clinics, again in the name of therapy, could become centers of sex-role control for nontranssexuals. Presently, some of them are "treating" children who are diagnosed as potential trans-sexuals. The U.C.L.A. Child Gender Program currently has four-year funding from the National Institute of Mental Health. The program so far has "treated" young boys with "gender disturbances"—especially those with "feminine-gesture mannerisms," voice inflections, and aversion to "masculine play." David Rorvik has asked:

> Why is there no U.C.L.A. program, for example, for the nonandrogy-nous supermale who is surely at least as crippled as the rigidly ef-feminate male and also surely in greater supply. . . . Who is qualified to decide which of us needs the new therapy and what that therapy should consist of?[7]

Such a program is already catering to parents who have strong ideas about the kind of masculine children they want their offspring to be. It could also be oriented toward female children who stray too far from the path of stereo-typical behavior.

Most fundamentally, a society that produces sex-role stereotyping functions as a primary cause of transsex-ualism. This, of course, is not acknowledged in the medical and psychological literature that purports to explain the etiology of transsexualism. These theories take the stereo-types as given, reducing the cause of transsexualism to such psychologized explanations as "dominant mothers" and "absent fathers." However, if causation theories con-tinue to measure a transsexual's adjustment or nonadjust-ment to masculine or feminine norms, then they miss the point completely. I would suggest that a patriarchal so-ciety and its social currents of masculinity and femininity is the *First Cause* of transsexualism. The organs and body of the opposite sex that the transsexual desires merely in-carnate the "essence" of the desired role.

Within such a society, the transsexual only exchanges one stereotype for the other, thus reinforcing the fabric

by which a sexist society is held together. This has an ultimate effect on the treatment aspects of transsexualism.
For within such a society, it then makes perfect sense to
adjust the transsexual's body to his or her mind if the
transsexual's mind cannot be adjusted to his or her body.

The transsexual who seems to contradict the stereotypically feminine behavior and role-playing of male-to-
constructed-females is he who claims to be a lesbian-feminist. Within the last five years, a number of transsexually
contructed lesbian-feminists have appeared within the
feminist community. By assuming the identity of feminist
and lesbian, these transsexuals give the impression that
they are fighting on both the personal and political fronts
against stereotyped limitations, while also challenging the
basic sex-role constructs of a patriarchal society.

It is important to recognize, however, that as patriarchy
is neither monolithic nor one-dimensional, neither is transsexualism. Although the transsexually contructed lesbian-
feminist does not exhibit a feminine identity and role, he
does exhibit stereotypical masculine behavior. Significantly, such transsexuals have inserted themselves into
positions of importance and/or performance in lesbian-
feminist circles.

What goes unrecognized, consciously or unconsciously,
by women who accept such transsexuals as women and as
lesbian-feminists is that their masculine behavior is dis-
guised by the castration of the male "member." Loss of
a penis, however, does not mean the loss of an ability to
penetrate women—women's identities, women's spirits,
women's sexuality. As Mary Daly has noted, their whole
presence becomes a "member" invading women's presence
to each other and once more producing horizontal violence.[8] Thus the transsexually constructed lesbian-feminist
not only colonizes female bodies but appropriates a feminist "soul."

Those women who doubt that men "without members"
are capable of colonizing feminists' energy, time, and space
should acquaint themselves with the history of eunuchism.
Etymologically *eunuch* means "keeper of the bed." Eu-

nuchs were men that other more powerful men used to keep their women in place—i.e., in women's apartments, harems, and the like. In this way, some eunuchs rose to positions of patriarchal power and influence. In a similar way, will transsexually constructed lesbian-feminists be used to keep lesbian-feminists in place?

Empires, of course, become empires by spreading their dominion to include seemingly quite disparate territories. Thus it should not be surprising that transsexualism has spread into the feminist community. The transsexual empire initially colonized women's bodies. Now it has extended to colonize feminist identification, culture, politics, and sexuality.

The spread of medical empires, and thus of patriarchal power, has not only occurred by intrusion into female and feminist *spaces*, but has expanded also at critical moments in feminist *time*. It is significant that the medical specialties of gynecology and obstetrics were consolidated during the rise of the so-called first wave of feminism.[9] Mary Daly has pointed out that another medicalized venture of social control through surgery—transsexualism— happened concurrently with the recent rise of feminism in America during the 1960s.[10] Finally the phenomenon of the transsexually constructed lesbian-feminist has occurred along with the 1970s movement of lesbian-feminism.

Ultimately, transsexualism is a very mythic phenomenon, unfolding a world view of patriarchy that explains its origins, beliefs, and practices. Transsexuals are living out two basic patriarchal myths: single parenthood by the father (male mothering) and the making of woman according to man's image. Both myths are writ large in all the religions of man-made civilization. They are archetypally illustrated in the birth of Athena from Zeus's head. Athena becomes the ultimate man-made woman who, once having sprung from Zeus's head (in order to be able to "think like a man") thereafter pronounces in favor of patriarchy.

All women have been created in man's image, in that our roles and identities have not been self-generated but have been originally defined for us. In this sense, one could say that all women who do not step out of such roles and identities are "transsexuals" or man-made females. Male-to-constructed-female transsexuals, however, extend the myths of single parenthood by the father and the making of woman according to man's image to their ultimate lengths. Here the therapeutic fathers *make* women, not only in their image, but *out of* men. The mythic deception comes full circle when one reads in the psychological literature, for example, that male-to-constructed-female transsexualism is "the result of too much mother and too little father."[11] This situation is then remedied through medicalized "rebirth." The list of father figures (single parents) who make "rebirth" possible is endless—from the therapeutic fathers who coach transsexuals into their proper roles to the medical fathers who "deliver" the transsexual body into existence.

How does the female-to-constructed-male transsexual fit into such a context? It is my contention that she functions as a token to promote the deception that transsexualism is a supposed *human* problem, instead of a uniquely male problem. The female-to-constructed-male transsexual promotes the "illusion of inclusion." She is assimilated into the transsexual empire in much the same way that women are assimilated into other male-defined realities—on men's terms.

This tokenism shows in several things. Initially, transsexualism was developed for men, by men, according to male-defined body and role stereotypes of women. Only later did medicine turn its attention to women who wished to be transsexed, and then in small numbers. Compared to studies on male transsexualism, there is a relative scarcity of female studies. The ratio of women to men obtaining the operation is one to four. Johns Hopkins did its first operation on a man, and along with other surgical centers, has continued mainly to service men.[12]

Recently, transsexual proponents have claimed that the incidence of female-to-constructed-male transsexualism is rising. This has not been documented, as far as I have been able to determine. With the recent publication of *Emergence* by Mario Martino, the subject of female-to-constructed-males may receive more attention and we may see an increase in their numbers.[13] However, it is important to note that tokenism is not just a matter of numbers. Even if the percentage of female-to-constructed-male transsexuals were augmented to the point where they would numerically equal male-to-constructed-females, they would still be tokens because they would be fashioned by a man-made empire, according to male designs.

Who is the female-to-constructed-male transsexual and what motivates her to undergo surgery? The few studies on female transsexuals tell us that they are less exhibitionistic, more emotionally stable, and more socially integrated than their male counterparts.[14] Mario Martino, in "his" autobiography, confirms these findings from "his" own experience as a female-to-constructed-male transsexual, and as a nursing supervisor in a hospital that performs transsexual operations.

The females-to-males I met seemed to fall into a constructive general pattern: Outwardly, they were more or less like anyone else. They set their life goals, completed their sex reassignments, continued their education, married, built homes and families. Most of these females who came for sex-change surgery made little fuss and, when discharged, quietly left the hospital without incident.

But the male-to-female patients were another story. Too few of them acted like any other female, either in speech or in manner. The extroverts among them referred to one another as closet queens, shrilled out their demands, showed their newly constructed vaginas to anyone who'd look, and used language I've never heard from a woman.[15]

From this description, and other more formal studies, it appears that in these behavioral aspects, the female-to-constructed-male transsexual is stereotypically feminine, and the male-to-constructed-female, typically masculine. This is not a contradiction of my statement that male-to-constructed-female transsexuals are, for the most part, more feminine than even the most feminine biological women. It is rather a commentary on the fact that although male transsexuals do everything possible to play the feminine part, they often unwittingly betray *both* sex-role stereotypes.

Why women want to become men is a more complicated question. If one reason men become constructed women is to capture female creative energy and power, women may become constructed men to attain what is perceived as male creative energy and power, patriarchy having deceived women into believing that maleness is necessary for real creativity and power. Like many women, female-to-constructed-male transsexuals have been forced to underestimate their own power and creativity and are not in touch with their own female energy source. Unlike many women who seek the expression of their own power and energy in men through marriage or other derivative situations, transsexuals *become* men.

If, as I have claimed, making men into constructed women is in the ultimate interests of men, because they can create their ultimate man-made woman, how do female-to-constructed-male transsexuals coincide with this theory? Conceivably, in a transition period during which the biological woman is in the process of being made obsolete by bio-medicine, the aim would be to assimilate those women who do not conform to male standards of femininity. It is important to understand that assimilation equals elimination. Not being able to assimilate would-be males into the feminine, patriarchy assimilates them into the masculine.

G. J. Barker-Benfield in *The Horrors of the Half-Known Life* has shown that female castration or *oophorectomy* (ovariotomy) was widespread in the late nineteenth and early twentieth centuries as a male mode of keeping women in place.[16] Keeping women in place was closely associated with control of female sexuality. Oophorectomy, as well as clitoridectomy, was used to check the supposed growing female "disease" of masturbation and the supposed boundless sexual desire and appetite of women. Advocates of sexual surgery saw themselves as restoring order to deviant women. Barker-Benfield notes

that any attempt by women to break out of their prescribed order was taken to signify that they wanted to
become men.[17] Thus female castration was an attempt
to ward off this "unsexing" of women, restoring her to
her normal feminine role.

There are several parallels that are useful here for understanding the female-to-constructed-male transsexual situation. Transsexual surgery, first of all, is the most recent
brand of medicalized female castration. As oophorectomy
was used to tame deviant women, transsexual surgery can
be viewed as taming potentially deviant women. What is
further attempted is to ward off potential lesbianism. It
is also noteworthy that female castration and clitoridectomy were employed to deprive women of sexual pleasure.
Likewise, the woman who is transsexed usually has no
sexual pleasure (in terms of phallic erection and orgasm),
in contrast to the male-to-constructed-female transsexual
whose artificial vagina is lined with the sensitive penile and
scrotal skin.

It is ironic that whereas previously a woman who did
not conform to her role was perceived as wanting to be a
man and was repulsed, some women today who explicitly
state they want to be men are encouraged by doctors.
However, these women are still castrated women, both in
the physical and in the wider senses of that word. If *castration* truly means "to deprive of power and potency," then
women who are transsexed are ultimately deprived of
female identification, power, and potency.

Furthermore, the real men can always afford to admit
a few fake men who conform to masculine standards. Like
token women, female-to-constructed-male transsexuals are
domesticated by peripheral status within the "men's club."
Men tame both groups of women by letting them be *like*
men. (Token women, instead of having constructed male
bodies have male diplomas, professional status, and derivative identities.)

Ultimately, female-to-constructed-male transsexuals are
the "final solution" of women perpetrated by the transsexual empire. Male-to-constructed-female transsexuals

attempt to neutralize women by making the biological
woman unnecessary—by invading both the feminine and
feminist fronts. Female-to-constructed-male transsexuals
neutralize themselves as biological women and also their
potentially deviant power. This is merely the most extreme
form of neutralization that is taking place also with unnecessary hysterectomies and with the movement toward
androgyny. With both, the biological woman is not only
neutralized but neuterized.

Finally, as Barker-Benfield has written: "Castrators and
clitoridectomists persistently presented their work as an
attempt to get woman to control herself. They demanded
woman's collusion."[18] To use Robin Morgan's phrase and
apply it in this context: female-to-constructed-male transsexuals are "the ultimate weapons in the hands of the
boys." For here, the woman herself "chooses" to become
one of them in an ultimate sense. Token women, at a minimum, still retain female body identity. Female-to-constructed-male transsexuals divest themselves of the last
traces of female identification. Their collusion crosses a
critical boundary, from which there is little hope of return.
They are truly "the lost women" to other women.

Transsexualism is often discussed in the context of
homosexuality and transvestism. Harry Benjamin, for
example, has a chapter in *The Transsexual Phenomenon*
in which he discusses the three states. In his language:
"The transvestite has a social problem. The transsexual has
a gender problem. The homosexual has a sex problem.[19]

Benjamin contends that homosexuality is not related
to transsexualism in the sense that transsexuals usually perceive themselves as heterosexual. Furthermore, most transsexuals detest being identified as homosexual. It is claimed
that some refrain from sexual relations until they have
undergone surgery.

According to Benjamin, the essential difference between
transvestites and transsexuals is that with the latter the
sex organs are objects of hatred and disgust which drive
them to seek sex conversion surgery. Transvestites have
no such drive or even desire. Transvestism may be a pre-

lude to male-to-constructed-female transsexualism if the
man involved decides that cross-dressing alone does not
relieve his gender discomfort. With women, as John Money
states, "the syndrome of transvestism without transsexualism apparently does not occur."[20]

While Benjamin, Money, and others have made definite
distinctions between transvestism, transsexualism, and
homosexuality, they have omitted differences (and similarities) that are critical. For example, commentators have
noted that the nonoccurrence of female transvestism is
due to the fact that society tolerates women who wear
pants and other clothing designated as masculine, whereas
men who wear dresses are not accepted. What is not mentioned is that only men are transvestites or "female im-
personators," because only what is culturally non-norma-
tive, abnormal, subnormal, and deviant can be mimicked—
in this case, women.[21] As Mary Daly has pointed out, it
is very difficult to imitate the norm.[22] Who ever heard of
a *white* minstrel show?

While some transsexual researchers have made feeble
attempts to differentiate among homosexuality, transvestism, and transsexualism, the gender clinics that treat
potential child transsexuals, homosexuals, and transvestites give the impression that the three are one. Indeed,
these states are lumped together in the popular mind.
A headline in a recent issue of the *Clinical Psychiatry
News* reported: "Children from Transsexual or Lesbian
Home are Heterosexual."[23] Thus the impression is conveyed, "They all look alike" and "Once you've seen one,
you've seen them all."

Furthermore, Richard Green, who reported these "findings" at the annual meeting of the Society for the Scientific Study of Sex, gives the false impression that both
surgical sex change and lesbian motherhood are relatively
recent phenomena. This masks the reality that while transsexualism is a recent phenomenon generated by the medical profession, lesbian motherhood is hardly a recent oc-
currence and is certainly not spawned by medical science.
Lesbians have been around from earliest known times, and
many were women who had married, borne children, and

had later chosen to separate from their husbands. What Green fails to state is that only recently have lesbian mothers been studied in the "gender laboratories."

Thus very real differences become obscured, and transsexualism is equated with lesbianism. Put this together with the phenomenon of the transsexually constructed lesbian-feminist, which I discuss in Chapter IV, and any genuine lesbian-feminist self-definition becomes beseiged from all sides. What this story finally points to is the infinite ability of clinics and researchers to absorb all "deviancies" with their "sponges" of study and observation. Medicalized transsexualism adds the further dimension of making such "deviancies" amenable to medical management and to medical technology.

INTRODUCTION

Some Comments

on Method

(for the Methodical)

TRANSSEXUALISM highlights, in a unique way, several key issues in feminist studies— among them sex-role socialization, "nature versus nurture," and definitions and boundaries of maleness and femaleness. Important issues in medical ethics, such as bodily mutilation and integrity, "nature" versus technology, medical research priorities, unnecessary surgery, and the inevitable issue of the medical model, are involved also.

Transsexualism touches the boundaries of many of the existing academic disciplines in such a way as to raise fundamental questions about the territorial imperatives of biology, psychology, medicine, and the law, to name but a few. Questions about the causes of transsexualism and the proper methods of treatment have been hitherto restricted to the domain of psychology and medicine. But as a feminist ethicist I maintain that these issues of causation and treatment are imbued with male-defined values and philosophical/theological beliefs—beliefs about the so-called natures of women and men. When John Money

1

states that the core of one's gender identity is fixed by the age of eighteen months, his statement is fraught with certain normative beliefs about the changeability of human existence. Such beliefs become invisible in the mounds of supposed scientific data that Money offers about sex differences. Or when transsexuals and transsexual specialists relegate sex-role dissatisfaction and a subsequent desire for the qualities ascribed to the opposite sex to the category of transsexualism, this very classification forms a type of medical belief system that resembles what has classically been called *theodicy*.

In this theodicy, as in all religious theodicies, the surrender of selfhood is necessary to a certain extent. In the medical theodicy, transsexuals surrender themselves to the transsexual therapists and technicians. The medical order then tells transsexuals what is healthy and unhealthy (the theological equivalents of good and evil). Thus the classification function of the term *transsexualism* analyzes a whole system of meaning that is endowed with an extraordinary power of structuring reality.

This book is concerned with how medicine and psychology, in particular, function as secular religions in the area of transsexualism. Chapter II is devoted to an analysis of the scientific data on sex differences, especially the work of John Money and his associates. Chapter V presents the "triumph of the therapeutic," the "medical model," and the medical-technical specialties as they function to generate values and beliefs concerning the cause, diagnosis, and treatment of transsexualism.

My main point is to show how so-called health values of therapy, hormonal treatment, and surgery have replaced ethical values of choice, freedom, and autonomy; how these same "health" values have diffused critical awareness about the social context in which the problem of transsexualism arises; how more and more moral problems have been reclassified as technical problems; and indeed how the very notion of health itself, as generated by this medical model, has made genuine transcendence of the transsexual problem almost impossible.

LANGUAGE: "SAY WHAT YOU MEAN
AND MEAN WHAT YOU SAY"

Words have meanings often undetected by those who use them. One graphic example of this is the use of the words *masculinity* and *femininity*, *male* and *female*, and *he* and *she* as they appear throughout the medical and psychological literature on transsexualism. Medical literature on transsexualism uses the words *masculinity/masculine* and *femininity/feminine* to indicate what its authors *perceive* to be real changes that take place, either through the administration of hormones and/or surgery. The psychological literature on transsexualism uses the same designations to talk about the gender identity and/or role of the transsexual, one of which the transsexual rejects in order to pursue the other, as if these stereotypes had some kind of ontological reality that was conferred by "feeling" that one is, for example, a "woman trapped in a man's body."

I use the terms *masculinity/masculine* and *femininity/feminine* to indicate that what really does take place when the transsexual is encouraged to pass as a woman, or when hormones and surgery are administered, is in fact the *feminization* of a man, or the *masculinization* of a woman. This is precisely what happens because masculinity and femininity are social constructs and stereotypes of behavior that are culturally prescribed for male and female bodies respectively, but that in the case of the transsexual, have nothing to do with a male or female body. Thus the male-to-constructed-female goes from one stereotype to the other. The words *masculine* and *feminine* are used throughout this work to indicate that a superficial, artifactual, and socially and surgically constructed change is what takes place rather than a deep intrinsic change that encourages existential development. The stereotypical language is used intentionally to highlight the superficiality of the transsexual process. To *feminize* or *masculinize* into a cultural identity and role is to socialize one into a constructed identity and role. Similarly, in the sex-conversion surgery itself, what takes place is a surgical construction of body appearance that is brought in line with the body stereotype of what a masculine or feminine body should look like in a gender-defined society; e.g., in a woman, a big bust, a curvacious figure, a small frame, etc. And indeed, as we shall note in Chapter I, transsexuals undergo an immense amount of polysurgery, much of it of a cosmetic nature, to bring themselves into line with the stereotype of their newly acquired body.

Since I am highlighting that a *superficial stereotyping* process of masculinization or feminization is precisely what does take place in the transsexual situation, I shall omit putting the stereotypes in quotation marks or italicizing them in order to grant these words their utmost validity as the fabrications that they genuinely are. At the same time, however, I have chosen to put the words "he" or "she" and "male" and "female" in quotation marks when they refer to a pre- or postoperative transsexual. This is to indicate that, while transsexuals are in every way masculine or feminine, they are not fundamentally male or female. Maleness and femaleness are governed by certain chromosomes, and the subsequent history of being a chromosomal male or female. Masculinity and femininity are social and surgical constructs.

Aside from the language of masculinity/femininity, male/female, and he/she in the medical and psychological literature, the term *transsexualism* itself is also problematical and fraught with certain normative assumptions. The term *transsexualism* was first used by Harry Benjamin in a lecture at a meeting of the New York Academy of Medicine in 1953. It is interesting to note, however, that the *Index Medicus* did not include a reference heading for transsexualism until 1965. Before this, any works dealing with surgical sex change were placed under the headings of transvestism, homosexuality, or some other deviant sexual category. But as transsexualism acquired its own terminological existence and independent classification, many normative assumptions began to gain ground.

First of all, the suffix *ism* is a clue to how transsexualism functions. Some authors use the word *transsexuality* as opposed to *transsexualism*, with a varied spelling of

the latter as *trans-sexualism*. But I have chosen to consistently employ the term *transsexualism*, because it is
one of the main contentions of this work that transsexualism operates as an ideology which the suffix *ism* is
meant to denote. Webster defines *ideology* in two ways,
both of which can be applied to transsexualism and the
ways in which it functions. The first definition Webster
gives for *ideology* is "visionary theorizing." In this sense,
transsexualism offers certain individuals a supposed futur-
istic vision of what they can become. (However, in reality,
instead of giving transsexuals an open and truly visionary
future, it restricts them unalterably to the present and
visionless context of cultural roles and stereotypes under
the *guise* of being ideologically visionary.) Webster's
second definition of ideology is threefold: (a) "a systematic body of concepts especially about human life
or culture," (b) "a manner or the content of thinking characteristic of an individual, group, or culture," and (c) "the
integrated assertions, theories, and aims that constitute
a sociopolitical program." Transsexualism functions as
ideology by defining a portion of human life as transsexual—using concepts such as "women trapped in men's
bodies," and the classic mind-body dichotomy to form
"integrated assertions, theories, and aims that constitute
a sociopolitical program." A perusal of the literature will
indicate that a popular as well as specialized vocabulary
has been built up. *Transsexualism at this point constitutes
a "sociopolitical program" that is undercutting the movement to eradicate sex-role stereotyping and oppression in
this culture.* Instead it fosters institutional bases of sexism
under the guise of therapy.

Many definitions of transsexualism have been put forth,
some differing from others in describing the phenomenon.
Benjamin states: "transsexualism is a sex and gender problem, the transsexual being primarily concerned with his
(or her) self only, a sex partner being of secondary although occasionally vital importance."[1] Donald Russell's
definition is among the more neutral, in that it attempts
to describe and not posit causal hypotheses:

The term "trans-sexual" refers to a person who is said to believe firmly, in spite of all physical or genetic evidence to the contrary, that he (or she) is inherently of the opposite sex. The transsexual has a fixed or apparently unalterable belief that he is of one sex "trapped" in the body of the other.[2]

Doctors Milton Edgerton, Norman Knorr, and James Callison who comprise part of the interdisciplinary team at the Johns Hopkins Gender Identity Clinic define transsexualism in a similar manner.

The term "transsexualism" has now been widely accepted in the medical literature as designating that psychiatric syndrome which is characterized by the individual's attempts to deny and change his (or her) biological sex and to thus achieve and permanently maintain the opposite gender identification.[3]

It should be pointed out, however, that the phrase *psychiatric syndrome* here does not refer to any psychotic causation theory. The authors later state: "Is any patient who seeks castration by surgery, by definition psychotic? We do not find this to be the case."[4] Rather the words *psychiatric syndrome* probably indicate that the authors do not consider transsexualism to be of biological origin.

Popular definition of transsexualism reveals a more value-laden content which raises a host of questions about the reality of transsexualism. In popular terms, transsexualism has come to mean a condition of "feeling trapped in the body of the wrong sex." This inevitably raises the question, is it biologically possible to convert a person surgically to the opposite sex? Is it possible to change sex— that is, to *transsex*? In order to answer this question, it is first of all necessary to discuss various meanings of the word *sex*—a word that has both a dismaying multiplicity and ambiguity of meanings.

The Six Sexes. John Money has distinguished various definitional levels of the word *sex* that are helpful in assessing whether it is biologically possible to cross-sex.[5]
1. *Chromosomal Sex.* This kind of sex determines biological maleness or femaleness, contrary to popular opinion

that anatomical sex is determinative. Normal males have a chromosomal pattern of XY with normal females being XX. In rare cases, chromosomal anomalies occur and constellations such as XXY or XXYY appear. The pattern of sex chromosomes is present and unchangeable in every body cell, including blood cells. Chromosomal sex can, however, conflict with anatomical sex, especially after transsexual surgery.

2. *Anatomical or Morphological Sex.* This kind of sex includes what are referred to as primary and secondary sex characteristics. The primary dimensions of anatomical sex are the testes in the male and the ovaries in the female. Secondary anatomical sex characters include the penis, scrotum, prostate, hair distribution, and a deeper voice in the male; and the clitoris, vulva, uterus, vagina, breasts, a wide pelvis, female voice, and hair distribution in the female. In the case of transsexualism, it is anatomical sex that is altered through hormonal and surgical procedures.

3. *Genital or Gonadal Sex.* This kind of sex is the collective term for the testes in the male or the ovaries in the female.

4. *Legal Sex.* Genital sex becomes the legal sex although this is not actually defined in the codes. It is in this area that errors of sex do occur and not too infrequently. By merely determining sex on the basis of genital sex, the obstetrician or midwife may be deceived. Biological anomalies, such as various hermaphroditic constellations, may escape them. Consequently the legal sex designated at birth is wrong, and complications often present themselves at a future time.

5. *Endocrine or Hormonal Sex.* This is determined by androgen in the male and estrogen in the female. Besides the sex glands, the pituitary or adrenal glands also supply hormones essential for both sexes. Endocrine sex is also mixed to various extents. Testes, as well as male adrenals, produce certain amounts of estrogen. Likewise, various amounts of androgen can be found in the ovaries and in the adrenals of women. To a certain extent, therefore, females and males are hormonally intersexed. Conse-

quently, hormonal products can be used to feminize a male or masculinize a woman. Hormonal treatments are preliminary measures used to alter the sex of a transsexual before the actual operation is undertaken.

6. *Psychological Sex.* Much of the literature uses this terminology to designate attitudes, traits, characteristics, and behavior that are said to accompany biological maleness or femaleness. I would prefer the term *psychosocial sex* to indicate the all-important factor that such attitudes, traits, characteristics, and behavior are socially influenced.

Robert Stoller uses the term *gender* to distinguish this kind of sex from biological sex. He differentiates between sex and gender in the following way:

Dictionaries stress that the major connotation of *sex* is a biological one, as for example, in the phrases *sexual relations* or the *male sex.* In agreement with this, the word *sex*, in this work will refer to the male or female sex and the component biological parts that determine whether one is male or female; the word *sexual* will have connotations of anatomy and physiology. This obviously leaves tremendous areas of behavior, feelings, thoughts, and fantasies that are related to the sexes and yet do not have primarily biological connotations. It is for some of these psychological phenomena that the term *gender* will be used: one can speak of the male sex or the female sex, but one can also talk about masculinity and femininity and not necessarily be implying anything about anatomy or physiology. Thus while *sex* and *gender* seem to common sense to be practically synonymous, and in everyday life to be inextricably bound together, one purpose of this study will be to confirm the fact that the two realms (sex and gender) are not at all inevitably bound in anything like a one-to-one relationship, but each may go in its quite independent way.[6]

The most striking example of sex and gender going in opposite directions is the transsexual. Transsexuals reject the gender that the culture has assigned to them and gravitate toward the gender assigned to the opposite sex. The transsexual literature stresses how confirmed the transsexual is in the gender identity of the opposite sex. "In the true transsexual there is no question of, or ambivalence about the gender preference, for the identification has been completed for some time at the point when they appear before the physician requesting sex reassignment."[7]

John Money and Anke Ehrhardt in *Man & Woman, Boy & Girl,* make a further distinction between gender identity and gender role.

Gender Identity: The sameness, unity, and persistence of one's individuality as male, female, or ambivalent, in greater or lesser degree, especially as it is experienced in self-awareness and behavior; gender identity is the private experience of gender role, and gender role is the public expression of gender identity.

Gender Role: Everything that a person says and does, to indicate to others or to the self the degree that one is either male, or female, or ambivalent; it includes but is not restricted to sexual arousal and response; gender role is the public expression of gender identity, and gender identity is the private experience of gender role.[8]

Thus they would distinguish between the psychological and sociocultural, or between private and public manifestations of gender.

The word *gender* has certain problems for the feminist critic. It gives the impression that there is a fixed set of psychosocial conditions that determines gender identity and role. When used in conjunction with other words such as *gender dissatisfaction, gender discomfort,* or *gender dysphoria,* it conveys that these can only be altered by very specialized therapy and/or sophisticated technical means. Feminists have described *gender dissatisfaction* in very different terms—i.e., as *sex-role oppression, sexism,* etc. It is significant that there is no specialized or therapeutic vocabulary of *black dissatisfaction, black discomfort,* or *black dysphoria* that has been institutionalized in black identity clinics. Likewise, it would be rather difficult and somewhat humorous to talk about *sex-role oppression clinics.* What the word *gender* ultimately achieves is a classification of sex-role oppression as a therapeutic problem, amenable to therapeutic solutions. Therefore, I prefer to use the word *gender* and the phrase, *gender dysphoria* and the like, when I am discussing the management of the transsexual issue in the therapeutic and/or technical

contexts. However, because of the nature of the subject
of transsexualism, there were times, while writing this
book, when I found the word unavoidable despite my
"dissatisfaction." In these places, I indeed used it with
reservation.

What does this delineation of the various kinds of sex
say about the reality of transsexualism? The most significant fact is that it is biologically impossible to change
chromosomal sex. If chromosomal sex is taken to be
the fundamental basis for maleness and femaleness, the
male who undergoes sex conversion surgery is *not* female.

Anatomically, transsexualism does take place, but
anatomical changes also happen in what is commonly
termed plastic surgery. Transsexualism most intrinsically
affects *genital* or *gonadal* sex. For example, it is possible
surgically to remove a woman's ovaries, and it is also
possible to construct an artificial vagina in a man whose
penis and testes have been removed. The question then
becomes how much value we would give to this kind of
alteration in terms of changing the totality of a person's
sex. Georges Burou, a Casablancan physician who has
operated on over 700 American men, expressed the superficiality of sex-conversion surgery in these words: "I don't
change men into women. I transform male genitals into
genitals that have a female aspect. All the rest is in the
patient's mind."[9] Moreover, the change in genital sex does
not make reproduction possible. Maybe with the development of various forms of reproductive technology, this
will be feasible in the future, but as yet, a change in genital
sex is not accompanied by reproductive capacity.

Endocrine or *hormonal* sex is the most susceptible to
alteration. Change here, for the transsexual, occurs without any surgical intervention. Hormonal treatment for men
and women is the threshold of the transsexual odyssey.
These treatments have certain anatomical effects resulting,
for example, in breast development for men or a redis-
tribution of body hair for both women and men. But this
reality requires constant hormonal treatments.

In law, transsexualism can occur. It is legally possible to

change sex. However, the whole area of *legal* sex has been one of contention for the transsexual who wishes to have sex-conversion surgery validated. The postoperative transsexual has often faced long and costly legal battles concerning amendation of birth certificates, social security numbers, drivers' licenses, and the like. There are a few states that have promptly issued new birth certificates with the name and sex changed accordingly. In other states, a more complicated procedure, namely a court order, is required before official documents can be altered.

If it is impossible to change basic chromosomal structure, then it is necessary to take a more in-depth look at not only the terminology but also the reality of transsexualism. Can we call a person transsexed, biologically speaking, whose anatomical structure and hormonal balance have changed but who is still genetically XY or XX? If we don't recognize chromosomal sex as determinative, plus the subsequent history that attends being chromosomal female or male, what are we really talking about when we say female or male? Is there any such enduring reality as biological maleness or femaleness?

Words and More Words. Furthermore, what does the word *transsexualism* say to us? We use this word to speak of both pre- and postoperative individuals, but does it make sense to call a person transsexual if that person has not been anatomically altered in a surgical way? In applying the word *transsexual* to both pre- and postoperative persons, credence is given to the fact that the mere desire to change sex by surgical means determines transsexual status.

The transsexual experts, themselves, have been uncomfortable with the term *transsexualism*, although not for the reason I mentioned previously. Within the past few years, many have started to replace it with the term *gender dysphoria*. In 1975, for example, the Second International Conference on Transsexualism was renamed the Second International Conference of Gender Dysphoria. John Money and Paul Walker, in a review of the proceedings, point out that the new symposium title represented a major concern of the participants regarding nomenclature. Jon Meyer and John Hoopes state:

It must be recognized that the term "transsexual" is not an adequate label. It does not represent the clinical variance to be found among applicants for reassignment or allow for adequate description and classification of the differences.[10]

The authors go on the explain that the term *dysphoria* emphasizes the person's difficulty in establishing an adequate gender identification, and the pain and conflict surrounding masculinity and femininity. It encompasses, but is not restricted to, persons who request sex-conversion surgery. Finally they propose abandoning the terms *transsexual* and *transsexualism*, except to describe the *postoperative* person.[11]

I have chosen to retain the term *transsexualism*, however, because: (1) most of the professionals and lay populace still call it that; (2) *gender dysphoria* obscures many of the social and ethical issues that I wish to point to in this work and, in my opinion, really does not name the intent of the medical empire that generates and perpetuates the problem; (3) while the term *gender dysphoria* may resolve some of the preceding definitional problems that I have raised, such as the designation of the preoperative transsexual, it restricts the reality behind "gender dysphoria"—i.e., sex-role oppression—to those who seek sex reassignment. To make it the private property, so to speak, of the transsexual empire and its professionals is to superficialize the depths of the questions that lie behind "gender dysphoria." Therefore, I have chosen to retain the term *transsexual* to describe persons who *believe* that they are of the opposite sex, who *desire* the body and role of the opposite sex through medical intervention, who put themselves into the hands of the transsexual experts, who have started hormone therapy, and who have accepted the classification of *transsexual*.

As an abstract noun the word *transsexualism* effectively obscures the question of who is transsexing whom. In deleting both agent and object, the word *transsexualism* also becomes a state of being. It is granted the status of "state-hood" by its very terminological existence, perpetuating the ideology that if such a state of being actually does exist, there is a certain group of people who really need this surgery. Until, of course, the surgery was popularized, post-Christine Jorgensen, the specific need of surgery was not evident, although some people may have felt that they wanted to change sex. To what extent the availability of the surgery has generated a wider need for it is again masked by the terminology.

In deleting the agent, the word *transsexualism* cloaks the power of the medical empire to generate a unique group of medical consumers. Thus the actions of a primary *agent*, the medical establishment, are rendered invisible, and the so-called need of the transsexual, the *patient*, is highlighted. Put succinctly, the terminology of transsexualism disguises the reality that someone transsexes someone, that transsexuals "prove" they are transsexuals by conforming to the canons of a medical-psychiatric institution that evaluates them on the basis of their being able to pass as stereotypically masculine or feminine, and that ultimately grants surgery on this basis.

Furthermore, by placing all the disordered experiences of the gender-dissatisfied individual under the heading of *transsexualism* and giving it the force of statehood, the transsexual therapists and technicians are able to order and control that reality. All of this is accomplished by the inherent power of a classification system that has been given medical and psychological credibility. Once sex-role oppression is given the name of transsexualism, and institutionalized in the gender identity clinics, and realized by hormone and surgical treatment, the "condition" of transsexualism itself explains *why* one would have the wrong mind in the wrong body. Why? Because one *is* a transsexual. This classification bestows sense on all the disparate and atomic experiences that once seemed so unfathomable. It functions to mask ethical issues and normative statements that raise themselves very pointedly in the case of transsexualism.

Two further notes about my own use of language. First, in places where syntactical structure made it awkward to use the pronoun *they* when referrring to transsexuals, I have chosen to emphasize the pronoun *he.* I do not intend this usage in the commonly accepted, pseudogeneric sense. Rather the use of *he* is intended to reinforce the fact that the majority of transsexuals are men (see Chapter 1). Transsexualism is originated, supported, institutionalized, and perpetuated primarily by males and it directly affects mostly men. Second, I use the words *patriarchal society* to define my view of the social context in which the problem of transsexualism arises. Although in many places I have used more general terms such as a *role-defined society*, or a *gender-defined society*, there are other places where I felt it necessary to avoid the obscure and passive connotations of these more general words, especially as they have been developed in the idiom of the social sciences. These disciplines attribute the conditions of a sexist society to amorphous "roles" and "forces" that are unspecified. Nobody is blamed and everyone is blamed. Such words delete the agents of these "roles" and "forces"—that is, the society and institutions men have created.

Such words also lend credence to the idea that the problem of transsexualism and other "role-controlled" problems are so awesomely complex and due to such vague "forces" that even the best intentions and strategies won't be able to comprehend, never mind solve, them. This has the effect of taking the immediate focus and pressure off men and male-defined institutions. Additionally, they say that "role-defined forces" are all that must be coped with and not the agents who initiate and preserve those forces, and the institutions that reify them.

Thus it is that language generates reality. As Peter Berger has noted: "Reality hangs by the thin thread of conversation." But the reality that language generates is perpetuated and upheld by the persons and institutions who use that language. Thus we turn to the persons and institutions involved in the transsexual realm.

A TOUCH OF EMPIRICISM

I have used several kinds of empirical research. I talked with transsexuals themselves, with doctors and psychologists who are involved in transsexual treatment and therapy, with directors of gender identity clinics, and with other individuals, such as clergy, who interact with transsexuals. I also visited certain gender identity clinics and hospitals, where transsexual surgery is performed, and an institution that funded transsexual research.

Writers on moral issues frequently do little or no in-the-field research. They understand their discipline as a "library science," or they limit their empirical research to institutions that "treat" the problem, rather than also including those persons and individuals who are most immediately affected. (Daniel Callahan, for example, did a comprehensive medical, legal, and ethical analysis of abortion, yet nowhere in his study does he indicate that he spoke extensively with women who were in the process of choosing or had chosen abortions.)[12] It has been my experience that talking with transsexuals themselves, as well as with individuals involved in the study and treatment of transsexualism, especially in their occupational milieu, made a vast difference in what I came to know about transsexualism.

I spoke with fifteen transsexuals, thirteen of whom were male-to-constructed-females. (This total is numerically comparable to numbers of transsexuals who were interviewed in many other studies.) I used what sociologists would call the "unstructured research interview" employing open-ended questions.[13] This approach maximizes discovery and description. I chose this method also because I make no pretense of doing a "hard-core," systematic, sociological study of transsexuals. (My own interview data serves as back-up to other more formal studies.)

Besides transsexuals themselves, I interviewed many of the active figures in the field of transsexual research and therapy. At Johns Hopkins, I talked extensively with John Money, Paul Walker, and Eleanor Bagby. I also spoke with

several persons involved in gender identity clinics. I talked
extensively with Zelda Suplee, director of the Erickson
Educational Foundation, which has funded much transsexual research and activity. Finally, I interviewed several
doctors and counselors who are active in the area of transsexual treatment and counseling on a private basis. All this
helped form my belief that the issue of transsexualism is
basically one of *social ontology*—that is, an issue of what
society allows and encourages its constituency to *be*.

THE ONTOLOGICAL ARGUMENT

My main conclusion is that transsexualism is basically a
social problem whose cause cannot be explained except
in relation to the sex roles and identities that a patriarchal
society generates. Through hormonal and surgical means,
transsexuals reject their "native" bodies, especially their
sexual organs, in favor of the body and the sexual organs
of the opposite sex. They do this mainly because the body
and the genitalia, especially, come to incarnate the essence
of their rejected masculinity and desired femininity. Thus
transsexualism is the result of socially prescribed definitions of masculinity and femininity, one of which the
transsexual rejects in order to gravitate toward the other.

Thus I will argue, in Chapter III, that the *First Cause* of
transsexualism is a gender-defined society whose norms of
masculinity and femininity generate the desire to be transsexed. Many will ask how an obviously "personal" problem, such as transsexualism, can be primarily attributed to
a social cause. Some will probably say that society cannot
be a *cause* and that as psychological advocates reduce
transsexualism to personal causes, I am doing the reverse—
blaming society. I believe that the primary cause of transsexualism cannot be derived from intrapsychic attitudes
and/or behaviors, or even from family conditioning processes. One must begin with the roles of a gender-defined
society, as the *First Cause* of transsexualism (that which,
in the Aristotelian sense, sets all other causes in motion)

to gain insight into its psychological manifestations. Only through a societal starting point can we gain insight into the real subjective meaning of the problem.

Transsexualism relates to what society allows and encourages its constituency to *be*. Behind the transsexual quest for the body and the sex role and identity of the opposite sex is the *quest for deeper selfhood*. I would ultimately call this the *quest for transcendence* or the *quest for be-ing*. However, be-ing cannot be separated from the social context (as has been the case with much traditional ontology), and for this reason, it is perhaps imperative that I explain further just what I mean by ontology.

The ontological tradition has been rejected by many philosophers and theologians because of its static dimensions. Developed within a society that was encompassed by a static world view, it is seen as offering little or no basis for change. Yet the split between being and becoming is not a necessary one, as Mary Daly has demonstrated.[14]

Be-ing is the initial power of everything, the beginning "structure," if you will, of reality, not as unchanging but as process. I have therefore chosen to talk about transsexualism as most deeply a question of be-ing, which cannot be separated from the social context that generated the problem to begin with. In discussing integrity in Chapter VI, I attempt to demonstrate that what is needed is an ethic of *total* integrity grounded in be-ing. In this way one can clarify the genuine personal-social issues involved in transsexualism.

The words *ontological* and *natural* are very often used as synonyms. But my own ontological method is not a new natural-law approach. I am not arguing that what is natural is good, I am not polarizing technology against nature. Rather I am making an appeal to the integrity or harmony of the whole. Thus my development of an ethic of integrity in Chapter VI is not meant to state that transsexual treatment and surgery are violations of a static biological nature of maleness or femaleness but that they violate a dynamic process of be-ing and becoming that includes the integrity of the body, the total person, and the society. The chromosomal base of maleness or femaleness is one defining factor of *bodily* integrity. Chromosomes contribute to bodily integrity, and one clue to their importance is the fact that transsexuals must continually suppress their anatomical and morphological consequences by estrogen or androgen therapy. Yet my appeal here is not that chromosomal maleness or femaleness is natural. Rather, I am emphasizing that medicalized intervention produces harmful effects in the transsexual's body that negate bodily integrity, wholeness, and be-ing.

Furthermore, chromosomes are only one defining factor, in the context of the total history of what it means to be a woman or a man, in a society that treats women and men differently on the basis of biological sex. This means that the integrity of the body must also be placed in the context of the integrity of the total person, which includes the realization of such values as choice, awareness, and autonomy. Finally, if the transsexual answer reinforces the foundation of sex-role oppression, which is sex-role stereotyping, by encouraging the transsexual to conform to these stereotypes, then it is also violating the integrity of the *society*.

Transsexualism is a half-truth that highlights the desperate situation of those individuals in our society who have been uniquely body-bound by gender constrictions, but it is not a whole truth. While transsexualism poses the question of so-called gender agony, it fails to give an answer. I hope to show that it amounts to a solution that only reinforces the society and social norms that produced transsexualism to begin with.

CHAPTER I

"Everything

You Always

Wanted to Know

about Transsexualism"

THERE are many questions
that people often ask about transsexualism. When was the
first transsexual operation performed? Where was it done?
How did transsexualism first gain public recognition? What
is the cost of the surgery? How, medically speaking, is a
person transsexed? What are the legal ramifications of sex
conversion surgery? Is it possible to change birth certificates, drivers' licenses, and the like? Has transsexualism
been a phenomenon throughout history?

Transsexual operations have been surgically possible
since the early 1930s. The hormonal and surgical techniques, however, were not refined and made public until
the early 1950s. Since then, thousands of transsexual
operations have been performed both here and abroad.
Largely due to the support of individuals such as Harry
Benjamin, M.D., and institutions such as the Erickson
Educational Foundation and Johns Hopkins, transsexual
treatment and surgery has become a legitimate medical

area of research and activity. The medical specialties that it calls forth, or more correctly that call it forth, are varied and complex, beginning with hormone therapy and often ending in numerous operative procedures. Just as complicated are the legal intricacies of changing sex on birth certificates, licenses, and other certificates of personhood required to live one's life. Other legal issues also affect the institutions performing the surgery.

As a medical category that enlists many surgical specialties and as a transformed state of being that requires legal validation transsexualism is a relatively new phenomenon. Historical antecedents are found in certain mythological accounts, initiation rites, and certain modes of eunuchism and castration but, strictly speaking, transsexualism has no historical precedents.

RECENT HISTORY

The word *transsexualism* did not become part of the English language until the early 1950's. It was invented as a medical term by Dr. D. O. Cauldwell, who used it to classify a girl whom he described as obsessively wanting to be a boy. He called her condition *psychopathia transsexualis.*[1] Several years later, in 1953, Harry Benjamin used the English word *transsexualism* in a lecture before the New York Academy of Medicine. Before 1967, the *Index Medicus* did not list it as a subject heading. Prior to this, it was subsumed under such categories as *transvestism* and *sex deviation.* However, before the publication of the famed Christine Jorgensen case in 1953, most people had never heard of the word nor of the state of being that the word signified.

Christine, formerly George, Jorgensen was transsexed in Denmark in 1952 by a team of Danish physicians headed by Christian Hamburger. Their findings were published a year after the operation in the *Journal of the American Medical Association*, with the consent of Jorgensen. In 1967 Jorgensen wrote about "her" own experiences in

"her" autobiography.[2] However, the first book to relate
a probable case of transsexualism in a popular-scientific
style and content was Niels Hoyer's *Man Into Woman*
(1933). The fact that the introduction to this book was
written by a well-known British sexologist, Norma Haire,
gave Hoyer's book a certain scientific credibility. The book
is the story of a male Danish painter who became Lili
Elbe after several rather obscure operations.[3]

Although Christian Hamburger has been credited with
bringing together many of the surgical specialties for the
treatment of the transsexual, he was not the first physician
to perform transsexual surgery. This title belongs to a
German, F. Z. Abraham, who, in 1931, reported the first
case of sex-conversion surgery.[4] In the years between 1931
and 1952 sporadic and piecemeal reports of transsexual
operations came forth, primarily from Germany and Switzerland. Hamburger, however, seems to have been the first
to make use of hormonal castration and to follow up on
his patients.

At the time Jorgensen was transsexed, there were few
places where one could go to obtain such surgery. Casa-
blanca, Istanbul, and countries such as Denmark, Germany, and Switzerland, were the most frequent locations
to which transsexuals travelled, provided they could pay
the cost and were willing to risk little or no medical
follow-up. Today, however, the situation, at least in the
United States, is quite different.

In the late 1950s, Dr. Harry Benjamin of New York,
funded by grants from the Erickson Educational Foundation, began treating transsexuals and publicizing his
research, hoping for professional and public understanding of what he entitled *The Transsexual Phenomenon*.[5] Benjamin is the key American figure who aroused
the interest of medical and psychological professionals
especially, in the problems of the transsexual. With the
founding of the Harry Benjamin Foundation in 1964,
he brought together a group of professionals from many
specialties to do systematic research on transsexualism.
This research took the form of batteries of tests, studies

of transsexuals' sexual attitudes, and pre- and postoperative evaluations.

A major expansion of transsexual research and activity took place in 1967 with the formal opening of the Johns Hopkins Gender Identity Clinic in Baltimore, Maryland. The fact that a major medical institution, with the prestige of Johns Hopkins, had initiated a clinic of this nature catapulted transsexualism into the public and professional eye as a legitimate medical problem. It was not until Johns Hopkins began performing the surgery and had initiated its Gender Identity Center that sex conversion operations gained acceptance and were begun in other respected medical institutions. When Benjamin began his work in this country, there was no reputable hospital in America that would have permitted transsexual surgery. Now, post-Johns Hopkins, there are estimated to be at least thirty such hospitals; among them, university hospitals at Minnesota, Stanford, Northwestern, Arkansas, Michigan, Kentucky, and Virginia.

The Johns Hopkins Clinic has served as a model for others of the same nature. It consists of a team of psychiatrists, psychologists, plastic surgeons, gynecologists, urologists, and endocrinologists. It works in close concert with certain legal and religious professionals who are called in to offer relevant advice. The team has also devised methods of evaluating preoperative transsexuals to judge their candidacy for surgery and operates selectively on those individuals who meet the criteria. It continues to review criteria, mainly to determine whether surgery is warranted in all claims of transsexualism. It also continues to refine its methods of surgical treatment, and attempts to do systematic postoperative follow-ups. Various team members, individually and in concert, have published many articles about their work and are regarded as being in the forefront of transsexual research. Of all persons who have been engaged in this work at Johns Hopkins John Money, now Professor of Medical Psychology and Pediatrics at the Johns Hopkins Hospital, has been the foremost publicist of the transsexual phenomenon.

Since 1967, many so-called gender identity clinics for transsexuals have been established in various parts of the country. Some are directly associated with university hospitals where surgery is done, while others, separated physically from any hospital base, counsel transsexuals, start hormone treatments, and eventually make selective referrals of candidates to medical personnel who then proceed with the surgery. Although reports conflict as to how many transsexual operations have actually been performed in this country and how many persons seek the surgery, figures published in *Newsweek* magazine on November 22, 1976, indicated that there are about 3,000 transsexuals in the U.S. who have undergone surgery and 10,000 more who view themselves as members of the opposite sex. Because more Americans want surgery than are accepted by those hospitals performing it, many transsexuals have probably continued to seek such surgery abroad. In the spring of 1973, the *Erickson Foundation Newsletter* reported that only 10 percent of those individuals who go through evaluation for surgery eventually achieve it.

It is very difficult to obtain exact professional statistics concerning the number of preoperative and/or postoperative transsexuals. Various figures are given, at times, but they often conflict. Zelda Suplee, former director of the Erickson Educational Foundation and present head of the Janus Information Facility at the University of Texas Medical Branch in Galveston, has attested to this lack of vital statistics on transsexualism.[6] Money and Walker also confirmed this lack of statistics in a recent book review in which they state: "In the absence of any national directory of sex-reassignment applicants, data on patients for surgery are inconclusive."[7] Thus the nature and incidence of transsexual activity is not clear. This lack of data is very significant in light of the fact that other major surgery statistics seem readily available.

With respect to the cost, the various procedures and surgery involved differ from hospital to hospital. On the average, the male-to-constructed-female operation and hospital stay alone can cost from $3,000 to $6,000. The

female-to-constructed-male operation involves a series
of several operations before the results are achieved and
costs up to $12,000. There are, of course, many other
expenses besides the surgery and hospital bills. For male
transsexuals, electrolysis to remove a heavy beard or
stubble can cost as much as the surgery.

Although many medical insurance policies do not cover
the cost of surgery on the grounds that such surgery is cosmetic, many others consider it a "reconstructive" and
"therapeutic" measure and will pay for it. In some states,
Blue Cross and Blue Shield will finance the surgery. In
other areas, for example New York City, courts have ruled
that transsexual operations are to be included in medical
assistance provided by the city and state for persons on
welfare. In New Jersey, Medicaid payments have been
authorized in some cases.[8] Since federal funds that had
been allocated for abortions have recently been withdrawn, feminists are struck by the inequity of this situation. To paraphrase Jimmy Carter, life has been "fair"
to transsexuals.

A MALE PROBLEM

While it is clear that more men than women request and
obtain sex-conversion surgery, various ratios have been
cited by researchers. The lowest ratio of women to men
(one to eight) was reported by Benjamin in 1966. This was
based on his own clinical experience with 152 cases of male
transsexualism and twenty cases of female transsexualism.
The highest ratio (one to two) was reported by John Randell in 1959. Most reports fall in between these two. According to international medical literature the generally
accepted ratio is one to three or one to four.[9] Recently,
it has been claimed that the incidence of female-to-constructed-male transsexualism is rising. Canon Clinton Jones
of the Hartford Gender Identity Clinic and Dr. John
Money of Johns Hopkins both mentioned this increase
to me in personal interviews with them.[10] Both said that

they had seen, during the early seventies, almost as many women as men seeking surgery. However, the number of operations performed on men is still substantially higher. It is significant that this supposed increase has not been verified in print with the exception of a somewhat vague reference made by Dr. Anke Ehrhardt in a commentary on the article, "Transsexualism and Surgical Procedures," in which she states: "More and more females appear in doctors' offices and seek hormone and surgical treatment."[11] What actual number "more and more" specifically refers to is, of course, anyone's guess. Zelda Suplee stated that from her personal contact with would-be transsexuals the preponderance is still male-to-constructed-female.

In my own interview sampling, I talked with only two female-to-constructed-male transsexuals. Often, when I was given a female-to-constructed-male contact, I had great difficulty finding the person. It is reasonable to speculate that the extreme difficulty I had in finding female-to-constructed-male transsexuals, plus the scant mention of them in the literature, may be indicative of the fact that there are fewer of them than are claimed.

Christian Hamburger gives the more commonly claimed ratio of one to three. He cites the letters he received and continues to receive in the aftermath of the famed Christine Jorgensen case. Hamburger believes that the reason for this one to three ratio "may be biological in nature," whatever this may mean. He also stated that a "contributing factor may also be that the case we reported involved a change from man into woman."[12] John Money, however, has suggested that the preponderance of male transsexuals reflects the fact that men are more vulnerable to "psychosexual disorders" than are women. A similar view held that:

It may be that transsexualism, like other forms of sexual variations, is actually more frequent in the male than in the female and thus is in keeping with Kinsey's hypothesis that the male is more prone to conditioning by psychological stimuli in the sexual and gender sphere than is the female.[13]

There are many reasons male-to-constructed-female transsexualism is more predominant. Most obviously, the surgery is easier, less costly, and more developed and publicized. Second, but perhaps less obvious, is the fact that men have been much freer to experiment than women. Thus even in the area of transsexual treatment and surgery, it seems that men who desire to become female and to live out the gender role that is culturally prescribed for women are actually, in their assertiveness of seeking out and enduring the surgery, conforming much more to the masculine stereotype. Women, through a cultural conditioning that has generated less impulse to experiment, are likely to be much more reticent.

Third, male transsexualism may well be a graphic expression of the destruction that sex-role molding has wrought on men. Thus it could be perceived as one of the few outlets for men in a rigidly gender-defined society to opt out of their culturally prescribed roles. Women, on the other hand, since the recent rise of feminism, have been able to confront sex-role oppression on a sociopolitical, as well as personal, level. Thus women have realized that both masculine and feminine identities and roles are traps.

Fourth, transsexual surgery is a creation of men, initially developed for men. The research and literature is overwhelmingly oriented to the male-to-constructed-female transsexual and also overwhelmingly authored by men. I do not mean to say that women are not writing in the transsexual literature, are not working in the gender identity clinics, are not counseling transsexuals, or are not becoming transsexuals. It must be acknowledged that women are present in token proportions in all of these various areas. Many even happen to be in the foreground, directing gender identity clinics and co-authoring writings on the topic. However, I would suggest that those women who are engaged in transsexual legitimation, writing, and counseling are functioning as tokens who promote the illusion of comprehensive female inclusion. In this respect, they are like the well-publicized women who are always present in some way to validate male-defined realities. Women who write in support of transsexualism are usually co-authors (Anke Ehrhardt, Patricia Tucker), and female counselors of transsexuals are women who, for the most part, "assist" in the gender identity clinics. Thus the androcentric origin, control, maintenance, and legitimation of transsexualism becomes obscured. The fact that the overwhelming research interest, number of publications and medical state of the "art" are concerned with male-to-constructed-female transsexualism is also evidence of the male-centered nature of the transsexual phenomenon.

The female-to-constructed-male transsexual is the *token* that saves face for the male "transsexual empire." She is the buffer zone who can be used to promote the universalist argument that transsexualism is a supposed "human" problem, not uniquely restricted to men. She is the living "proof" that some women supposedly want the same thing. However, "proof" wanes when it is observed that women were not the original nor are they the present agents of the process. Nor are the stereotypes of masculinity that a female-to-constructed-male transsexual incarnates products of a female-directed culture. Rather women have been assimilated into the transsexual world, as women are assimilated into other male-defined worlds, institutions, and roles, that is, on men's terms, and thus as tokens. As Judith Long Laws has written: "Tokenism may be analyzed as an institution, a form of patterned activity generated by a social system as a means of adaptation to a particular kind of pressure."[14] I would maintain that, under the pressure of having to demonstrate that transsexualism is really not limited to men, the medical empire assimilates female-to-constructed-male transsexuals, but always on its own terms. "The Token is a member of an underrepresented group, who is operating on the turf of the dominant group, under license from it."[15] In tokenism, the flow of outsiders into the dominant group is usually restricted numerically but just enough so that the illusion of inclusion takes place. This is exactly what happens with transsexuals. The accepted four to one ratio of male-to-constructed-females seeking and achieving transsexual status is enough to register the appearance of sufficient inclusion of women. Further, the token female presence in all aspects of the transsexual world is enough for the transsexual experts to claim that transsexualism is sex-blind.

Yet it is most important to note here that tokenism, as Mary Daly has pointed out, is not merely a matter of numerical restriction.[16] For example, the United States Senate could be composed of 50 percent women, and these women senators would still be tokens if their consciousness and legislation were still controlled by a patriarchal ethos, if they did not initiate and legitimate activities, and if they did not have a controlling power. Thus if the included group is not the controller of its own ethos and the initiator or legitimator of action, no matter how numerically present it may be, it is still a token group. Six million Jews could go to their death in the Nazi camps, not because there were too few of them but because they were not in control and thus their numbers were impotent. In the same way, the percentage of female-to-constructed-male transsexuals could be numerically increased to the extent where they would equal men, yet if they were still being transsexed by a "transsexual empire" whose social and body stereotypes were conceived by men, they would still be tokens.

Part of the syndrome of tokenism is to make women *seem* important. John Money, whose work will be discussed in Chapter II, is very careful to co-author his articles and books with a woman. It is an irony that women are getting authorship credit in the area of transsexualism when they have gotten so little credit in other fields for what work they really have initiated.[17]

A fifth reason why more men want to be women, than women men, can be hazarded from other feminist analyses of biomedical issues. Simply put, it is that men recognize the power that women have by virtue of female biology and the fact that this power, symbolized in giving birth,

is not only procreative but multidimensionally creative.
Various observers have called this recognition by various
names. Karen Horney reversed Freud's theory of penis
envy calling it womb envy.[18] Ralph Greenson, in an address to a clinical meeting of the A.M.A., gave this interesting analysis:

It is horrifying—a danger to the future of the human race. . . . Our
only hope is that basic instincts will eventually win out, that a true
equality of the sexes will emerge. Always before people thought it
was the woman who envied the man. But we have found that more
than two-thirds of those who wanted to change their gender were
males. What is shocking is that this is more widespread than was believed. These people are not psychotic; they are not crack-pots. . . .
Men have contempt for women only on the surface. Underneath is a
repressed envy, and repressed envy arouses fear. . . . One reason the
male envies the woman so much is that she is always sure of herself
as a woman. A man is never quite sure he is a man—he has to prove it
over and over again. [19]

Barbara Seaman and others have called this kind of envy
and desire "male mothering."[20] Barbara Ehrenreich and
Dierdre English in their ground-breaking works on the history of medicine in the West discuss the same phenomenon
on a more political level when they talk about the male
takeover of women's healing functions, especially during
the medieval and Reformation periods (the obliteration of
the witch-midwife) and the modern period (the consolida-
tion of orthodox medicine, particularly in this country).[21]
Transsexualism can be viewed as one more androcentric interventionist procedure. Along with male-controlled cloning, test-tube fertilization, and sex selection technology, it
tends to wrest from women those powers inherent in female biology. In a very real sense, the male-to-constructed-
female transsexual not only wants female biological capacities but wants to *become* the biological female.

Finally, and I think most important, there are more
male-to-constructed-female transsexuals because men are
socialized to fetishize and objectify. The same socialization
that enables men to objectify women in rape, pornography,
and "drag" enables them to objectify their own bodies.

In the case of the male transsexual, the penis is seen as a "thing" to be gotten rid of. Female body parts, specifically the female genitalia, are "things" to be acquired. Men have always fetishized women's genitals. Breasts, legs, buttocks are all parts of a cultural fixation that reduces women not even to a whole objectified nude body but rather to fetishized parts of the female torso. The *Venus de Milo* symbolizes this as well as the fact that it has never been restored to its original integrity. "Cunt," "ass," "getting one's rocks off," "balling," are all sexist slogans of this fetishized worldview where even "chicks" and "broads" are reduced to the barest essentials. Male-to-constructed-female transsexualism is only one more relatively recent variation on this theme where the female genitalia are completely separated from the biological woman and, through surgery, come to be dominated by incorporation into the biological man. Transsexualism is thus the ultimate, and we might even say the logical, conclusion of male possession of women in a patriarchal society. Literally, men here possess women.

Definitions of fetishism are revealing in this context. Webster's Dictionary defines *fetish* in several ways: First, as an object believed among a primitive people to have magical power to protect or aid its owner; *broadly:* a material object regarded with superstitious or extravagant trust or reverence; an object of irrational reverence or obsessive devotion; an object or bodily part whose real or fantasied presence is psychologically necessary for sexual gratification and that is an object of fixation to the extent that it may interfere with complete sexual expression. Second, as a rite or cult of fetish worshipers. Third, fetish is simply defined as fixation.

From these definitions, it is clear that the process of fetishization has two sides: *objectification,* and what might be referred to as *worship* in the widest sense. Objectification is largely accomplished by a process of fragmentation. The fetish is the fragmented part taken away from the whole, or better, the fetish is seen to contain the whole. It represents an attempt to grasp the whole. For example, breasts and legs in our society are fetish objects containing the essence of femaleness. Thus the fetish contains and by containing controls.

However, the other side of fetishization is worship or reverence for the fetish object. In primitive religions, fetish objects were worshiped because people were afraid of the power they were seen to contain. Therefore primitive peoples sought to control the power of the fetish by worshiping it and in so doing they confined it to its "rightful place." There was a recognition of a power that people felt they lacked and a constant quest in ceremonies and cults to invest themselves with the power of the fetish object. Thus to worship was also to control. In this way, objectification and worship are two sides of the same coin.

In this sense transsexualism is fetishization par excellence—a twisted recognition on the part of some men of the creative capacities of the female spirit as symbolized and incarnated in the usurped female biology. This usurpation of female biology, of course, is limited to the artifacts of female biology (silicone breast implants, exogenous estrogen therapy, artificial vaginas, etc.) that modern medicine has surgically and hormonally created. Thus transsexual fetishization is further limited not even to the real parts of the real whole, but to the artifactual parts of the artifactual whole.

In summary, then, since men have been socialized to fetishize women, it is not surprising that this fetishization process is one more explanation of why there are more male-to-constructed-female transsexuals. What could be perceived as an initial protest against sex-role stereotyping (i.e., the transsexual's initial gender discomfort and gender rebellion) becomes short-circuited.

THE MEDICALIZED "FEMALE"

The medical procedures involved in transsexualism are puzzling to laypersons; most cannot begin to imagine what is physically involved in changing sex or how the change is accomplished.

The medical odyssey of the transsexual is a long one, often beginning years before surgery is completed. For men it usually starts with the administration of the female hormones estrogen and progesterone. This is referred to as "hormonal castration." Hormonal treatment has two effects: it suppresses the existing physiological sex characteristics; and it develops and maintains the opposite anatomical sex characteristics.[22] Benjamin explains:

> The feminization of the male patient can be accomplished by female hormones, both estrogen and progesterone, which develop the breasts, soften the skin, reduce body hair, diminish erections and decrease libidinous conflict by suppressing testicular androgen production.[23]

In addition, the gonads are inhibited, the testes atrophy, the distribution of subcutaneous fat is changed in a female direction, and muscular strength diminishes. Very often, however, beard growth diminishes only slightly, and other areas of male hair growth also remain generally unchanged. For this reason, many transsexuals resort to electrolysis. As far as voice is concerned, there is little change.[24] (Many transsexuals seek out speech therapy.)

Hormones are administered in various ways. For men, the estrogens of 17β-estradiol and estrone can be given orally. Estradiol monobenzoate, another estrogen, can be injected intramuscularly twice a week. Numerous artificial compounds with estrogenic activity have also been synthesized for oral administration, besides the steroids. DES (diethylstilbesterol), for example, has been widely used. Estrogenic hormones can also be applied as ointments or alcoholic solutions and absorbed through the skin. Estradiol, in combination with progesterone, has also been administered in the form of rectal suppositories. The treatment of male transsexual candidates is almost totally dependent on estrogen to induce hormonal castration and feminization. Such treatment is long-term—in many cases, lifelong.

The next step is the surgery itself, which requires the combined techniques of the urologist, gynecologist, and the plastic surgeon. The total procedure takes place in four steps, although all of them may or may not be desired by a particular patient. The four steps are penectomy, castration, plastic reconstruction, and formation of an artificial vagina (vaginoplasty). Some transsexuals have only the first and second steps performed, and indeed, some writers recommend this approach.[25]

The vagina is constructed by creating a cavity between the prostate and the rectum. An artificial vagina is formed from a skin graft from the thigh and lined with penile and/or scrotal skin.[26] Thus orgasmic sensation is possible. The shape of the artificial vagina is maintained by a mold that is worn continuously for several weeks following surgery. Once healing has occurred, manual dilation or penile insertion two or three times weekly is necessary to prevent narrowing, which can result through the contraction of scar tissue.[27]

The next, most common, procedure is enlarging the breasts, usually with inserted implants. This is often followed up with increased estrogen therapy. However two cases of breast cancer that occurred about five years after such treatment have been reported.[28] The author suggests that the malignancy was entirely due to the hormonal imbalance created by excessive estrogen therapy and orchidectomy (removal of one or both testes). Leo Wollman has commented: "The degree of risk may well be a function of the amount of hormone used. . . . The most likely possibility is that the hormonally feminized male transsexual conservatively treated with estrogen, runs the same risk of breast malignancy as does a normal female."[29] However, in light of the recent evidence about estrogen replacement therapy and also evidence linking cancer and birth control pills, Wollman's position is hardly reassuring. Normal women, even on conservative doses of estrogen therapy, "run a great risk" of incurring cancer.[30]

Following surgery, transsexuals receive oral maintenance doses of estrogen thus becoming medically managed individuals. Usually, this treatment is administered biweekly, although longer intervals do occur. The hormones used are the same as those given preoperatively. Such hormones are said to play an important role in general metabolism, particularly with regard to bones, skin, blood vessels, and muscles. Interestingly, it has been said that, "without these hormones, postoperative patients would experience climacteric symptoms, including hot flashes and deterioration of general body tone."[31] These are, of course, the classic menopausal symptoms. It is now seriously suggested, in the light of evidence linking estrogen replacement therapy and cancer, that such symptoms, if indeed they are really experienced by women, could best be treated by other means (e.g., calcium and phosphorous replacement to prevent bone deterioration).

Surgery, however, often does not end with vaginal construction. Secondary operations are often sought by the transsexual, usually for esthetic reasons and/or to correct real or psychologically felt complications. This cosmetic surgery frequently has nothing to do with refashioning the genitalia themselves. It ranges from limb surgery, to eye surgery, chin surgery, ear surgery, scar revision, and even tattoo excision. Some transsexuals also seek reduction of the Adam's apple. All these procedures are undertaken by the transsexual in the hope of conforming more to the fashionable, stereotypical feminine body image. Many transsexuals go to great lengths to fit themselves to the prescribed body measurements and gestalt of a man-made woman.

Surgery to correct complications centers on the breasts and genitalia. Bleeding can be a problem in the breast area, and care must be taken to control this completely. Otherwise, postoperative hematoma (extravascular collection of blood, usually clotted and forming a mass) can occur. Also, the lack of overlying breast tissue covering an implant offers little protection from even the slightest injury. The breast is vulnerable to injury that may cause subsequent expulsion of the prosthesis, again requiring corrective surgery. As far as the genitalia are concerned, correctional problems can occur here also. It has been reported that surgical complications are not common, but the most recurrent ones include narrowing of the vagina, rectovaginal fistulas, and narrowing of the urethra.

Overall, it has been said that "the final external appearance of the genitalia varies—not only from patient to patient, but with the surgical technique employed. Few patients are truly satisfied. Many seek further corrective changes."[32] Here, however, there is some conflicting evidence. On the one hand, Milton Edgerton and his colleagues have reported that of nine patients operated on by their group all were dissatisfied with the surgery, although all stated that they "would do it again."[33] Conversely, Fogh-Andersen reported in his series that most patients were satisfied with their surgery and did not regret having made the change.

Several authors have commented on the surgical demands and needs of transsexuals. For example: "The surgeon must be prepared to combat the tendency of these patients to desire 'polysurgery.'"[34] This can be responded to in several ways. First of all, *all* transsexual surgery, from the primary operative procedures through the secondary surgical adjustments and cosmetic procedures, can be regarded as "polysurgery," or "unnecessary surgery." (I will discuss the issue more extensively later in this book.) Secondly, it is hard to see how the surgeon can "be prepared to combat the tendency of these patients to desire 'polysurgery'" if surgeons are the ones who are creating all the different varieties and kinds of polysurgery, by developing the surgical specialties, which in turn create the demand.

THE MEDICALIZED "MALE"

The female-to-constructed-male transsexual also begins the sex conversion odyssey with hormone treatment. Androgen is injected to arrest menstruation, to stimulate some hair growth on the face and body, possibly to lower the voice slightly, and to accomplish some reduction of breast tissue. This also causes the muscles and body appearance in general to become progressively more masculine (e.g., the shoulders widen). Long-term administration of testosterone often increases the size of the clitoris. However, menstruation is not always suppressed by hormone treatment. In some cases, radiation had to be used, because breakthrough bleeding occurred after androgens were injected. In the medical literature, this is called *radiation menopause.*[35]

One of the ill effects of long-term androgen therapy has been attacks of acne. Some observers also report a libido increase that they regard as undesirable and troublesome, but whether or not this is caused by biological or social-psychological influences is debatable. One of the more serious consequences of androgen is that all its effects are not always reversible. If a woman decides to stop hormone treatment, her voice may retain its low pitch and her facial hair may remain.

Surgery involves several steps, all of which are not necessarily undertaken. Mastectomy, hysterectomy, and oophorectomy (removal of the ovaries) are surgical procedures that most transsexuals undergo. As the penis is a constant reminder to the male transsexual of his rejected male body, so are breasts and menstruation to the female.

The female transsexual patient, perhaps considerably more than the male, feels quite strongly that something is wrong internally. The menses are regarded as loathsome and often are described as being exceedingly painful. Many patients will seek and perhaps obtain exploratory laparotomy and hysterectomy firmly convinced that testes and other male organs will be discovered.[36]

Since testosterone causes only a moderate reduction of a woman's breasts, female transsexuals usually obtain mastectomies. Hysterectomies and removal of the ovaries constitute the second step in female-to-constructed-male transsexual surgery.* The vagina remains. Phallus construc-

---

*The removal of ovaries was used to tame deviant women during the nineteenth and early twentieth century rash of sexual surgery. This mode of female castration has now been superseded by hysterectomy. If one regards the female-to-constructed-male as a potential deviant, as a potential lesbian and woman-identified woman, the comparison between these castrated women and female-to-constructed-male transsexuals is significant.

tion, when undertaken, begins in conjunction with a hysterectomy. It is technically possible to construct a penis surgically by rotating a tube flap of skin from the left lower quadrant of the abdomen and closing the vaginal orifice. A urinary conduit can be led through such a phallus, so that the constructed penis may be used for urination. However, because of complications, many surgeons have decided against constructing the phallus so it can be used to urinate. Instead, the female urethra is maintained in its existing position beneath the constructed penis. But the new penis lacks sensitivity, and can become erect only through the insertion of certain stiffening material that remains in the penis all the time, or can be put in and out through an opening in its skin.[37]

Many female-to-constructed-male transsexuals, however, stop after obtaining hormone therapy, mastectomy, and hysterectomy, feeling that they do not wish to undergo the multistaged procedures required for the construction of a phallus, which is often also accompanied by scrotal construction. Some transsexuals recognize that the phallus will serve little, if any, role in sexual activity, since the technique of creating an erect penis has not been developed.

Some female transsexuals, however, do undergo the number of hospitalizations required for phallus construction. They are convinced that the rodlike stiffener, inserted into the skin of the constructed member, can put pressure on the original clitoris (which still remains) during intercourse, making an orgasm possible. Therefore, some transsexuals are willing to endure the multiple procedures that are necessary for this. One female-to-constructed-male transsexual underwent thirty-three plastic operations to obtain a satisfactory penis.[38] Furthermore, the "fear of discovery" becomes a strong pressure, pushing both male and female transsexuals to undergo every possible kind of surgery. All transsexuals express profound anxiety about being placed in an uncontrolled environment, through accident or illness, and thereby being "unmasked."[39] For the female-to-constructed-male transsexual, "toilet trauma," as Zelda Suplee calls it, is a particular fear. Public lavatory facilities for men often require the kind of exposure that women do not meet, and this alone increases the female transsexual's anxiety about phallus construction.

THE LEGAL LANDSCAPE

Problems for the transsexual, however, are not limited to the medical-surgical realm. For most transsexuals, there are legal difficulties that must also be resolved, and a corresponding legal journey that must be travelled. In fact the legal odyssey, for most transsexuals, begins long before the operation takes place.

Legally, there are many constraints on the transsexual and on both the institution and the doctors performing the operation. In addition, there are several state statutes that have been invoked against preoperative transsexuals who have been caught in the act of cross-dressing. Many of these same statutes have been used against transvestites, and in some cases against homosexuals, in the past. Section 887, subdivision 7, of the New York State Code of Criminal Procedure is typical of some state female impersonation statutes that have been used in the past against transvestites and homosexuals, and are now being invoked against transsexuals. Although the preoperative transsexual is not having sexual relations at the time of arrest, nor attempting to solicit or defraud as a female, he is arrested on the grounds of masquerading as female. In such situations, the transsexual has often presented medical certification attesting to his transsexual status, and has still been arrested and convicted under this statute. Furthermore, doctors have been warned against issuing such certification on the grounds that such documents might be judged illegal and/or improper medical conduct by the local, unsympathetic medical association.[40]

In many states, there is no hesitation on the part of the police to arrest under a disorderly conduct statute.[41] This is done despite the fact that the transsexual was in no way being disorderly at the time of arrest and does not perpetrate the usual acts (e.g., crowd-gathering, loud commotion, etc.) that cause disorderly conduct arrests. Various "catch-all" statutes are also invoked. Under these statutes, persons can be taken into legal custody for acts that outrage public decency and for which there are no other specific and covering statutes. Thus catchall statutes make it very difficult to predict what kind of behavior is defined as criminal, and they leave much discretion to the arresting officer.[42] Under catchall statutes, transvestite, homosexual, and transsexual persons have been frequently arrested, and many have been jailed, convicted, and fined.

Legal difficulties are not solved for the transsexual even after sex-conversion surgery has taken place. The postoperative transsexual, in many states, faces long legal battles in trying to change personal papers. Some states have been quick to grant such changes; others have been more gradual; and some have refused altogether.

In many areas, transsexuals and their advocates have asked the courts to define sex, and to thereby set a precedent for other legal decisions on the matter. Johns Hopkins Hospital followed a fundamentally different procedure. The medical community there took the initiative on behalf of their clients to guide the city and state in setting an administrative precedent for birth certificate changes. In 1967, one of the Johns Hopkins Gender Identity Committee members spoke with an official of Baltimore's Bureau of Vital Statistics. This official allowed that the name on a transsexual's birth certificate could be amended and also that the sex could be changed to conform to the new legal name. A shortened birth certificate with only new information on it was then issued to the transsexual. The old certificate with emendation was kept in a sealed envelope on record and could be produced, if necessary, to insure continuity of legal identity, which might be needed for the purposes of proving past schooling, social security, and inheritance rights. Most of the transsexual's everyday needs would be met by the short-form certificate carrying no evidence of sex reassignment.[43]

With respect to the surgery itself, there are several statutes that may be invoked against both transsexuals and the institution that performs the operation. Looming largest is the threat of legal mutilation, which is embodied in so-called mayhem statutes, still on the books in a majority of states. These statutes forbid the willful and permanent deprivation, crippling, and/or mutilation of a bodily organ. They could be used to prosecute the transsexual who undergoes sex-conversion surgery, the surgeons performing the operation, and the institution in which the operation is done. Surgeons have been warned by district attorneys' offices throughout the country of impending prosecution under this law, when they have inquired about the legality of transsexual surgery.[44]

In contrast to the risk of criminal liability, a physician may also be exposed to liability in tort, if the individual's consent to the operation should be declared invalid. (A case in Argentina ruled that a transsexual's consent to sex-conversion surgery was unnatural, and therefore invalid, and the surgeon became liable in tort for assault.)[45]

In the United States, however, where no such legal decisions have been rendered concerning the operation itself, the institutions that are performing such operations have followed various legal courses. With a mayhem statute hovering over it, the U.C.L.A. Medical Center decided not to initiate such operations on their own but instead asked the law if it could find some legal precedent to guide them. One of the university's legal advisors cautioned against what he termed a legally risky surgical venture. Thus the U.C.L.A. Gender Identity Clinic presently performs sex-conversion surgery on only those individuals who have definite and provable biological sexual anomalies.[46]

A second group of medical personnel at the University of Minnesota acted similarly to the U.C.L.A. team in asking the law for guidance in this area. However, the absence of a mayhem statute in the state of Minnesota was the key factor that encouraged its decision to proceed with transsexual operations.[47] Had they been faced with the presence of a mayhem statute, it is likely that the Minnesota group might have followed U.C.L.A.'s course.

Strikingly different from the preceding two cases is that

of the Johns Hopkins Gender Identity Clinic. This group, instead of asking the law for guidance, as we noted previously in the birth certificate situation, again set a precedent for the law to look to. When the case of G. L., a seventeen-year-old boy, arose and transsexual surgery was sought by the boy and his parents, the specialists involved, confident of their medical decision about sex-reassignment surgery for the boy, proceeded on the basis of their own medical judgment. The boy, the boy's parents, his probation officer (the boy had been involved in repeated delinquencies supposedly linked to sexual dissatisfaction with his body), two specialists from the Hopkins Clinic, and a judge joined together to form a liaison among the petitioners, medicine, and the law in the event that sex conversion should be challenged in the future. Furthermore, the judge signed a court order for the surgery. This court order would set no legal precedent unless challenged by a higher court, but the very act of procuring a court order placed the whole procedure within the scope of the law. The judge himself attended several meetings of the Johns Hopkins Gender Identity Committee and said he would be available should his advice be needed. This, of course, is a highly unusual procedure. The University's lawyer also worked closely with the team, discussing various legal issues with them and advising them on such aspects as consent and legal name changes. Thus confrontation between law and medicine was avoided so that no lawyer or judge would be put in the position of interpreting Hopkins's policy. Acting on the basis of professional judgment, the Hopkins medical group defined the problem as a medical one and acted accordingly, getting the law to affirm its judgment.[48]

In assessing the legal position of the transsexual, various factors come into play. First of all, it can be demonstrated that statutes invoked against the preoperative transsexual who cross-dresses are plainly unjust, not applicable, or too widely construed to be legitimately enforced. Section 887, subdivision 7, of the New York State Code of Criminal Procedure is a case in point. This statute expressly forbids female impersonation, but should only be invoked when impersonation is used to defraud or solicit. As Robert Sherwin has stated, there is no law that expressly forbids males to wear female clothing, per se. There are laws that forbid males from doing so for the purposes of defrauding when, for example, one tries to gain illegal entry or attempts to acquire money by such impersonation.[49] However, the statute has not been adhered to, and wide discretionary powers are given to arresting officers.

Arresting officers in some states have used also a wide and broadly applied disorderly conduct statute or other catchall statutes to pull cross-dressers off the streets or out of public, and even private, places. Given the latitude of application here, such statutes should be revised or eliminated altogether. Impersonation statutes should be invoked precisely for the purposes they were intended, i.e., to stop fraud; disorderly conduct should include only obvious disorderly conduct. Transvestism cannot of itself be demonstrated to be disorderly conduct.

At this point, the causes of transsexualism need to be examined. The medical and psychological literature has focused on two areas: (1) prenatal critical hormonal factors that supposedly set "the direction but not the extent of sex differences"; and (2) individual and family influences that are claimed to condition transsexual development. Both theories warrant a close examination, yet, as I shall argue, both neglect the wider and more primary influence of sex-role stereotyping in a patriarchal society, and both ultimately conclude by blaming the mother.

CHAPTER II

Are Transsexuals

Born or Made—

or Both?

THE causes of transsexualism
have been debated for years. Perhaps the earliest commentator was Herodotus. He explained the origin of what he referred to as "the Scythian illness" by resorting to divine causation. Venus, enraged with the plundering of her temple at Ascelos, changed the Scythian males and their posterity into women as her divine punishment for their misdeeds.[1]

Herodotus notwithstanding, most theories fall into two camps—biological and psychological. Biological theories have tended to focus on neuro-endocrine factors. In this chapter I will mainly be concerned with these biological aspects, especially as they are developed as part of an interactionist theory in the writings of John Money and his associates. Chapter III will be devoted to psychological theories of transsexualism, which highlight factors of imprinting, family conditioning, and general psychoanalytic hypotheses.

In both chapters I will demonstrate that while biological and psychological investigations seek different causes, they both utilize the same theoretical model—i.e., both seek causes within the individual and/or interpersonal matrix. In such investigations, social, political, and cultural processes tend to be relegated to a subsidiary or nonexistent role, because the model focuses attention on individual or interpersonal gender differences and similarities rather than upon the gender-defined social system in which transsexual behaviors arise. For example, psychological theories measure a transsexual's adjustment or nonadjustment to the cultural identity and role of masculinity or femininity. They seldom question the social norms of masculinity and femininity themselves.

This chapter will be concerned mainly with the work of John Money and associates. There are many reasons I have chosen to do an extensive analysis of Money's work. First of all, his theories on sex differences have gained wide acceptance, both in academic and lay circles. They have also been widely cited by feminist scholars. No other researcher in this area has developed any comparable body of research. Thus most discussions of sex differences refer to Money's work as a kind of bible. Second, no one has done a comprehensive analysis and critique of Money's work, especially as it relates to issues surrounding transsexualism. For example, Money's much-publicized theory that core gender identity is fixed by the age of eighteen months forms one critical basis for the justification of transsexual surgery, and therefore deserves special attention. Finally, inherent in Money's proclaimed scientific statements about sex differences are many normative and philosophical statements about the natures of women and men. Under the guise of science, he makes normative and prescriptive statements about who women and men are and who they ought to be. It is one task of this chapter to expose these assertions.

Money's theories about sex differences are based on the supposition that the nature-nurture debate is obsolete. Instead he proposes an interactionist theory of sex differences that claims to unite biological and environmental factors into a unique, sophisticated gestalt. At times he sounds like a biologizer and, at other times, like an environmental determinist. It is very difficult to get a precise grasp on exactly what Money is stating. Thus while it may seem that I am equivocating with the explanation and critique of Money's theories, this is because Money himself consistently equivocates.

In discussing the importance of biology, Money is no biologizer of the *ancien régime* in which, for example, hormonal determinists linked anatomy directly with destiny. (I am reminded here of theories about female behavior that were based on "raging hormonal imbalances" [Edgar Berman] or male bonding theories based on reductionistic endocrinology and selective anthropology [Lionel Tiger].) Rather, what makes Money's theories on sex differences so attractive to those who should know better is that he *claims* to unite biological and environmental factors into a unique, sophisticated whole.

On the environmental side, Money's statements about the effects of socialization or learning are just as deceiving. Possibly to avoid the charge of biologizer, Money emphasizes that the socialization side of the coin is more significant than the biological. In fact, it is so significant that "core" gender identity is fixed during the first eighteen months of life. Here the theme changes from "biology is destiny" to "socialization is destiny." Yet many of those who accept Money's theories seem not to notice this switch, which takes on all the force of a new natural law. The seductiveness of Money's work resides in the fact that he comes close to the truth in postulating that the interaction of biology and environment *may* explain certain facets of sex differences. But it is my contention that he has failed to show us that they do. Thus he tells us very little about the origins of transsexualism.

THE NATURE-NURTURE DEBATE IS OBSOLETE

In my opinion, there are five main aspects to Money's theory of sex differences:

1. The distinction between nature and nurture, or innate traits versus acquired traits, is obsolete. Biology *combined* with socialization determines sex differences.
2. A most critical period in the development of sex differences is the prenatal stage. At this point hormones activate the brain and set the *direction* but not the *extent* of sex differences.
3. The development of gender identity can be compared to the development of native language.
4. The "locking tight" of gender identity occurs by the age of eighteen months. After this, it is very difficult, if not impossible, to reverse psychosexual orientation.
5. Social change will come about, not by doing away with cultural definitions of masculinity and femininity, but by bringing more *flexibility* to the stereotypes to meet present and future changes.

Money dissociates himself from early theorists of biological determinism by accusing them of using simplistic methods. He purports to take a more solidly scientific approach using new information. (One way in which he has been able to escape the label of simplistic biologizing is by what I have termed his pseudo-interactionism or pseudo-organicism.)[2] Compared to earlier theorists, Money appears to be a very astute and careful researcher of gender identity. For example, the earlier, more reductionistic theorists linked anatomy *directly* to destiny. Straightforward links between hormonal factors and supposed behavioral results were simplistically set forth. In Money, however, the connection between the two is *indirect*. There is a mediating structure, the human brain—more specifically, the hypothalamus—which when activiated by specific sex hormones sets up neural pathways for gender identity that postnatal socialization later develops.

As early as 1963, Money was saying that the dichotomy between innate and acquired traits was conceptually outdated.[3] This assertion has continued to form the philosophical underpinning for all of his work on sex differences and is reiterated as the basis of *Man & Woman, Boy & Girl*.

In the theory of psychosexual differentiation, it is now outmoded to juxtapose nature versus nurture, the genetic versus the environmental, the innate versus the acquired, the biological versus the psychological, or the instinctive versus the learned. Modern genetic theory avoids these antiquated dichotomies, and postulates a genetic norm of reaction which, for its proper expression, requires phyletically prescribed environmental boundaries. If these boundaries are either too constricted, or too diffuse, then the environment is lethal, and the genetic code cannot express itself for the cells carrying it are nonviable.[4]

The interaction of biological and social factors is explained by using the concept of a program and by comparing that program to the development of native language. There are certain parts of the program that exert a determining influence, particularly in the prenatal period, and leave a permanent imprint. These are hormonal influences that act on the brain to set up supposed neural pathways to receive postnatal, social, gender identity signals. After birth, the biological program shifts to one of psychosexual conditioning, and gender identity now becomes largely a matter of biographical history, especially social biography. Once written, the social biography program leaves its imprint, as did the biological. Money and Ehrhardt admit that of the two, the social factors are the most influential part of gender identity differentiation but that prenatal hormonal factors are necessary to set the direction, if not the extent, of sex differences. They "predispose."

Such theories have an attraction because they seemingly reconcile opposing factors. They achieve instant reconciliation, so to speak. However, it is important to examine organic theories, especially those that claim to have a scientific base, to see if the connection is made by fiat rather than by demonstrable and credible evidence. I believe that there is a series of missing links in Money's approach.

For example, let us examine the biological "program." Money and Ehrhardt's assertions about the importance of prenatal hormonal factors influencing behavior rest on statements such as the following.

Testicular secretions, their presence or absence or their intrusion
from exogenous sources, account not only for the shape of the
external but also for certain patterns of organization in the brain,
especially *by inference* in the hypothalamus, pathways that will
subsequently influence certain aspects of sexual behavior. Thus
they pass on the program, dividing it between two carriers, namely
the genital morphology and that part of the central nervous system,
peripheral and intracranial, which serves the genital morphology
[Italics mine].[5]

Put simply, if a person, for some reason, has more androgen prenatally, it will take *less* stimulus to orient that
person toward strenuous physical activity (certain designated masculine activities) and *more* stimulus to evoke
a response to helpless children (and other designated
feminine activities). To prove this, Money draws on data
from animal experimentation and from certain groups
of females who were androgenized *in utero*.

There is something missing, however. How do hormonal
secretions account not only for physical genital formation
but for "certain patterns of organization in the brain"
which influence "certain aspects of sexual behavior"? The
connection between hormonal determinants and subsequent brain patterns is never made clear. *How* does the
central nervous system, insofar as "prenatal hormonal
factors make it sexually dimorphic," pass on its program
in the form of behavioral traits, which are "culturally
classified as predominantly boyish or girlish"?[6] Money
and Ehrhardt are cautious enough to say: "These traits
do not automatically determine the dimorphism of gender identity, but they exert some influence on the ultimate pattern of gender identity."[7] This is precisely the
question, however. *How* do they exert even "some influence," and what is the content of this specific influence?
Money admits that the precise answer to this question is
not yet known. "In human beings the pathways have not
yet been anatomically identified."[8] If this is Money and
Ehrhardt's ultimate conclusion, then it is reasonable to
ask why they spent so many pages discussing the *prob-
ability*, at best, of especially the animal findings being
extrapolated to human behavior. Money and Ehrhardt

appear to be forcing the parallel between animal behavior and females androgenized *in utero*. It is just as credible that the so-called masculine behavior of the androgenized girls could be *entirely* due to postnatal socialization.

In summary, the point is should *any* significance be claimed for biological factors in the development of gender identity? Just because Money and Ehrhardt proclaim that the nature-nurture debate is outmoded and that there is an organic interaction between biology and socialization should not dissuade us from asking for the specific evidence in a work that makes great pretensions to using scientific modes of inquiry. Is science, in John Money, reducible to hidden pseudometaphysical statements about the nature and behavior of men and women? Or as Ann Oakley has pointed out, why do these alleged prenatal hormonal factors that set the course for gender identity differentiation so exactly parallel the course that society sets for masculine and feminine gender identity and role? Is what is at stake in Money's work not science, but a world view, ideology, or faith commitment of an ontological sort? It appears that Money has only negated the *idea* that it is either/or, but has not proven the reality that it is both/and.

HORMONAL HAPPENINGS IN THE WOMB

According to Money in the case of transsexualism *possibly* something goes wrong during the prenatal critical period. Specifically, Money and Ehrhardt list a number of prenatal abnormal determinants, not all of which necessarily influence the development of transsexualism.

The phyletic program may be altered by idiosyncrasies of personal history, such as the loss or gain of a chromosome during cell division, a deficiency or excess of maternal hormones, viral invasion, intrauterine trauma, nutritional deficiency or toxicity, and so forth. Other idiosyncratic modifications may be added by the biographical events of birth.[9]

Of all such "idiosyncratic modifications," however, Money and Ehrhardt devote themselves most explicitly to hormonal factors. They are careful to assert, nevertheless, that these hormonal factors and how they relate to transsexualism are "imperfectly understood."

There may well be an as yet undiscovered fetal metabolic or hormonal component which acts to induce a predisposition to ambiguity or incongruity of postnatal gender identity differentiation. There may be a special disposition in the organization of the brain toward the acquisition of roles and their dissociation in the manner of multiple personality or fugue state. In either case, a prenatal disposition is probably insufficient in itself, and needs to be augmented by postnatal social history.[10]

Thus the authors are careful to appeal again to their interactionist theory of sex differences, being cautious about overstressing the hormonal.

The Overriding Effects of Androgen. According to Money, male and female hormones are not equally significant in affecting "the hypothalamic pathways that will subsequently influence certain aspects of sexual behavior." Rather, it is the presence or absence of androgen that is most determinative. Until about the sixth week after conception, the embryo does not begin to differentiate sexually. (Or, as some would phrase it, all human fetuses are female up to this point.) Biological femaleness results from the *absence* of androgenic hormones. Money and Ehrhardt state it this way: "In the particular context of neonatal (or prenatal) hormonal effects, the antithesis of androgen is not estrogen, but nothing."[11] In Money's opinion, androgen regulates both the development of external genitalia and certain forms of behavior and intelligence. As far as the external organs are concerned, "feminine differentiation requires only the absence of androgen. It does not require the presence of a feminizing substance."[12]

Likewise the presence or absence of androgen affects behavior. Here again, "the antithesis of androgen is not estrogen, but no gonadal hormone at all—in fact no substitute whatever."[13] The absence of androgen either at the prenatal critical period or at other critical periods

of development (whether absent normally as in the genetic
female, or artificially through castration or antiandrogen
treatment in the genetic male) results in a brain "organized" to produce so-called feminine behavior and response. Thus it is Money and Ehrhardt's contention that
there is a fetal organization of neural structures essentially
of the hypothalamus, which makes parts of the brain essentially male or female. Portions of the fetal brain affect
not only hormonal and reproductive functions but also
behavior—especially lovemaking and coitus. However,
other behavior patterns are affected as well. For example,
Money and Ehrhardt cite so-called tomboy conduct. Their
causal explanation of tomboyism is grounded in fetal hormonal activity.

The most likely hypothesis to explain the various features of
tomboyism in fetally masculinized genetic females is that their
tomboyism is a sequel to a masculinizing effect on the fetal brain.
This masculinization may apply specifically to pathways, most
probably in the limbic system or paleocortex, that mediate dominance assertion (possibly in association with assertion of exploratory and territorial rights) and, therefore, manifests itself in com-
petitive energy expenditure.[14]

Originally the authors also made a positive correlation,
although tenuously, between increased fetal androgen
and increased I.Q. Money and Ehrhardt stated that there
is "some preliminary evidence to suggest that an abnor-
mally elevated prenatal androgen level, whether in genetic
males or females, enhances I.Q."[15] The authors claim that
this finding of I.Q. elevation in females exposed to excessive androgen was not a finding that was looked for. It was
a "serendipitous one" and one that also occurred in genetic males similarly exposed.*

*Ehrhardt has subsequently discredited the I.Q. findings herself.
In conjunction with Susan Baker, she has stated that it is highly
unlikely that increase in I.Q. is an effect of hormone treatment.
Rather it is a construct of inadequately matched controls. See
Anke A. Ehrhardt and Susan W. Baker, "Prenatal Androgen, In-
telligence, and Cognitive Sex Differences," in R. C. Friedman,
R. M. Richart, and R. L. Vande Wiele, eds., *Sex Differences in
Behavior* (New York: Wiley, 1974).

In order to prove that androgen affects the kinds of
behavior referred to above, Money and Brennan cite
studies with two human control groups who were accidentally androgenized *in utero.* The first was done on
a group of girls with the so-called adrenogenital syndrome.
The second study researched another group of girls with
the progestin-induced syndrome. (These syndromes are
explained further in the following pages.) Money and
Brennan connect both syndromes with transsexualism.
Basically, their words speak for themselves.

Tomboyishness in the progestin-induced and the adrenogenital
syndromes is a matter chiefly of physical energy expenditure and
outdoor athletic interests of the type customarily assigned to
boys. . . . This description of tomboyishness in childhood applies
fairly well to what the transsexual patients reported of themselves,
except that they grew up to discover they were lesbian-oriented
in their erotic disposition. One may, therefore, legitimately pose
the question of whether a tendency to tomboyish energy expenditure is not a primary trait in incipient female transsexuals, and one
that somehow facilitates the subsequent differentiation of a transsexual gender identity, provided various prerequisite postnatal
conditions . . . are encountered.[16]

Always careful, however, never to stress the biological side
of the coin alone, Money and Ehrhardt explain transsexual
development further by reverting to their interactionist
approach.

These traits may interact with postnatal social influences that shape
gender identity. Prenatally induced tomboyish traits, for example,
may make it easy for a genetic female to have not simply a tomboyish version of a feminine gender identity, but, if postnatal
circumstances so conspire, to differentiate a transsexual gender
identity and want a sex reassignment. The same might happen in
reverse for a genetic male.[17]

One may legitimately ask, however, how many female-
to-constructed-male transsexuals have either the progestin-
induced or the adrenogenital syndromes and how many
"tomboys" become transsexuals. Anticipating these questions and others like them, Money and Brennan admit

that, after all is said and done, "The most economical conclusion to draw from all the foregoing is that female transsexualism is a disorder of psychosexual differentiation
and is, regardless of its still unknown etiology, a psychologic manifestation."[18]

"Monkey See, Mammals Do." Much of Money's theorizing
concerning hormonal activity *in utero*, specifically with
respect to androgen, is based on animal experimentation.
Rats, hamsters, and monkeys, in particular, who were an-
drogenizd prenatally or neonatally, were studied under
mating conditions.

Citing the so-called masculine behavior of the prenatally
androgenized, hermaphroditic, female rhesus monkey,
Money and Ehrhardt state that her activities are reminiscent of tomboyism in girls. Like male monkeys, she shows
an increased amount of play initiation, rough-and-tumble
activity, chasing behavior, and playful threats. It is important here to note that "tomboyism" is never specifically
defined by Money, but always described in this kind of behavior. Mounting play is increased compared to other female monkeys, who present hind-end stances of sexual
invitation. Moreover, the patterns of mounting of such
masculinized monkeys also take on a masculine stance. All
of this is by way of demonstrating that the human clinical
syndromes concerning the influence of prenatal hormones
on gender behavior that are reviewed in *Man & Woman,
Boy & Girl*, have their counterparts in experimental animal
data. The authors caution, however, that these prenatal
hormones only set "the direction" which later interaction
with the social environment completes. They also caution
that in the final analysis, "little can be said regarding the
various structures of the brain that supposedly are subject
to prenatal hormonal organizing influences."

A Two-Way Critique. On a scientific level, several commentators have made major criticisms of gender identity and
behavior theories that rely on animal findings, with particular reference to Money's work. Ann Oakley, for one,

has stressed that animal research can only be applied hypo-
thetically to humans. Particularly in the field of sexual
behavior, she has noted that animals are subject to a much
more direct control mechanism than humans. Humans impose an additional control of learning.

Oakley cites Rose's work, which reached the conclusion
that although androgen may be significantly related to sexual behavior the social context of the monkeys themselves
is of great importance. For example, female rhesus monkeys injected with androgen show an increase in the
"male" practice of "mounting," but only if they are dominant members of their group to begin with before they
are injected. If subordinate females are injected, the
incidence of mounting behavior remains the same. Likewise, when dominant male monkeys who secrete testosterone in excess are placed in a social environment
where their dominance is not recognized, they become inferior members of the group and their testosterone output
lessens considerably.[19]

Thus it can be seen that the role of sex hormones in
generating signals that are relayed to the brain and converted into sexual arousal is clearly outweighed by environmental factors. In the latter example of the male monkeys
(to reverse the Freudian adage), it is destiny that determines anatomy, or at least determines hormone levels.
The testosterone output itself varied enormously depending on how the male monkey perceived his environment
and his place in it. Further research has shown how aggressive behavior in animals is significantly dependent on how
it is reinforced. Mice and dogs can be trained to relative
passivity by altering the type of reinforcement that aggressive behavior is usually activated by. But in the animal
world, study of the way in which environmental factors
may be able to affect behavior has been neglected.[20]

Elizabeth Adkins has pointed to a number of factors in
the animal experiments that make human comparisons or
extrapolations from animal data highly dubious. She reinforces the role of environment and its impact on rhesus
monkeys. Researchers have found that there are discrepan-
cies between those animals reared in the laboratory and

those reared in the wild. The latter are less aggressive, and thus Adkins suggests that some of the sex differences and early hormone effects may have been influenced by the artificial social and physical environment of the monkeys.[21]

Furthermore, the majority of the animal experiments use copulating behavior as an example of sex differences. None of the human experiments do.[22]

The primary effect of early exposure to androgen in the female rat is that the capacity to display lordosis (the receptive posture) is impaired. Yet there is no human behavior homologous to lordosis, and in fact human female sexual behavior is not particularly controlled by sex hormones at all.[23]

It is also difficult to sex-type animal behavior from one species to another, since there is marked species differentiation. Adkins cites Kleiman's findings, which showed that in some mammals, males are more aggressive than females; in others, females are more aggressive. Thus it is very difficult to generalize anything about animal behavior, whether within a species, or cross species. The analogies to human behavior are all the more difficult to make.

What do such findings ultimately indicate about the pertinence of animal behavior in assessing human behavior? Humans, to an even greater degree, impose additional controls on any hormonal experiments—that of sociocultural factors in general—and it is the human ability to learn and to rationalize, or even to be affected by sociocultural factors that are not necessarily learned, that make generalizations from other species difficult and of dubious value.

The analogy becomes increasingly ridiculous when we add that the nonhuman female primate has no hymen, menopause, [or] artificial feeding bottle. . . . The males of these species are dominant, aggressive, and show no desire or ability to give the female pleasure. This is equally absurd in its application to human culture, enabling the patriarchal world to be supported in its very foundation, justifying the aggressive acts of the male, in the bedroom, by reference to the jungle, and providing a rationale for aggressive acts in the distinctly human world of social, economic, and political affairs.[24]

We might also add here that as it is absurd to extrapolate human data from animal activity in the jungle, it is as absurd to extrapolate such data from animals in cages.

The only human contexts where the effects of outside androgen increase in females could be studied were the progestin-induced syndrome and the adrenogenital syndrome. Money and Ehrhardt studied both groups. In the first case, ten girls had been androgenized accidentally *in utero* as a result of the drug progestin, which their mothers took during pregnancy. In the adrenogenital syndrome, the adrenal cortex in the normal XX female fails to synthesize cortisone and, instead, releases an incomplete product that has the biological masculinizing properties of androgen. Money and Ehrhardt studied a group of fifteen girls with this syndrome whose androgen level was reduced gradually after birth. They ranged in age from four to sixteen years. In both groups (the progestin-induced and adrenogenital), each girl's androgen excess levelled off postnatally. They developed normal-looking female genitalia and appearance, and they were raised as females. However, Money and Ehrhardt found, in contrast to a control group of females who had not been excessively androgenized *in utero*, that they showed so-called opposite sex behavior—e.g., tomboyism, rough-and-tumble play.

Elizabeth Adkins has asked, however, if this is the only interpretation that can be made. Upon closer examination, she finds many problems with the method and design used by the experimenters. First of all, the adrenogenital girls had been treated with cortisone since infancy, which itself can have behavioral effects that would differentiate these girls from others. Adrenogenital girls who were not receiving cortisone were never tested. More importantly, parental treatment may have produced less sex-typed behavior, since such parents may have been more willing to tolerate "tomboyish" actions because they knew their girls were different. Most significant, Adkins states that what then was looked upon as deviant girlish behavior is now the norm.[25]

Finally, observers have pointed out that human hormone levels, as well as animal hormone levels, vary according to environmental circumstances. For example, many forms of stress have been correlated with a drop in testosterone.[26] "Moreover, hormone levels in a given individual vary according to environmental circumstances (a study of American soldiers in Vietnam, for example, showed a sharp drop in testosterone levels); we are apparently dealing with a fluctuating process, not a fixed state."[27]

Aside from the critical commentary that has already been directed at Money's work on sex differences from a scientific level, there is a more philosophical critique that can be made at this point. Money and Ehrhardt's statements about the "overriding effects of androgen" have strong suggestions of Aristotelian/Thomistic biology. In Aristotle and Thomas, the male principle was seen to be the active power of generation and the female principle the passive power, or worse, the totally nonaffecting power (read nonpower or even nonbeing). According to Thomas Aquinas:

Among perfect animals the active power of generation belongs to the male sex, and the passive power to the female. . . . As regards the individual nature, woman is defective and misbegotten, for the active force in the male seed tends to the production of a perfect likeness in the masculine sex; while the production of woman comes from defect in the active force or from some material indisposition, or even from some external influence; such as that of a south wind which is moist, as the Philosopher observes.[28]

Money and Erhardt say much the same thing in the language they choose to describe the power of androgens: "the antithesis of androgen is not estrogen, but nothing." In Money's theories of sex differences, androgen is the activating principle—"feminine differentiation requires *only* the *absence* of androgen. It does not require the *presence* of a feminizing substance." (Italics mine.) However, it is not only estrogen, or other female hormones such as progesterone, that are said to be passively present. What remains obscured in Money and Ehrhardt's work is the initial female development of all embryos.

Money's "overriding effects of androgen" statements

can be thrown into bolder relief by contrasting his words
with those of endocrinologist Estelle Ramey, who phrases
the "androgen principle" in this way:

For the little it is worth as commentary on Adam's Rib, it is the female sex that is primal. The early embryo is female until the fifth
or sixth week of fetal life. A testicular inductor substance must be
generated at this point to suppress the growth of ovaries. No ovarian
inductor is required for female differentiation because all mammalian embryos of either genetic sex have the innate capacity for
femaleness. Eve and not Adam appears to have been the primeval
human that God had in mind.[29]

This wording projects quite a different picture than
Money and Ehrhardt's assertion about the insignificance
of estrogen. Indeed Ramey presents the initial female
momentum of sex differentiation as being so powerful
that it must be "suppressed." Warren Gadpaille, M.D.,
states the same principle in this way:

Nature's prime disposition is to produce females; maleness only
results from something added—androgen. In the absence of androgens, whether the fetus is of XX or XY genotype, differentiation
will proceed as female (though in the genotype XY in mammalian
species at least, ovaries will not differentiate). The converse is not
true; the absence of ovaries, and thus of estrogenic and progestinic
substances, does not interfere with female internal and external sex
structure development though such individuals will naturally be
infertile.[30]

Thus initial embryonic female differentiation is so powerful that even without the presence of female hormones,
female internal and external sex structure will result
whether in an XX or XY genotype. Furthermore, as Eileen
van Tassell has pointed out, the male needs the X chromosome in order to survive. There is no YO chromosomal
anomaly. The female, however, does not need a second X,
and XO females have been born and survived.[31]

    Both Ramey and Gadpaille's statements suggest that, in
opposition to Money and Ehrhardt's interpretations, it
would be more correct to say that genetic XX-ness is the

primordially activating substance. As Robert Stoller has said: "The genital anatomic fact is that, embryologically speaking, the penis is a masculinized clitoris; the neurophysiological fact is that the male brain is an androgenized female brain."[32]

Why is it then that Money and his associates have not pointed out that it is essentially a female anatomy and a female brain that sets the course of biological development that male hormones *only* turn in a different direction? If there is a biological basis or force for masculine and feminine behavior, as Money asserts, which sets "the direction" but not the extent of sexual behavior and psychosexual differentiation, then this biological force may be initially female. Or more importantly, why pick an arbitrary period of androgen onset, and speculate that this is *the* critical period when the equally critical period might be the "original" fetal female state?

In the book *Sexual Signatures*, Money has taken note of what he and Patricia Tucker call the "Eve base view." (It is significant that this interpretation appears in Money's more popularized work on sex differences, and not in *Man & Woman, Boy & Girl.*)

When it comes to male and female, the Bible tells of Adam as the base with something—a rib—taken away to make Eve. In the light of modern research you might take Eve as the base and think of something—male hormone—added to make Adam, or you could keep Adam as the base with something—again male hormone—decreased to make Eve. We have adopted the Eve base view, and will refer to the something that must be added for male differentiation as the Adam principle.[33]

It is certainly not evident throughout *Man & Woman, Boy & Girl* that Money and Ehrhardt have "adopted the Eve base view." Nor does Money follow through on the statement in view of his belief about the "overriding effects of androgen."[34]

Money's use of *masculine, feminine, tomboy, sissy* is revealing. The language of *masculinization* and *feminization* is applied equally to biologizing processes and psychosocial processes. The explanation of tomboyism stands out here very strikingly. For example, Money states: "The most likely hypothesis to explain the various features of tomboyism in fetally masculinized genetic females is that tomboyism is a sequel to a masculinizing effect on the fetal brain."[35]

In several places, Money talks about genetic males and females failing to develop normal *masculine* or *feminine* gender identities. Obviously, Money and his associates accept the stereotypes to some extent. To consistently term assertive and rough-and-tumble behavior on the part of girls *tomboyish* and to persist in naming certain behavioral qualities as *masculine* or *feminine* is to support patriarchal history's assertion that such behavior and qualities *are* and *should be* sex-specific. Here the language of inadequate science becomes subtly transferred to the language of ethics.

While it is true that many cultures define certain behaviors, personality characteristics, tasks, and activities as male or female, masculine or feminine (a point that Money and associates highlight), these same cultures define masculinity and femininity in vastly different ways, emphasizing various qualities, interests, and occupations as sex-linked. (Anthropologists such as Mead, Malinowski, and Devereux have written extensively on this subject.) It appears that the language of masculinity and femininity varies so widely throughout the world that the only reason for maintaining it seems to be an implicit belief that societies must link some behaviors and qualities to biological sex in order to be orderly and functional. This, as will be developed later, is Money's contention (within suitable boundaries of flexibility).

GENDER IDENTITY DEVELOPMENT COMPARED TO DEVELOPMENT OF NATIVE LANGUAGE

A third main point in Money's theory of sex differences is an analogy with language. Money and Tucker remark that it is no accident that the years of language develop-

ment (the first few years after birth) are also the years of
gender identity formation.

> You were born wired for language, so to speak, but not programmed
> for any particular language. . . . The environmental trigger that
> enabled you to start talking was the use of language by those around
> you during that critical language-learning period, the first few years
> after birth. It was the interaction between your prenatally pro-
> grammed disposition for language and the postnatal, socially pro-
> grammed language signals you heard that made it possible. You
> couldn't have become a talking person unless somebody talked a
> language to you. Furthermore, the language that was talked to you
> then put its mark on the way you could think ever after. It becomes
> your native language and will always be your native language, even
> if you never use it afterward.[36]

In the same way, Money and Tucker talk about the development of gender identity. Supposedly, persons are
born with "something that was ready to become your
gender identity. You were wired but not programmed
for gender in the same sense that you were wired but
not programmed for language."[37]

The analogy between development of native language
and formation of gender identity is flawed. First of all,
Money confuses a general ability to speak any language,
depending upon cultural factors, with a specific ability to
differentiate according to one gender only, i.e., either the
so-called masculine or feminine gender. According to
Money, as we have seen, gender identity is predisposed
by prenatal, rather specific, hormonal factors and later
added to by postnatal environmental influences. It is quite
a different thing to say that one is "wired" for language
and that one is "wired" for gender. While we are not
"wired" for any particular language, as Money readily admits, we are "hormonally wired" for a specific gender
identity—within flexible limits of the stereotype (if all goes
well).

A more suitable analogy would be that we are "wired"
to exercise a variety of behavioral qualities in the same
way that we are "wired" to speak a variety of languages,
both very dependent on postnatal learning and cultural

factors. If Money simply said that we are "wired" to develop some sexual identity, i.e., some awareness of ourselves as sexual beings, then there would be no argument with him. It is ironic that Money should choose the analogy of native language when, in other instances, he has remained so insensitive to his own "syntactic exploitation."

THE "LOCKING TIGHT" OF GENDER IDENTITY

If biology begins the program of gender identity, social factors set the direction of that behavior in an even more determined way. In Money's work, the gender of assignment and rearing transcends all other determinants. He cites instances of children with identical genotypes, hormones, gonads, and other internal structures, some of whom were reared as girls and others as boys. In almost every instance the child came to regard her or himself as female or male, depending on the way in which she or he was reared. The gender of rearing remained, even in the face of contradictory pubertal changes. Most dramatic of all are cases in which even the external genitalia were obviously more similar to the opposite sex than the child was assigned to and in which she/he was reared. Even in these cases, gender identity remained unequivocably that of assignment and rearing.

Money is very specific about the critical period for gender identity—that is, between the ages of twelve and eighteen months—asserting that gender identity is pretty well fixed by the age of eighteen months. In the case of hermaphrodites, "It is ill-advised to impose a sex reassignment on a child in contradiction of a gender identity already well advanced in its differentiation—which means that the age ceiling for an imposed reassignment is, in the majority of cases, around eighteen months."[38] This is so, because child-rearing in our culture is sexually distinctive, and from the day that an infant is picked up out of a crib, that child begins to get gender identity signals (by the way she/he is touched, spoken to, etc.).

The minute you were born, society took over. When the drama of
your birth reached its climax, you were promptly greeted with
the glad ritual cry, "It's a boy!" or "It's a girl!" depending on
whether or not those in attendance observed a penis in your crotch.
. . . The label "boy" or "girl," however, has tremendous force as
a self-fulfilling prophecy, for it throws the full weight of society
to one side or the other as the newborn heads for the gender identity fork. . . . Parents react differently to the signal "son" or "daughter" from the first moment.[39]

There are some exceptions, of course, to this age ceiling,
but this is due to confused gender-rearing practices. For
example, when parents are given conflicting diagnoses of
their infant's sex, perhaps by different physicians at different times, they may express their uncertainty in confused gender-rearing practices. But on the whole, in the
"normal" (read culturally prescribed) process of gender
identity and role development, the "locking tight" of this
process occurs at an incredibly early age. Furthermore,
according to Money, once more girls are defined by the
absence of a penis, not by the presence of female genitalia.
This corresponds to his theory of prenatal development,
where it is the absence of androgen, not the presence of
estrogen, that is responsible for female differentiation.
    This "locking tight" of gender identity almost takes
on the tone of a new "natural-law" theory in Money.
"When the gender identity gate closed behind you it
locked tight. You knew in the very core of your consciousness that you were male or female. Nothing short of disas-
ter could ever shake that conviction . . ."[40] Freudian "natural law" dictated that anatomy was destiny, and Erik
Erikson, a more contemporary Freudian, polished this
"simplism" into an inner- and outer-space analogy, where
the "inner" sexual apparatus of the female and the "outer"
sexual apparatus of the male were seen to be the prime
determinants of feminine "inner"-directed and masculine
"outer"-directed behavior. However, Money has reversed
the classical "anatomy is destiny" theory into a "neo-
natural law" theory of social determinism. He continues:
"Once a sex distinction has worked or been pressured into

the nuclear core of your gender schema, to dislodge it is to threaten you as an individual with destruction. The gate is as firmly locked there as it is on your chromosomes and gonads."[41] Obviously, no one would deny that socialization is a very powerful factor, but to make it deterministic, as Money does, is to make it absolute and immutable. He and his associates have constructed a pseudometaphysics, which derives its "natural" value from societal processes instead of from classical "nature." In effect, they have created a new theory of the social "nature" of sex-role differences that is just as immutable as older biological natural law theories.

Money's dismissal of the importance of social influence after the stage of early childhood demonstrates that he has not looked seriously at authors who write about socialization. As Berger and Luckmann point out: "Everything that has been said so far on socialization implies the possibility that subjective reality can be transformed. To be in society already entails an ongoing process of modification of subjective reality."[42] Money's response to this would probably be that while relative transformations are possible the "core" of one's gender identity schema is "locked tight." However, as Berger and Luckmann state: "there are instances of transformation that appear total if compared with lesser modifications."[43] They refer to such transformation as "alterations," and assert that they "radically reassign reality accents."

The "radical reassignment of reality accents" of "core gender identity" has become a lived reality in the past and present history of feminism. However, Money does not allow this history or its consequences to affect his "core gender identity" theories and their immutability. If women had not been able to alter the nuclear "core" of our gender programming, we would not be doing many of the things that we are. One of the primary tenets of the women's movement has been that so-called gender identity differences are not natural or immutable. And as such, they are amenable to change. However, as *Time* magazine reported: "Despite his evidence of the importance of environment in molding sex roles, Money holds out little hope to feminists that there can be significant breakdown of sex-role stereotypes in the current generation of adults."[44] What Money does not see is that the hope of feminism is already being realized in feminists themselves, who are living contradictions of everything that Money is saying about the immutability of "core gender identity."

Obviously, the theory that "core" gender identity is "locked tight" by the age of eighteen months has utmost relevance for causation theories of transsexualism. It enables Money to suggest that transsexual gender identity is possibly fixed at a very early age.

FLEXIBLE STEREOTYPES

Although Money's final position on gender identity appears to be ethically neutral, it has profound social and ethical consequences, especially with respect to the whole issue of transsexualism. In the last chapter of *Sexual Signatures*, Money and Tucker begin by stating that the stereotyped differences between the sexes will always remain. They censure both the right and the left for respectively wanting to keep the stereotypes rigidly circumscribed or wanting to abolish them altogether. (Feminists might justifiably wonder which leftist movement has ever wanted to abolish sex-role stereotypes altogether.) Seemingly, they advocate the *via media*.

Many of the pioneers maintain that the stereotyped differences between the sexes should be done away with, and many nonpioneers fear that relaxing gender stereotypes will do away with all differences and homogenize the sexes. Both groups are tilting at windmills. As long as there is a human race, there almost certainly will be differences between the sexes in sexual behavior, work, and play.[45]

What they stand for is flexibility. Individuals must "bring more flexibility into the cultural stereotypes so that those who are growing up today need not be handicapped by

having obsolete sex distinctions driven into the core of
their gender schemas by the pressure of stereotypes that
are unnecessarily rigid."[46] Nevertheless, the stereotypes
themselves should remain. Abolishing them would violate
Money's canon that socialization is destiny.

In *Sexual Signatures*, Money and Tucker assert: "The
healthy society is one that tolerates experimentation with
a variety of adaptive responses within its stereotypes."[47]
The major criticism I would make of this "adaptive responses" or "flexibility" position, is that a "flexible stereotype" is a contradiction in terms. Webster's *New Colle-
giate Dictionary* defines *stereotype* as "to repeat without
variation." A stereotype that admits a "variety of adaptive
responses" within it is no longer a stereotype. A fixed pattern admits no flexibility or else it is no longer fixed. Furthermore, it should also be noted that on a historical level,
it is within the nature of stereotypes to give the illusion of
flexibility.

Interestingly, Money and Tucker state: "People can no
more be expected to decode behavior that has been locked
into the core of their gender schemas than a Chinese woman
whose feet were bound in childhood could be expected to
walk naturally."[48] It would seem that the authors do not
realize that stereotypes do mutilate personal development,
just as foot-binding mutilated Chinese women's development. To advocate a *flexibility within the range of stereotypes*, yet not do away with the stereotypes completely, is
similar to giving a woman whose feet have been bound and
mutilated crutches or a chair to be carried in, yet not the
ability to completely and freely move about.

The language of flexibility is deceiving. On the one
hand, it gives Money's biologism and social determinism
the appearance of openness and variability. But, in fact, he
makes a hidden and rather subtle ontological assumption
that social change *cannot* affect the core of gender identity
and is definitely limited to undefined parameters of "flexibility."

However, the *cannot* changes to *should not*, the *ontol-*

ogy changes to *ethics.* From the position that adult individuals cannot alter the nuclear core of their gender
schemas, Money moves to the stance that "if society or
your early environment drove that distinction into the
core of your gender schema so that it has become an integral support for your gender identity, society has no
right to demand that you drive it out again."[49] Would
Money assert that if "society" has driven racist attitudes
into the "core" of one's identity, it has no right to expect
that one should drive them out?

Money's ethics thus boil down to prescribing the con-
tinuation of sexist roles, modified in some undefined and
arbitrarily "flexible" manner. In fact, the sexist nature
of his ethical prescriptions becomes evident in his advice
about child-rearing practices.

The ideal is for a child to have parents who consistently reciprocate
one another in their dealings with that child. Then a five-year-old
daughter is able to go through the stage of rehearsing flirtatious
coquetry with her father, while the mother appropriately gives recip-
rocal directives as to where the limits of rivalry lie; conversely for
boys.[50]

This is an incredible piece of sexist advice, advocating
some of the worst aspects of sexual stereotypes. Why
should a five-year-old girl be encouraged to rehearse "flirtatious coquetry" with her father while her mother stands
on the sidelines permitting such behavior within suitable
"limits of rivalry"? Once more, little girls are taught to
identify with men and men's ideals of them while, at the
same time, learning to see other women as their rivals for
male affection.

In conclusion, what does this advocacy of stereotyping,
albeit "flexible," mean for transsexuals? If people not only
"cannot" but "should not" change their core gender identity, and if "society has no right" to demand that they do,
then transsexualism becomes an adequate and morally
right solution to so-called gender identity dissatisfaction
and confusion. In this perspective, if one cannot adjust the

mind to the body, it becomes perfectly reasonable to adjust the body to the mind. Since core gender identity is fixed by age two, in Money's schema, then the body and not the psyche must be changed.

CHAPTER III

"Mother's

Feminized Phallus"

or Father's

Castrated Femme?

T HE TITLE of this chapter is
meant to suggest the distance between the alleged dominant mothers blamed in the psychological literature for
causing transsexualism, and the truly dominating medical/
psychiatric fathers who *create* artificial women (femmes).
The distance is great. "Blaming the mother," in the psychological literature, which proposes that transsexualism is
the result of "too much mother and too little father," obscures the real cause of transsexualism—patriarchy and the
legions of therapeutic fathers who create transsexuals according to their man-made designs and specifications.

This chapter will consider major psychological theories
about the causes of transsexualism and suggest a more fundamental cause. It is my contention that all of the causal
theories that have been discussed so far accept patriarchal
norms of masculinity and femininity. Many psychological
theories, for example, measure the transsexuals' conformity to, and deviation from, these stereotypes during
their process of maturing, or they assess family interactions, such as "dominant mother and absent father,"

"mother-son symbiosis," only within the context of these same stereotypes. I believe that the First Cause, that which sets other causes of transsexualism in motion (such as family stereotypes and interactions), is a patriarchal society, which generates norms of masculinity and femininity. Uniquely restricted by patriarchy's definitions of masculinity and femininity, the transsexual becomes body-bound by them and merely rejects one and gravitates toward the other. The sexual organs and the body of the opposite sex come to incarnate the essence of the desired gender identity and role,and thus it is not primarily the body that is desired, but what a female or male body means in this society.

According to these psychological theories, if the individual fails to adjust to his native body and role, then she/he should be treated. If all forms of personal and family therapy fail to adjust the would-be transsexual's mind to the would-be transsexual's body, then the *individual* answer is to adjust the transsexual's body to his mind. In this perspective, hormonal treatment and surgery become a humane and logical solution to the transsexual problem. Meanwhile, the social factors that continue to reinforce transsexualism go "untreated." And transsexual treatment and surgery becomes the ultimate "Individual Solution."

To understand how sexual stereotypes are the First Cause of transsexualism, we should look at how transsexuals think and speak of themselves and how they "prove" they are "real" transsexuals by "passing" as masculine or feminine. In fact, they must prove they are real before they are accepted for treatment. Thus the role of the medical-psychiatric establishment in reinforcing sex-role stereotypes is significant, and one that affects the deepest dimensions of the transsexual issue.

PSYCHOLOGY CONSTRUCTS THE CONSTRUCTED FEMALE

Robert Stoller, a psychoanalyst, has probably done the major work in developing psychological theories about the

causes of transsexualism in a study of nine cases of male-
to-constructed-female transsexualism.[1] Here he develops
his basic conditioning approach, which he refers to as
"mother's feminized phallus" or what can be more simply
phrased as "blaming the mother." In summary, Stoller attributes male transsexualism to a classic mother-child relationship that occurs within the context of a disturbed marriage. In the clinical cases as he relates them, the mothers
were generally unhappy women, who often in early life
wanted to be males themselves, and who in their marriages
were dominant and assertive. Indeed, Stoller claims that
such mothers suffer from a marked case of classic Freudian
penis envy. The child serves the mother as the phallus for
which she has supposedly yearned. The child himself does
not pass through the "normal" male formative stage of
separation from the mother and consequent individuation.
Masculinity is not developed in the transsexual boy, and
there is no fear of castration (which Freud posited as necessary to developing masculinity). Transsexuals' fathers
were allegedly passive men who were consistently absent
from their homes or, if present, were as good as absent.
They exerted little influence on their sons and had practically no father-son rapport. Given this state of affairs, the
mother turned to her son, for continuing fulfillment, con-
centrating totally on him and encouraging the boy to identify with her and with her body by constant physical contact (involving continuous holding and touching, carrying
and cuddling).

According to Stoller, given this extreme mother-son
symbiosis, which sometimes lasted into prepubertal years,
the boy began to feel that he was a woman despite the evidence of his senses that he was anatomically male. Having
developed a core feminine gender identity in the early
years of life, the boy cannot develop, later on, along culturally dictated masculine lines. Stoller sums up his evidence from the clinical case studies in this way:

The similarities of the findings are probably beyond coincidence; it
appears, as has been noted often before in other males with strong
feminine identifications, that the femininity of these males is the

result of too much mother and too little father. These data do not point to a genetic, hormonal, or other physiological element significantly contributing to the boy's gender identity. . . . My thesis, to be better tested in the future, is that the degree of femininity that develops in a boy and the forms it takes will vary according to exactly (not approximately) what is done to him in earliest childhood.[2]

Stoller goes on to state the importance of searching for "detailed descriptions" of these mother-son relationships. He emphasizes that while there are obviously males who have had strong symbiotic relationships with their mothers in early childhood and who do not emerge as transsexuals, the quality of the symbiotic relationship was quite different in the nontranssexual cases. Here the mother probably did not have the same kind of *physical* relationship with her male child. And Stoller does relate, "in detail," in case study after case study, the physical interactions of mothers and sons—sons who were permitted to sleep with their mothers well into prepuberty, sons who had visual and tactile access to their mothers' bodies up to a relatively late age, as well as mothers and sons who were continually in each other's presence in other ways. The fathers of these boys were weak, passive, and distant, and fatherly influence was usually absent in all ways. Most of these marriages were held together in name only. Divorce was rare in transsexual families. However, although parents existed under the same roof, the marriages were sexless and generally emotionally empty.

In his latest book, *The Transsexual Experiment*, Stoller also reveals a study of ten cases of female transsexuals. While there are differences between male and female transsexuals, Stoller again focuses on blaming the mother.[3] The female infant, who lacks feminine graces and is not "cuddly," has a mother unable to show any emotional tone due to depression. Again the father is rather passive and has little or no emotional rapport with his wife and child. As a result, the girl is used by both parents as a father-substitute to alleviate the mother's depression. Her acting out of masculine characteristics is encouraged by both parents, and becomes self-perpetuating as a sense of masculine identity.

"Blaming the mother" appears in theories even beyond the psychological realm:

Typically, the mother keeps this male infant to herself. She gratifies his wishes instantly whenever possible. She enjoys and encourages actions which keep the child close to her and discourages attempts to move away. However, as the child grows, the mother may not be able to handle aggressive and active play and directs the male child to quieter activities and to quieter companions, possibly girls. Gradually the child learns that feminine actions bring a positive response from the mother and other members of the family.[4]

These authors go on to state that such actions may even include cross-dressing as a female. They also discuss the absent father syndrome, either in fact or in effect.

John Money also cannot avoid the charge of "blaming the mother" in his discussion of transsexualism. He finds that all available evidence on the subject points to the conclusion that transsexualism is directed by "undercover signals from society, usually represented in early postnatal life by the mother."[5]

While accepting major premises of Stoller's theory of transsexualism in boys, Richard Green, a past associate of Stoller's at U.C.L.A., and a former student of John Money's, puts much less emphasis on certain psychoanalytic concepts, such as the symbolic meaning of the boy to his mother and her own supposed bisexuality. Green gives more weight to peer-group interaction. Thus his work, while certainly being primarily psychological, acknowledges socialization factors outside of the intrafamily sphere. "Blaming the mother," however, is a part of Green's theorizing. He agrees with Stoller that a mother's response, physical contact, perceptions, and time given to her son often contribute to transsexual development. The father again is an absent figure and, as the son's feminine proclivities develop, alienation between father and mother increases. The mother continues to encourage her son's cross-dressing while the emotional distance between father and son widens.

Green is also sympathetic to biological causes. "Currently the most provocative signpost is the linkage between prenatal male hormone levels and postnatal masculine activity."[6] However, as we noted in examining Money's work, biological and psychological theories go well together, and it is often difficult to decide where one leaves off and the other picks up.

Green takes a more positive approach in the questions he poses at the end of *Sexual Identity Conflict in Children and Adults.* "What if the social consequences of evolving in an atypical lifestyle were radically modified? Would the motivation for sex-change surgery be as great for males if the society were fully tolerant of their deviant sexuality?"[7] He continues:

A question to be answered though, would be the degree to which the desire for genital change in an adult male is derived secondarily from social sanctions against homosexuality or femininity, or springs primarily from a female identity. If from the former, requests for surgery might be related to the extent to which the culture becomes more tolerant.[8]

These questions, however, when combined with his former psychological hypotheses, seem contradictory. Significantly, they are raised in question form and parenthetically, whereas "blaming the mother," peer interaction, and hormonal factors all seem to have the full force of facts.

The syndrome of "blaming the mother" in each of these theories raises some fundamental critical responses. Most important, each of these theories of "blaming the mother" is indicative of a fundamental reversal. The biological and psychological theorists blame the mother for both female and male transsexualism. Neither asks who is actually transforming transsexual bodies into the desired sex and instructing them in the rudiments of cultural femininity and masculinity. The irony is that mothers are blamed, yet it is transsexual "father figures" (the fathers of the psychiatric and medical domains) who are performing the operations and coaching into roles. One way of perceiving this reversal is to view such "fathers" as "male mothers" who see themselves redeeming the biological mothers' defective handiwork, whether that defective process is regarded as biological (failing to give enough of the right hormone or giving too much of the wrong hormone *in utero*), or as psychological (failing to rear the child correctly).* The inherent irony here is that the mother is blamed when in fact it is the psychological and medical fathers who are the omnipresent agents of transsexualism. The agency of such medical and psychological fathers is much more certain and dominating than the doubtful and psychologized role of the supposed dominant mother. Without them, transsexualism would not be a reality.[9]

Are we to suppose that it is mainly the mother who is concerned with the stereotypical behavior of the child? All of these theorists who blame the mother for the transsexual behavior of their children do not even allude to studies indicating that fathers are usually more concerned with encouraging sex-typing than are mothers. These studies suggest that fathers play a very significant role in the gender identity development of their child, perhaps in the case of the transsexual even coercing the boy into masculine behavior which the child rejects because such behavior has been forced upon him.

Three other theories should be noted concerning the causes of transsexualism. N. Lukianovicz, like Stoller, raises the whole issue of castration anxiety as one possible cause of transsexualism. But, in contrast to Stoller, he maintains that the transsexual does possess castration fear. The male transsexual attempts to overcome the anxiety

---

*"Male mothering," discussed in Chapter I, is a very ancient and familiar theme in the history of patriarchal civilization in which men have attempted, in various ways, to supplant the role of women in mothering. There are religious male mothers who give spiritual rebirth in baptism; the Dr. Spocks and other child-rearing specialists who tell women the best means of bringing up their children; the male obstetricians who took over the function of midwifery and "deliver" the child into existence; and more recently the technocratic progenitors who are attempting to bring human life into existence through genetic technology with little or no female instrumentality.

of castration by creating an imaginary "phallic woman" and subsequently identifying with and becoming her. The fantasy of a "phallic woman" is a substitute for phallic exhibition, which is inhibited by castration anxiety.[10]

Another psychoanalytic explanation gives weight to separation anxiety. Transsexuals develop this anxiety early in life, before "object differentiation" occurs.

To alleviate this anxiety, the child resorts to a fantasy of symbiotic fusion with the mother. In this way, mother and child become one and the danger of separation is nullified. We believe this reparative fantasy to be the psychodynamic basis for transsexualism in the male, and the transsexual phenomena can be understood clinically as attempts to ward off any threats to the psychic fusion with the mother.[11]

In this interpretation, the transsexual literally *becomes* the mother. To sustain this fantasy, he attempts to reverse his anatomical sex. Ovesey and Person cite clinical evidence to support this causal hypothesis and distinguish between a transsexual's first experience of cross-dressing as opposed to a transvestite's. The transvestite often experiences sexual excitement in cross-dressing. For the transsexual, however, the mother's clothes "are a symbolic representation of the pregenital mother. Wearing them, he re-establishes the early symbiotic relationship with her. It is no surprise, therefore, that a frequent adult transsexual fantasy is of mothering, particularly mothering a girl child."[12]

Finally, we consider the psychological hypothesis of Henry Guze, who speaks of "experience deprivation" during critical periods of childhood development. Guze thinks that, as a rule, boys will psychologically develop in a feminine direction unless a male model is present in some way. "Thus a boy child is superficially more like a girl child or a woman until he reaches pubescence."[13] (Note the parallel here to prenatal biological male differentiation, in the sense that all fetuses are originally female until androgen activates male morphological development.) Guze seems to be saying that nature's disposition is to orient genetic males in a female behavioral direction until male role model influence is added. Thus, as Guze reiterates, "I should like to hypothesize that during the periods when a boy child is least developed in the masculine direction, he needs both contact and identification with a male in a manner that is not exploitative."[14] The same holds true for girl children, except that girls escape the severe gender problems, on the whole, that occur in the male.

In examining the various theories of psychological causation, one factor becomes very evident. All of them measure the degree of conformity to culturally defined norms of masculinity and femininity. In most of these theories, male transsexuals who were feminized and failed to become masculine were assessed by prevailing norms of masculinity and femininity. The psychological literature obviously regards this as not only deviant behavior but as undesirable for "healthy" male development. A negative judgment is attached to so-called feminine qualities expressed by boys and men. The stereotypes, the cultural norms of masculinity and femininity themselves, are never criticized.

If the stereotypes themselves are not confronted but are only frowned upon when acted out by persons of the "wrong" sex, then the origins of transsexualism will be individualized and psychologized. What will go unexamined is patriarchy's norms of masculinity and femininity and how these norms, if allowed to contain persons within such rigid boundaries, may generate such a phenomenon as transsexualism.

TRANSSEXUALISM AND SEX-ROLE STEREOTYPES

It is important to examine the web of patriarchally prescribed stereotypes that surround all facets of the transsexual issue: the way transsexuals speak about themselves and the reasons they give for wanting surgery; the accounts of family interaction; the gender identity clinic requirements that prescribe "passing" as masculine or feminine to "prove" transsexual status; psychological advice and treatment of adjudged child transsexuals; and testimony from acknowledged "experts" in the field, regarding the stereotypical behavior of transsexuals.

How transsexuals think and speak of themselves is very revealing. In preparation for this writing, I personally interviewed a sampling of fifteen transsexuals. In the interviews, thirteen of which were with pre- and postoperative male-to-constructed-female transsexuals, I consistently asked why they wanted to be women. How, in other words, did they define themselves as female? Most of the transsexuals responded in terms of the classic feminine stereotype. Some wanted to be women because all their lives they had "felt" they were women trapped in men's bodies. One expressed this "feeling" in terms of "absolute knowledge" as opposed to mere desire. More specifically, many transsexuals said they viewed themselves as passive, nurturing, emotional, intuitive, and the like. Very often, many expressed a preference for female dress and make-up. Others saw their feminine identification in terms of feminine occupations: housework, secretarial, and stewardess work. Some expressed feminine identification in terms of marriage and motherhood—wanting to "meet the right man," "have him take care of me," "adopt kids," and "bring them up." One expressed very definite views on child-rearing that were quite ironic in this context: "I would definitely teach my kids that boys should be boys and girls should be girls."

These kinds of overt stereotyped statements have been reiterated by many of the more well-known transsexuals (e.g., Jan Morris, Christine Jorgensen) who have been interviewed on the talk shows and in other media. Allen Raysdon, in the process of undergoing hormonal treatment in preparation for surgery, states: "When I was a child, all I could think about was the [girls'] clothes and parties and things and that I didn't like sports and fighting and things like that." He added that women are more emotional and sensitive; men are more cold and insensitive. Men play more active roles usually, he said, and called himself passive.[15] Paula, formerly Paul, Grossman has sketched a similar portrait of himself. Previously married and the father of three children, Grossman recently lost a test case in the New Jersey courts to postoperatively retain his former public-school teaching status. According to a newspaper reporter:

In many ways—and in the traditional sense of the word—Paula Grossman is extremely feminine. She is proud of her impressive bustline, a result of her monthly hormone shots. She has her hair done regularly at a beauty shop, and wears bright red lipstick and matching nail polish. ("I only wear eye-shadow at night.") She prefers dark sleeveless blouses with a single strand of pearls worn with tailored skirts. Her favorite shoes are Mary Janes, size 13.[16]

Sexual objectification becomes a recurring theme also in the interviews and case studies. A male prisoner who requested a sex-change operation revealed his stereotype of femininity to be at this level: "I have this problem, like all women do. I flirt a lot."[17] For others, prostitution becomes related to their new feminine status. Many, in order to pay the medical costs, turn to this source of income.* "Frequently, they cannot get jobs as women, or cannot keep them; the street becomes the breadwinner, and principal place of social contact."[18] Several transsexuals in my own survey were prostitutes both before as well as after their operations.

It is significant that very little of the transsexual literature has highlighted the stereotyping problem as either causally or therapeutically important. Very little notice has been paid to the fact that most transsexuals conform more to the feminine role than even the most feminine of natural-born women. One of the few exceptions to this is Thomas Kando's study, *Sex Change: The Achievement of Gender Identity among Feminized Transsexuals*.

THOMAS KANDO'S STUDY OF SEX CHANGE

Thomas Kando investigated seventeen postoperative male-to-constructed-female transsexuals who had received sur-

---

*Recently a male-to-constructed-female transsexual charged with prostitution had "her" case dismissed in New Orleans. It was found that "she" had been a man and, in Louisiana, only a natural-born woman can be convicted of prostitution. (*Ms.*, January 1978, p. 21.)

gery at the University of Minnesota Gender Services. His methods included open-ended interviews, structured questionnaires formally submitted and conducted in the hospital offices, and participant observation of the Minneapolis transsexual subculture, which included visits to bars, stripjoints, and nightclubs, "first to contact transsexuals known to circulate or to work there, later to fraternize and observe the milieu."[19] Kando also visited several transsexuals at home and thus became acquainted with their family contexts.

In contrast to the psychological and biological theorists, Kando spotlights the social problem immediately. "Unlike the feminists who argue that the social structure is unjust with respect to women and therefore needs reform, transsexuals decide to alter their own physical sex in order to legitimately conform to cultural expectations" (p. 5). He affirms that transsexuals aim primarily to achieve the desired sex roles and not merely the anatomy of the opposite sex. In answer to the question of what is the "ultimate criterion of being a woman," transsexuals emphasized mostly "social-psychological" criteria. (Ten out of seventeen mentioned such things as "being attracted to men," "being loved and needed by the family," and "behaving like a woman.") It is significant here that most of the transsexuals questioned did not see biological criteria, that is, the female organs themselves, as ultimate reasons for changing sex.

In examining the attitudes of these seventeen transsexuals, Kando compared them with "normal" females and males. Using such a comparison, he found that transsexuals are more what the culture expects women to be than are those who were born female. Kando measured this cultural conformity by using questionnaires that included a "masculinity-femininity" scale. The transsexuals were questioned in several areas:

1. *Attitudes toward cultural definitions of masculinity and femininity.* Certain questions measured the transsexuals' endorsement of society's dominant sex and gender norms. Male, females, and transsexuals were asked to agree

or disagree with normative statements such as: "Ultimately, a woman should submit to her husband's decisions." Here, Kando found that transsexuals were more conservative in their support of traditional sex-role ascriptions than either the men or the women (pp. 22–24).

2. *Role strain.* Transsexuals were asked about the conflict between the sex roles one is expected to play in society and the roles one is most willing and most able to play. Again, transsexuals experience very little role strain with respect to sex roles. In comparison, Kando noted that natural-born women experienced great role strain in relation to the cultural demands placed on them. Men experienced very little role strain. Thus although transsexuals acted out a feminine stereotype that was more feminine than most women, they were more like men in not experiencing much role strain.

These are interesting observations when compared with female-to-constructed-male transsexuals. Although female-to-constructed-male transsexuals conformed to many aspects of the masculine stereotype (in childhood they had no girlish interests, were "tomboys," etc.), a study of five female-to-constructed-male transsexuals revealed some significant data. Money and Brennan found that, "as compared to normal males, only two patients obtained an average rating for masculinity. The other three were rated less malelike in their responses than the normal male."[20] Although this writer interviewed only two female-to-constructed-male transsexuals, my assessment was that they were much less masculine than were the male-to-constructed-females feminine. Since roles have been male-created, and evidence points to the fact that men are relatively comfortable in their self-created masculine roles, then one would expect that male-to-constructed-female transsexuals would experience little role strain.

A person experiences role strain only if she or he has a self that is separate from the role. Put differently, role strain can be a healthy phenomenon. Using Peter Berger's definition of alienation as "the process whereby the dialectical relationship between the individual and his world is lost to consciousness,"[21] we might say that men and male-to-constructed-female transsexuals are most alienated. They *become* the role, and in so doing lose their individuality and self-definition. Berger's use of the word alienation, of course, is different from that of some existentialists who regard alienation as a basic split with the norms and mores of a culture. However, Berger's definition seems more adequate in understanding the deeper meaning of alienation—that is, "the individual 'forgets' that this world was and continues to be coproduced by him."[22] Women have not been so quick to "forget" that society has been created by men, and it is noteworthy that female-to-constructed-male transsexuals have also had a difficult time "forgetting," at least to some extent.[23]

A sampling of some of the statements of Kando's interviewees bears out the strong role conformity of male-to-constructed-female transsexuals.

Elizabeth: "I feel that everything should be distinctly masculine or feminine. My boy friend has to look like a real man."

Elinor: "The ultimate criterion of being a woman is being a good wife, being able to make a man happy."

Maryjo: "I feel that a man should make more than a woman!" (pp. 24–26).

This latter statement contradicted many of my own interviews where the "equal pay for equal work" ethic was generally subscribed to, not for any feminist reasons but because of the economic straits in which many transsexuals found themselves. Two transsexuals in my survey, R. and S., were willing to join "women's lib" only to this point. However, many of the transsexuals in Kando's sample seemingly would not even go this far in deviating from traditional feminine norms. Jane, for example, didn't want women to be in business at all. "Woman has no business being in business, unless there is something wrong with her. . . . Men should be the leaders" (p. 25).

Kando makes the important point also that, for transsexuals, most feminine socialization is anticipatory. Little postoperative coaching into feminine mannerisms and etiquette is required. One transsexual in Kando's study passed so effectively as a female that even "her" husband did not know. Not even the sex act betrayed "her" true identity (p. 41).

An occupational breakdown of Kando's sample revealed that among seventeen transsexuals interviewed, four proudly proclaimed being housewives and nothing but housewives. Of those who worked outside the home, most had stereotypical feminine jobs: secretaries (three), waitress (one), dancers (four), hairdressers or beauticians (two), actresses (two), university-affiliated research scientist (one).

As John Money has admitted: "Most transsexuals embrace the stereotype of their identity, even a person as sophisticated as Jan Morris."[24] Transsexuals "cling to the conventional stereotypes; they seek only the right to exchange one stereotype for the other."[25] Yet, as we have seen, Money does not follow through on this insight. He continues to encourage transsexual role behavior, which requires preoperative transsexuals to "pass" as feminine before they can be admitted for surgery.

Kando has evolved a typology of transsexuals that breaks down into four categories: housewife type (overwhelming orientation to straight, middle-class values and living); show business type (includes strippers, dancers, prostitutes); aspiring housewife type; and career woman type. My own data, as well as that of others, supports this breakdown.

The three factors most important to the transsexuals in Kando's study were marriage, nonemployment, and "passing." All male-to-constructed-female transsexuals shared middle-class ambitions as well as exhibitionistic tendencies. These findings confirmed my own interview data, particularly the factor of exhibitionism. Those male-to-constructed-female transsexuals I interviewed were only too happy to talk with me about all of the details of their transsexual odyssey, including a live demonstration of the results of surgery. This exhibitionism was in direct contrast to female-to-constructed-male transsexuals whom I contacted—who did not want to talk about their experiences, even in confidence (hence the inclusion of only two female-to-constructed-male transsexuals in my own interviewing).

Most of the transsexuals perceived their sexual relationships (even preoperatively) as heterosexual. One transsexual, Sally, phrased this in rather direct language. "I hate homos! I never wanted sex with them. I had homosexual affairs in grade school and in high school, but only with normals." As Kando summarizes, "transsexuals are reactionary, moving back toward the core-culture rather than away from it. They are the Uncle Toms of the sexual revolution. With these individuals, the dialectic of social change comes full circle and the position of greatest deviance becomes that of greatest conformity" (p. 145).

Thus far, I have noted overt acting out of stereotyped behavior by transsexuals. Kando's study, however, examines other not-so-commonly noted aspects of sex-role socialization and patriarchal values. For one thing, Kando noted transsexuals' attitudes toward women and men. Sally, for one, expressed a dislike toward women that was not expressed toward men. "Women . . . are more fearful of us than men. They fear that we'll be able to please a man better than they would, since we were men ourselves" (p. 41). Both male-to-constructed-females and female-to-constructed-male transsexuals strongly identify with men; this is one of the major similarities between both groups. A recent article on transsexualism in the *Boston Phoenix* quoted a female-to-constructed-male transsexual who, in speaking of "his" preoperative life as a woman said: "I had no hostilities toward men. I liked men—99% of my friends were men."[26]

Some of the transsexuals that Kando interviewed felt also that women were more intolerant of them than men. *Why* women tend to be less tolerant of the transsexual phenomenon is an interesting question. It is my belief that this is because more women than men perceive the destructiveness that is inherent in sex-conversion procedures. Having experienced on an everyday existential level the destructive elements of sex-role stereotyping in a patriarchal society, many women perceive that transsexualism does nothing to alter this society but merely reinforces it. Robin Morgan, in her speech to the Lesbian Conference in Los Angeles in 1973, addressed herself to this issue in responding to transsexual intrusion into the conference. "If transvestite or transsexual males are oppressed, then let them band together and organize against that oppression, instead of leeching off women who have spent entire lives *as women* in women's bodies."[27] Such a critique, of course, proceeds from a feminist perspective. However, what is important to note here is that what many transsexuals are saying, in stating that women are less tolerant of them than men, is that many women who probably would not call themselves feminists have an instinctual understanding of the destructiveness of transsexualism.

Another reason transsexuals identify strongly with men may be because it is men who have been helpful to transsexuals in their attempts to cross-sex. For the most part, these men were what Kando called "professional coaches." All of them—priests, counselors, psychiatrists, psychologists, M.D.s, surgeons—had played a professional role in the transsexual's sex passage, "not only when they sought out the operation but also at the earlier stages of their alienation" (p. 101).

"Blaming the mother" also functions to identify transsexuals with men. In noting that many of the transsexuals blamed others for what had happened to them, Kando states that the mother was by far the most frequent target.

Many have worked out an etiology for their gender condition, often borrowing vulgarized psychoanalytic motives that stress faulty childhood socialization, particularly the alleged unresolved Oedipal relationship. The mother may then alternatively be described as rejecting or overly protective, as either too feminine or too masculine. The main point is that she is given an important role in the sad series of events that lead to transsexualism.[28]

However, Kando also points out the contradiction between this "constructed etiology" of one's transsexualism and the insistence that one has always been a "woman." This repetition of "sad tale" accounts only reveals that transsexuals do, in fact, consider themselves victims of faulty socialization and not healthy women who need nothing but corrective surgery.[29]

There is, however, one major shortcoming in Kando's study. It is not clear that Kando recognizes the significance of his own findings. While he perceives that transsexuals incarnate role-defined behavior and subscribe to cultural stereotypes, he never makes clear that these same normative roles and stereotypes generate transsexualism to begin with.

TRANSSEXUAL REARRANGEMENTS OF THE STEREOTYPES: JAN MORRIS AND OTHERS

Not all transsexuals reveal their acceptance of stereotypical roles and behavior in the same obvious way as these examples. Some transsexuals, for example, deny identification with the stereotypes on a verbal level but their actions or subsequent contradictory statements betray them.

Perhaps the most publicized version of this kind of contradictory evidence is the Jan Morris case. Morris denies the stereotypes, yet, on the other hand, lives them out. Morris also deviates from most transsexual accounts in that he found the masculine role exhilarating before he was transsexed. As a top correspondent for *The London Times*, Jan, then James, Morris accompanied the Mt. Everest climbing team and scooped the story. He describes that experience in a remarkable variation on the theme of "anatomy is destiny."

There is no hardship to it, for it is not imposed upon him. He is the master. . . . It is *this feeling of unfluctuating control, I think, that women cannot share*, and *it springs* of course not from the intellect or the personality, nor even so much from upbringing, but specifically *from the body*. . . . I look back to those moments of supreme

male fitness as one remembers champagne or a morning swim. . . .
I was brilliant with my knowledge of the event, brilliant with muscular tautness, brilliant with conceit, brilliant with awareness of the
subterfuge, amounting very nearly to dishonesty, by which I hoped
to have deceived my competitors and scooped the world. . . . *I never
mind the swagger of young men. It is their right to swank, and I
know the sensation.*[30] (Italics mine.)

What such words basically illustrate is the contradiction
between Morris's claim that he was always a woman, and
his quite overt revelling in his male body and masculinity.
By the same token, if "women cannot share" such feelings
of "unfluctuating control," then how is it that Morris who
claimed to have always been a woman—who had "no
doubt about my gender since that moment of self-realization beneath the piano," while listening to his mother
play Sibelius—could have experienced the sensations of
"supreme male fitness," "muscular tautness," and the
swank and swagger of young men?

Henry Guze's insight may be of some interest here. He
notes that the male-to-constructed-female transsexual in
some ways puts masculinity on a pedestal. In doing so,
he responds as if he were unworthy of this esteemed role.
Since he feels he does not really fit the cultural concept
of a male, a concept he fears but also loves and admires,
he must be a female. I would add to this that he must be
a female in order to participate in what is basically a male,
heterosexual culture, and that sex-conversion surgery is
his only entrance into this world that he basically loves
and admires but doesn't totally fit into as a man. This
also explains his repugnance against homosexuality, which
would prohibit his fitting into the "straight" world. Furthermore, in order to identify completely with this world,
he must identify with everything that men have defined
this world to be, among which is the gender identity and
role behavior of a woman. Thus Rebecca West, in her review of Morris's *Conundrum*, notes that the author sounds
not like a woman, but like a man's idea of a woman. And,
of course, this is what is basic to the whole cultural stereo-

type of femininity itself; that is, it is a male-imposed definition of femaleness.*

After describing the heights to which masculinity can
soar, almost in the very next paragraph, Dr. Jekyll (James)
becomes Ms. Hyde (Jan). It is, of course, somewhat con-
fusing to read in *Conundrum* that it was this very putting
of one's masculinity to the test that deepened Morris's
desire for sex transformation. With all the fervor used to
espouse the masculine, he now espouses the feminine.
"Her frailty is her strength, her inferiority is her privilege"
(pp. 167–68). Thus in one surgical stroke, Morris accepts
the woman-on-a-pedestal myth. "She" extolls eternal
womanhood in the same way "she" extolls "male swank
and swagger." Now it seems only "common sense" to
want to be a woman rather than a man. Not only does
"she" like being a woman, but "she" likes all of the proclaimed "benefits" of womanhood. "I like being a woman,
but I mean a *woman.* I like having my suitcase carried. . . .
I like gossiping with the lady upstairs. . . . And yes, I like
to be liked by men."[31]

"Her" first experience of "being liked" by a man was
in a London taxi cab where the driver "boldly" kissed her
"roughly and not at all disagreeably on the lips," after
which he said, "There's a good girl," and "patted her
bottom." "She" loved it because it gave "her" a first experience of what it was to be loved and "cherished" by
a man as a woman.

---

*Zelda Suplee, in the same personal interview cited earlier, had an
interesting insight, which applies in this context. In trying to explain
to me why male-to-constructed-female transsexuals talk to the point
of exhibitionism about their transsexual odyssey, and female-to-constructed-male transsexuals seldom grant interviews or want to talk
about their sex changes, she noted the following. Male-to-constructed-female transsexuals "go down" on the social scale when
they become women. They basically realize this and thus constantly
talk about their new status and the journey involved. Such talk is
emotional compensation for the change downward. To carry this
a bit further, constant extolling of the feminine stereotype is one
more self-validating act that confirms that transsexuals "fit in" to
a male world that has constructed these stereotypes.

I'm 47. I think most women of my age, if they're honest, really accept the idea of helping men, and of being cherished by them. I've always had that feeling. If I could have my life over I suppose I would have been happiest being someone's second-in-command. Lieutenant to a really great man—that's my idea of happiness.[32]

This from the man who scaled Mt. Everest and basked in the glory, competition, and vigor of stereotyped masculinity. On the other hand, there is no *real* contradiction here, because if one finds one's identity in stereotypical behavior, it is very logical to switch from one stereotype to the other.

As a final apparent contradiction, Morris adds a note of disdain for those who would treat women as inferior. Here, Morris claims to be a "militant feminist."

I have seen life from both sides, and I know what prejudice survives. I know that by the very fact of my womanhood . . . I am treated in many petty situations as a second-class citizen—not because I lack brains, or experience, or character, but purely because I wear the body of a woman.[33]

Yet this feminist sentiment is rare in this book, for again, in the very next paragraph, Morris admits to frankly enjoying the compensations for being thought inferior—that is, "the small courtesies men now pay me, the standing up or the opening of doors, which really do give one a cherished or protected feeling" (p. 178). What Morris never seems to recognize is that the "second-class citizenship," the inferior position in which women are put by men, is the logical consequence of their acceptance of femininity as a stereotype and mode of relating.

Another way of viewing Morris's acceptance and seemingly contradictory extolling of both stereotypes is to say that Morris squeezed out of his male status all the vigor of young manhood. However, at the age of forty-seven—in the decline of his male vigor—he latched on to the status of a woman. Since women are often more vigorous when they are older and the cultural pressures have subsided, Morris captures "the best of both worlds," so to speak. Transsexualism thus allows him to fully exploit both stereotypes.

Furthermore, what Morris and other transsexuals exhibit in their acceptance of both identity and role artifacts is not unique to transsexual males. This psychology of acceptance has been noted in other male contexts. For example, Susan Brownmiller in her ground-breaking work, *Against Our Will: Men, Women, and Rape*, cites rape in male prisons as a means of transforming tough and masculine men into what are called "gal-boys."[34] Brownmiller, in her section on male rape in prison, gives us one more example of how the change from one role to another is managed in an astonishingly brief time.

Precisely what Morris and other transsexuals depict, in a most graphic way, is the easy replacement of one role by the other. Ernest Becker made the important observation that the sadistic and masochistic postures can be easily interchanged because they are "terms which describe one and the same thing: weakness and felt limitation in oneself; sharp duality of spirit and matter in people."[35] Likewise, the stereotypes of masculinity and femininity are similarly related. Each can exist, in fact, only in relationship to the other. Neither has anything essentially to do with maleness or femaleness. Because the split is so artifactual and because one cannot exist without the other, it is not difficult to understand how essentially to do with maleness or femaleness. Because the split is so artifactual and because one cannot exist without the other, it is not difficult to understand how a person may easily flip from one to the other. This is precisely what the transsexual does. Instead of moving out of both roles, the transsexual, as Jan Morris expresses so well, substitutes one for the other, under the illusion that she/he is entering into a state that is radically different from the role she/he rejects.

Another recent example of the apparent contradictions that Jan Morris represents is described in an article that appeared in the *Gay Community News*,[36] reporting on three male-to-constructed-female transsexuals—Carolyn, Heather, and Sandy. Most of the questions that were asked in this interview seemed devised to judge the degree of stereotypical identification of the three with dominant feminine norms. The contradiction in Carolyn's statements about sex-role stereotyping is fairly obvious. Carolyn identified "herself" as a feminist. When asked what attributes "she" would ascribe to a woman, "she" refused to comment on the grounds that it was sexist to limit certain characteristics to a certain sex. However, when pushed further on what is essential to being a woman, "she" responded with a classic stereotyped answer: "being willing to be sincere and loving and being able to just . . . give a great deal . . . get it back, too . . . care for somebody . . . put together a nice home." A second transsexual, Sandy, rejected macho men but then admitted that "she" desired to be dominated by men in bed. The third, Heather, also considered "herself" a feminist, disliked macho men, considered "herself" aggressive and independent but on the other hand, was reduced to selling "her" body to men.

My own interview data confirms the same kind of contradictions. R., for example, said "she" didn't believe in *part* of the stereotypically feminine role, such as doing housework, wanting kids, staying around the house, but "she" delighted in wearing profuse make-up and frilly feminine clothes. R. also made the very important point that one of the reasons transsexuals may seem to conform exaggeratedly to the stereotype is that they have to prove to the gender identity clinics that they can pass (i.e., live, work, dress, and be accepted) as women. This, of course, raises the significant issue of to what extent the medical and psychiatric professions contribute, perpetuate, and reinforce the stereotyping syndrome.

GENDER IDENTITY CLINICS AND SEX-ROLE STEREOTYPING

The role of the gender identity clinics and the medical-psychiatric establishment in general in reinforcing sex-role stereotypes is a significant one. Gender identity clinics have been instituted to counsel and to refer for surgery those candidates judged to be "real" transsexuals. One of the criteria in evaluating "true" transsexualism at Johns Hopkins, among other clinics, is an assessment of

the patient's current sociocultural role status and a con-
sideration of the vocational and economic transformations
she/he is making preoperatively.

The transsexual cannot have accurate knowledge or feeling of the
experience of living and being treated as a member of the opposite
sex until he spends sufficient time living in that role. . . . Present
data indicate that the length of time spent by the patient in actual
experience in the opposite sex role prior to surgery is of critical importance in our determining the extent of possible future crises.[37]

While this requirement is made for supposedly practical
and humanitarian reasons, it is important to point out that
its social effect is to reinforce conformity to certain cultural norms of masculinity and femininity, since it evaluates everything from dress to body language and to
positions in intercourse.

At Johns Hopkins, candidates for surgery are required
to live out opposite-sex roles for at least six months. Many
times, however, a longer period is required, and the average
length of time demanded by the clinics is two years. During this time, hormonal treatments usually begin.

Harry Benjamin has written that in evaluating the
"true" transsexualism of persons who came to him, "Most
important for my own satisfaction and consent to the
operation was the belief that a reasonably successful
'woman' could result."[38] It is precisely here that doctors'
views of the cultural stereotypes are revealed, and transsexual candidates are judged on the basis of what a man's
view of a "real woman" is. Concomitantly, of course,
female transsexual candidates are also judged on the basis
of what a man's view of a man should be. But either way,
men are perpetuating, judging, and reinforcing the cultural
stereotypes. Consider, for example, this account:

Marriage is the foremost ambition of a converted transsexual. This
is easily understood when one realizes that it is the most complete
affirmation of femininity. Prostitution sometimes becomes a
tempting substitute for marriage. There is no greater confirmation
of femininity than that of having normal heterosexual men again
and again accept her as a woman and even pay her for sex services.[39]

The sexual objectification of such a perspective is obvious. Or consider the following view of womanhood: "A true feminine identification, for instance, would result in warm and continued relationships with men, a sense of maternity, interest in caring for children and the capacity to work productively and continuously in female occupations."[40]

In an advice column to transsexuals that was published in *Sexology Magazine*, the following was specified:

You have to learn how to behave like a woman, how to walk, how to use your hands, how to talk, how to apply make-up, and how to dress. . . . Finally, but highly important, how do you know you can make a living as a woman? Have you ever worked as a woman before? I assume that so far, you have only held a man's job and have drawn a man's salary. Now you have to learn something entirely new.[41]

What this "advice" conveys, aside from confirming the economic oppression of women in a patriarchal society, is uncritical acceptance of this situation—distinguishing a "man's job" and earnings from a woman's, encouraging transsexuals to also accept this distinction, and indeed *requiring* that they do so before they are recommended for surgery. Moreover, this conformity on the part of the transsexual is often labeled by doctors, psychiatrists, and clinics as "high motivation."

The Erickson Foundation has published several pamphlets about transsexualism that attempt to inform the public about the subject in a readable and nonacademic way. In one of these, "Counseling the Transsexual," five male therapists are interviewed. Dr. R. strongly emphasizes the importance of cross-dressing consistently, getting a job in the new gender role, and seeing how people react to the transsexual in his new gender role.

These reactions, positive and negative, are part of his education: they reinforce convincing behavior and stimulate him to modify behavior that elicits doubtful or negative responses from others. . . . Any conscientious doctor will require that prior to surgery and while receiving hormone therapy the patient submerge himself in the chosen role for a considerable time—and I would recommend the full two-year term—until he is absolutely at ease in it, personally and socially.[42]

In the same pamphlet, Dr. N. talks about the necessity to explore the gender stereotypes with transsexuals. What it really means to be a man or a woman should be talked about to assure that the transsexual's conception is not idealized, exaggerated, or distorted in one way or another. Dr. N. indeed recognizes the more superficial aspects of of stereotypical behavior and attempts to dissuade his clients from such. For example, he would ask:

Does femininity mean going to the supermarket drenched in perfume and wearing gauzy organdies and make-up an inch thick—now this sounds like a caricature, but very frequently this is the male transsexual's honest conception of appropriate feminine attire.[43]

However, Dr. N's criticism of the stereotype is merely "skin-deep." In the next paragraph, he maintains that "being a woman" has to do more with "an inner quality, a way of feeling: something less obvious, more intangible."[44]

The web of stereotyping is woven also on the hospital ward following surgery. A nurse's account of "The Transsexual Patient After Surgery" advises that nurses should serve as feminine role models for transsexuals and that indeed it may be the demeanor of nurses and their interaction with transsexual patients on the wards that is most important to the future of the postoperative transsexual.

The nurse who is comfortable with her feminine role can be a non-threatening female role model for her patient. . . . The nurse can offer the way she walks, talks, sits, and dresses as a resource for her patient.[45]

Here, of course, we have the ultimate form of sex-role oppression. The woman herself becomes the funnel through which men's ideas of women are perpetuated and reinforced.

What is most disconcerting is the treatment of what is termed childhood transsexualism. Here again, the roles of the doctor, psychiatrist, and gender identity clinics in so-

cializing young children—this time to the prescribed role
of their anatomical sex—id disturbing. The Gender Identity
and Research Program at U.C.L.A. is working with a number of preadolescent boys who are termed "effeminate"
and are judged to have many of the childhood patterns
described by adult transsexuals. "Young boys with normal
male physical status who manifest feminine gender role
behavior and verbalize a cross-gender identity are high risk
for later adult sexual adjustment problems, e.g., transsexualism and homosexual conflicts."[46] The aim of the
program and treatment has been to work intensively with
the boys and their families so that the boys may come
to "voluntarily" accept themselves as masculine. An in-
terim report[47] divulged the following treatment measures:
(1) Development of a relationship of trust and affection
between the male therapist and the boy; (2) heightening
parental concern about the problem so that parents begin
to disapprove of feminine[48] interests and no longer covertly encourage them; (3) Promotion of the father's or
a father-substitute's involvement in the boy's life; (4) sen-
sitization of the parents to the interpersonal difficulties
which underlie the tendency of the mother to be overly
close with the son and for the father to emotionally divorce himself from family activities.

The development of the therapist-boy relationship illustrates some of the worst aspects of masculine sex-role socialization. The authors describe a nine-year-old boy whose
feminine propensities began to look like a case of boyhood
transsexualism. After two years of treatment, the boy
began to emulate his male therapist. The first sign of the
boy's conversion to masculinity was his narration of horror
stories in which murder and physical aggression took place.
Gradually the therapist began to point out to the boy his
own fear of aggressiveness, and eventually he became
more aggressive. At home, the boy acted this out by striking both his sister and his mother. "The development was
supported by the therapist and the mother's fears of it
were allayed. (If the therapist had not intervened strongly
at this point, it is likely that the mother's covert pressure

against such behavior would have resulted in the boy again returning to a passive posture.)"[49]

Another case is related which involved sessions with the parents. This mainly consisted of coaching the mother into a more passive familial position and assisting the father to emerge as the dominant parent. Prior to therapy mother and son spent great amounts of time together. The father's business commitments took him away from the family constantly and when he was home, his exhaustion precluded spending time with the boy. Moreover, the authors state that the father's image was frequently undermined by his wife. The parents, with the help of therapy and a "high motivation" to change and help their son, gradually reversed roles. The father became increasingly active with his son. The mother "channeled her assertiveness" elsewhere.

In both of these cases, each boy made a considerable shift in his gender-role orientation to a much more masculine posture. This shift was termed "appropriate gender behavior" by two doctors at Johns Hopkins.

Involvement of the parents in the treatment program may be helpful, if one can get their approval and support of appropriate gender behavior by the child, and a continuous effort by the parent of the same sex toward bolstering the correct sex role of the dysfunctioning child.[50]

A focus on the family and the father as dominant is by no means a new idea, of course, nor is it restricted to the field of psychology. The idea of the family as the locus of behavior and the father as instructor was legitimated in the philosophy of ancient Greece. Aristotle, for example, justified the family as a school of conduct and preparation for the larger world, particularly for the state. He saw the father as inspiring his children (and slaves) toward a life of virtue. Indeed, as Ernest Barker remarks, "There are times when Aristotle seems almost ready to think that the father may suffice for the moral instruction of his children."[51] In the family counseling sessions and practices of the gender identity clinics, we witness a

modern variation on this Aristotelian theme as the transsexual counselors attempt to nip the transsexual condition
in the bud. Having faulted the mother for her fostering of
the syndrome in her child, transsexual family therapy focuses on the father as the redeemer of his son's masculinity. Employing father substitutes (male therapists
as role models) and encouraging the "real" father to
assert his "rightful" fatherly and masculine role in the
family, the transsexual experts motivate and educate the
developing deviant boy to be culturally masculine.

Both the U.C.L.A. and Johns Hopkins professionals de-
fend the use of a male therapist. "By the nature of his
authority, prestige, and capacity for providing approval
and disapproval, he will be available to the boy as an appropriate object for identification."[52] The Johns Hopkins
group merely asserted that, "treatment of such a child
may be done best by a psychiatrist of the same sex, to
serve as an appropriate gender model." What is never analyzed is "appropriate" by whose standards? Such judgments are based on an invisible, yet culturally accepted,
standard of sex roles.[53] The therapists/authors cited never
once question the "appropriateness"[54] of behavior such
as the physical abuse of one's mother or sister. Indeed
many men, as evidenced by the incidence of rape, sexual
abuse, wife-beating, and violent crimes, do believe that
the perpetuation of violence against women is "appropriate" behavior. But perhaps, finally, there is a certain
uneasiness about the ultimate appropriateness of such
behavior:

Lest it be misunderstood that we have ascribed an inherently higher
value to masculine over feminine behavior, in closing, we will emphasize that it is rather the deleterious effect on social interaction,
with the considerable resultant distress emanating from a cross-
gender identity which motivates us.[55]

Thus, sympathy for the boys' social unacceptance becomes
the professed reason for the advocacy of certain therapeutic measures. This is reminiscent of the disapproval of
interracial marriages on the ground that the children of

such a union would be socially unacceptable in a white society. More important, the authors do not choose to recognize that while social unacceptance may be given as a reason, the therapeutic context itself conveys to these boys that there is an "inherently higher value" to masculine behavior. Moreover, another "deleterious effect on social interaction" results—the encouragement and perpetration of male violence against women.

In conclusion, while the authors admit that society's attitudes toward cross-gender behavior may be wrong, they create a social-individual split and opt for an individualistic ethic.

While privately, one might prefer to modify society's attitudes toward crossgender behavior, in the consultation room with an unhappy youngster, one feels far more optimistic about modifying the behavior of that one child than the entire society.[56]

Thus the task of social change becomes relegated to a "private preference" and has no significant place in therapeutic situations. Changing society's attitudes becomes secondary in the immediacy of the therapeutic moment.

In the final analysis, it is imperative to note that what has been termed an individualist or personalist position does not foster genuine individualism. The kind of individualism that transsexual therapy promotes is really an individualism that serves a role-defined society and thus it is more realistic to say that it is an ethic of social conformity.[57]

CHAPTER IV

Sappho by Surgery:

The Transsexually Constructed

Lesbian-Feminist

TRANSSEXUALISM is
multifaceted. From all that has been said thus far, it is
clear that it raises many of the most complex questions
feminism is asking about the origins and manifestations
of sexism and sex-role stereotyping.* While regarded by
many as an obscure issue that affects a relatively minute
proportion of the population, transsexualism poses very
important feminist questions. Transsexually constructed
lesbian-feminists show yet another face of patriarchy. As
the male-to-constructed-female transsexual exhibits the
attempt to possess women in a bodily sense while acting
out the images into which men have molded women, the
male-to-constructed-female who claims to be a lesbian-
feminist attempts to possess women at a deeper level, this
time under the guise of challenging rather than conforming
to the role and behavior of stereotyped femininity. As

---

*For a long time, I have been very hesitant about devoting a chapter
of this book to what I call the "transsexually constructed lesbian-
feminist." In the order this book was written, it was actually the

99

patriarchy is neither monolithic nor one-dimensional, neither is transsexualism.

All men and male-defined realities are not blatantly macho or masculinist. Many indeed are gentle, nurturing, feeling, and sensitive, which, of course, have been the more positive qualities that are associated with stereotypical femininity. In the same way that the so-called androgynous man assumes for himself the role of *femininity*, the transsexually constructed lesbian-feminist assumes for himself the role and behavior of *feminist*. The androgynous man and the transsexually constructed lesbian-feminist deceive women in much the same way, for they lure women into believing that they are truly one of us—this time not only one in behavior but one in spirit and conviction.

---

last chapter I wrote. The recent debate and divisiveness that the transsexually constructed lesbian-feminist has produced within feminist circles has convinced me that, while transsexually constructed lesbian-feminists may be a small percentage of transsexuals, the issue needs an in-depth discussion among feminists.

I write this chapter with the full realization that feminists look at the issue of the transsexually constructed lesbian-feminist from the vantage point of a small community in which transsexuals have been able to be very visible—not because there are that many of them, but because they immediately have center stage. Thus focusing attention on this particular aspect of the transsexual issue may only serve to inflate the issue and their presence all the more. It may also distract attention from the more central questions that transsexualism raises and the power of the medical empire that creates transsexualism to begin with.

Because the oral and written debate concerning the transsexually constructed lesbian-feminist seems to be increasing out of proportion to their actual numbers, I think that feminists ought to consider seriously the amount of energy and space we wish to give to this discussion. However, if any space should be devoted to this issue, it is in a book that purports to be a feminist analysis of transsexualism. Furthermore, most of the commentary thus far has been limited to letters to the editor and editorial comments in feminist papers, as well as a few scattered articles in various journals. Because of limited space, these analyses are necessarily restricted. I would like, therefore, to provide an extensive and intensive analysis of the issue and to address the deeply mythic dimensions that the transsexually constructed lesbian-feminist represents.

CONTRADICTIONS OR CONFIRMATIONS?

It is not accidental that most male-to-constructed-female transsexuals who claim to be feminists also claim to be lesbian-feminists. In fact, I don't know of any transsexually constructed feminists who do not also claim to be lesbians. It is this combination that is extremely important. Lesbian-feminists have spent a great deal of energy in attempting to communicate that the self-definition of lesbian, informed by feminism, is much more than just a sexual choice. It is a total perspective on life in a patriarchal society representing a primal commitment to women on all levels of existence and challenging the bulwark of a sexist society—that is, heterosexism. Thus it is not a mere sexual alternative to men, which is characterized simply by sexually relating to women instead of men, but a way of being in the world that challenges the male possession of women at perhaps its most intimate and sensitive level. In assuming the identity of lesbian-feminist, then, doesn't the transsexual renounce patriarchal definitions of selfhood and choose to fight sexism on a most fundamental level?

First of all, the transsexually constructed lesbian-feminist may have renounced femininity but not masculinity and masculinist behavior (despite deceptive appearances). If, as I have noted earlier, femininity and masculinity are different sides of the same coin, thus making it quite understandable how one could flip from one to the other, then it is important to understand that the transsexually constructed lesbian-feminist, while not exhibiting a feminine identity and role, still exhibits its obverse side—stereotypical masculinity. Thus the assumption that he has renounced patriarchal definitions of selfhood is dubious.

Masculine behavior is notably obtrusive. It is significant that transsexually constructed lesbian-feminists have inserted themselves into the positions of importance and/or performance in the feminist community. The controversy in the summer of 1977 surrounding Sandy Stone, the transsexual sound engineer for Olivia Records, an "all-women" recording company, illustrates this well. Stone is not only crucial to the Olivia enterprise but plays a very dominant role there.[1] The national reputation and visibility he achieved in the aftermath of the Olivia controversy is comparable, in feminist circles, to that attained by Renee Richards in the wake of the Tennis Week Open. This only serves to enhance his previously dominant role and to divide women, as men frequently do, when they make their presence necessary and vital to women. Having produced such divisiveness, one would think that if Stone's commitment to and identification with women were genuinely woman-centered, he would have removed himself from Olivia and assumed some responsibility for the divisiveness. In Boston, a transsexual named Christy Barsky has worked himself into a similar dominant position, this time coaching a women's softball team, coordinating a conference on women and violence, staffing a women's center, and performing musically at various all-women places. Thus, like Stone, he exhibits a high degree of visibility and also divides women, in the name of lesbian-feminism.

Pat Hynes has suggested that there is only an apparent similarity between a strong lesbian, woman-identified self and a transsexual who fashions himself in a lesbian-feminist image.[2] With the latter, his masculinity comes through, although it may not be recognized as such. Hynes especially points to the body language of transsexuals where she notes *subtle but perceptible* differences between, for example, the way lesbians interact with other women and the way transsexuals interact with women. One specific example of this is the way a transsexual walked into a women's restaurant with his arms around two women, one on each side, with the possessive encompassing that is characteristically masculine.

Mary Daly in explaining *why* this difference is perceptible points out that the transsexually constructed lesbian-feminist is able to deceptively act out the part of lesbian-feminist *because* he is a man with a man's history; that is,

he is free of many of the residues of self-hatred, self-depre-
ciation, and self-contradiction that attend the history of
women who are born with female bodies—all of which is
communicated both subtly and not so subtly in gestures,
body language, and the like.[3] Thus it is precisely *because*
the transsexually constructed lesbian-feminist is a man,
and *not* a woman encumbered by the scars of patriarchy
that are unique to a woman's personal and social history
that he can play our parts so convincingly and apparently
better than we can play them ourselves. However, in the
final analysis, he can only *play the part*, although the
part may at times seem as, or more, plausible than the real
woman (as is also the case with the male-to-constructed-
female transsexual who appears more feminine than most
feminine women).

What is also typically masculine in the case of the transsexually constructed lesbian-feminist is the appropriation
of women's minds, convictions of feminism, and sexuality.
One of the definitions of *male*, as related in Webster's, is
"designed for fitting into a corresponding hollow part."
This, of course, means much more than the literal signifi-
cation of heterosexual intercourse. It can be taken to
mean that men have been very adept at penetrating all of
women's "hollow" spaces, at filling up the gaps, and of
sliding into the interstices. Obviously, women who are
in the process of moving out of patriarchal institutions,
consciousness, and modes of living are very vulnerable and
have gaps. I would imagine that it would be difficult, for
example, for Olivia Records to find a female sound engineer and that such a person would be absolutely necessary
to the survival of Olivia. But it would have been far more
honest if Olivia had acknowledged the maleness of Sandy
Stone and perhaps the necessity, at the time, to employ
a man in this role. As one woman wrote of Sandy Stone
and the Olivia controversy: "I feel raped when Olivia
passes off Sandy, a transsexual, as a real woman. After
all his male privilege, is he going to cash in on lesbian
feminist culture too?"[4]

Rape, of course, is a masculinist violation of bodily integrity. All transsexuals rape women's bodies by reducing the real female form to an artifact, appropriating this body for themselves. However, the transsexually constructed lesbian-feminist violates women's sexuality and spirit, as well. Rape, although it is usually done by force, can also be accomplished by deception. It is significant that in the case of the transsexually constructed lesbian-feminist, often he is able to gain entrance and a dominant position in women's spaces because the women involved do not know he is a transsexual and he just does not happen to mention it.

The question of deception must also be raised in the context of how transsexuals who claim to be lesbian-feminists obtained surgery in the first place. Since all transsexuals have to "pass" as feminine in order to qualify for surgery, so-called lesbian-feminist transsexuals either had to lie to the therapists and doctors, or they had a conversion experience after surgery.[5] I am highly dubious of such conversions, and the other alternative, deception, raises serious problems, of course.

Deception reaches a tragic point for all concerned if transsexuals become lesbian-feminists because they regret what they have done and cannot back off from the effects of irreversible surgery (for example, castration). Thus they revert to masculinity (but not male body appearance) by becoming the man within the woman, and more, within the women's community, getting back their maleness in a most insidious way by seducing the spirits and the sexuality of women who do not relate to men.

Because transsexuals have lost their physical "members" does not mean that they have lost their ability to penetrate women—women's mind, women's space, women's sexuality. Transsexuals merely cut off the most obvious means of invading women so that they *seem* noninvasive. However, as Mary Daly has remarked, in the case of the transsexually constructed lesbian-feminists their whole presence becomes a "member" invading women's presence and dividing us once more from each other.[6]

Furthermore, the deceptiveness of men without "members," that is, castrated men or eunuchs, has historical precedent. There is a long tradition of eunuchs who were used by rulers, heads of state, and magistrates as *keepers of women*. Eunuchs were supervisors of the harem in Islam and wardens of women's apartments in many royal households. In fact, the word *eunuch*, from the Greek *eunouchos*, literally means "keeper of the bed." Eunuchs were men that other more powerful men used to keep their women in place. By fulfilling this role, eunuchs also succeeded in winning the confidence of the ruler and securing important and influential positions.

Moreover, the word *eunuch* is also related to the word *scheme*. (Eunuchs schemed to obtain political power.) In Mesopotamia, many eunuchs became royal officers and managers of palaces, and "others emerge on the pages of history as important and often virile figures."[7] Some were famous warriors and statesmen, as well as scholars. One finds eunuchs associated with temples dedicated to the goddesses from at least 2000 B.C. until well into the Roman period.[8] In fact the earliest mention of eunuchs is in connection with the Minoan civilization of Crete, which was a transitional period from an earlier gynocentric society. It thus appears that eunuchs, to some extent, always attached themselves to women's spaces and, most frequently, were used to supervise women's freedom of movement and to harness women's self-centeredness and self-government. "It is stated that entree into every political circle was possible for eunuchs even if barred to other men."[9]

Will the acceptance of transsexually constructed lesbian-feminists who have lost only their outward appendages of physical masculinity lead to the containment and control of lesbian-feminists? Will every lesbian-feminist space become a harem? Like eunuchs, transsexuals have gained prominent and dominant access to feminist political circles "barred to other men."[10] Just because transsexually constructed lesbian-feminists are not only castrated men, but have also acquired artifacts of a woman's body and spirit, does not mean that they are un-men, and that

they cannot be used as "keepers" of woman-identified
women when the "real men," the "rulers of patriarchy,"
decide that the women's movement (used here as both
noun and verb) should be controlled and contained. In
this way, they too can rise in the Kingdoms of the Fathers.
The political implications of historical eunuchism and its
potential for female control should not be lost upon
woman-identified women.

MYTHIC DIMENSIONS OF TRANSSEXUALISM

Transsexuals are living and acting out a very ancient myth,
that of single parenthood by the father. This myth was
prevalent in many religious traditions, including the Jewish, Greek, and Christian. Eve was born of Adam; Dionysus
and Athena were born of Zeus; and Jesus was generated
by God the Father in his godly birth. (Mary was a mere
receptacle used to conform Jesus to earthly birth standards.) When this myth is put into the context of transsexualism, the deeper dimensions of how transsexually
constructed lesbian-feminists reinforce patriarchy can be
perceived.

Simone de Beauvoir has remarked that "if [woman] did
not exist, men would have invented her. They did invent
her. But she exists also apart from their inventiveness."[11]
Men, of course, invented the feminine, and in this sense
it could be said that all women who conform to this invention are transsexuals, fashioned according to man's
image. Lesbian-feminists exist apart from man's inventiveness, and the political and personal ideals of lesbian-feminism have constituted a complete rebellion against the
man-made invention of woman, and a context in which
women begin to create ourselves in our own image. Thus
the transsexual who claims to be a lesbian-feminist *seems*
to be the man who creates himself in *woman's* image. This,
however, is deceptive, for note that he is still created in
man's image since he is essentially a child of the Father
(in this case, the medical fathers), renouncing his mothered birth.

Mary Daly has written at length in her most recent work, *Gyn/Ecology: The Metaethics of Radical Feminism,* about the myth of Dionysus.[12] She also cites various versions of the myth along with some scholarly commentaries on it. These can shed much light on the mythic implications of the transsexually constructed lesbian-feminist. First of all, Philip Slater points out the very interesting fact that, "Instead of seeking distance from or mastery over the mother, the Dionysian position incorporates her."[13] In the most popular version of the myth, Semele, the mother of Dionysus while pregnant with him, is struck by Zeus with a thunderbolt and is thus consumed. Hermes saves the six-month fetal Dionysus, sews him up in Zeus's thigh, and after three more months, Zeus "births" him. Thus Zeus exterminates the woman and bears his own son, and we have single-parent fatherhood (read motherhood). Moreover, Jane Harrison has pointed out that "the word Dionysus means not 'son of Zeus' but rather Zeus-Young Man, i.e., Zeus in his young form."[14] Thus Dionysus is his own father (read mother) and births himself into existence.

Whether we are talking about being born of the father, or the self (son), which in the myth are one and the same person (as in the Christian trinity), we are still talking about male mothering. At this level of analysis, it might seem that what men really envy is women's biological ability to procreate. Transsexuals illustrate one way in which men do this, by acquiring the artifacts of female biology. Even though they cannot give birth, they acquire the organs that are representative of this female power. However, it is the transsexually constructed lesbian-feminist who illustrates that much more is desired than female biology—that much more is at stake than literal womb envy. He shows that female biology, whether exercised in giving birth or simply by virtue of its existence, is representative of female creativity on a profound mythic level. Thus the creative power that is associated with female biology is not envied primarily because it is able to give birth physically but because it is multidimensional, bearing culture, harmony, and true inventiveness.[15]

The transsexually constructed lesbian-feminist feeds off woman's true energy source, i.e., her woman-identified self. It is he who recognizes that if female spirit, mind, creativity, and sexuality exist anywhere in a powerful way, it is here, among lesbian-feminists. I am not saying that the lesbian-feminist is the only self- and woman-identified woman. What I mean to express is that lesbianism-feminism signals a *total* giving of women's energy to women, and that it is this total woman-identified energy that the transsexual who claims to be a lesbian-feminist wants for himself. It is understandable that if men want to become women to obtain female creativity, then they will also want to assimilate those women who have withdrawn their energies from men at the most intimate and emotional levels.

This, of course, is not the usual way in which lesbian living has been harnessed. Most often, lesbian existence is simply not acknowledged, as evidenced in the laws against homosexuality, which legislate against male homosexuals, but not lesbians. It has been simply assumed that all women relate to men, and that women need men to survive. Furthermore, the mere labeling of a woman as "lesbian" has been enough to keep lesbian living harnessed or, at best, in the closet. "Lesbian is the word, the label, the condition that holds women in line. When a woman hears this word tossed her way, she knows that she . . . has crossed the terrible *boundary* of her sex role."[16] (Italics mine.)

Whereas the lesbian-feminist *crosses* the boundary of her patriarchally imposed sex role, the transsexually constructed lesbian-feminist is a *boundary violator*. This violation is also profoundly mythic, for as Norman O. Brown writes of Dionysus, he as the "mad god who breaks down boundaries."[17] Thus exhibiting qualities that are usually associated with femininity, he appeared to be the opposite of the masculine Apollo.

While the super-masculine Apollo overtly oppresses/destroys with his contrived boundaries/hierarchies/rules/roles, the feminine Dionysus blurs the senses, seduces, confuses his victims—drugging them into complicity, offering them his "heart" as a love potion that poisons.[18]

It is, however, the *feminist* Dionysus who appears in the transsexually constructed lesbian-feminist. But he "blurs the senses, seduces, and confuses" in much the same way as the *feminine* Dionysus. He not only violates the boundaries of women's bodies but of our minds and spirits. What is more tragic, however, is that he is able to make women break down our boundaries of self-definition. Elizabeth Rose in a letter in response to my article in *Chrysalis*, "Transsexualism: The Ultimate Homage to Sex-Role Power," illustrates well this tendency of feminists to be seduced by Dionysian boundary violation.

Raymond's article encourages us to set our "bottom line" (about whom we will allow the privilege of self-definition).

I am upset that a magazine "of women's culture" . . . is basically encouraging the elitist/separatist attitude that self definition [is] . . . subject to the scrutiny and judgments of those who, in the name of political purity, claim the power to define who is allowed entry into the feminist community . . . and, now, who is or is not female.[19]

Rose would encourage us to set no boundaries by employing the analogy of how boundaries have been used oppressively against lesbians in the past/present. "There are so many painful parallels between how the world has treated strong women and lesbians and how Raymond and others categorize and discount transsexuals."[20] But the analogy is false. The boundaries that have been and are used against lesbians are the boundaries of the Fathers:

The contrived Apollonian boundaries—such as the false divisions of "fields" of knowledge and the splits between "mind" and "heart." But in this process we do not become swallowed up in male-centered (Dionysian) confusion. Hags find and define our own boundaries, our own definitions. Radical feminist living "on the boundary" means this moving, Self-centering boundary definition. As we move we mark out our own territory.[21]

Rose and other women who have been confused/seduced by Dionysian transsexually constructed lesbian-feminist boundary violation would have us believe that all boundaries are oppressive. Yet if feminists cannot agree on the boundaries of what constitutes femaleness, then what can we hope to agree on? The Dionysian "Final Solution," as Daly points out, produces confusion in women—"inability to distinguish the female Self and her process from the male-made masquerade."[22] It encourages the leveling of genuine boundaries of self-preservation and self-centering.

THE SEDUCTION OF LESBIAN-FEMINISTS

It is not hard to understand why transsexuals want to become lesbian-feminists. They indeed have discovered where strong female energy exists and want to capture it. It is more difficult to understand why so many feminists are so ready to accept men—in this case, castrated men—into their most intimate circles. Certainly Dionysian confusion about the erasure of all boundaries is one reason that appeals to the liberal mind and masquerades as "sympathy for all oppressed groups." Women who believe this, however, fail to see that such liberalism is repressive, and that it can only favor and fortify the possession of women by men. These women also fail to recognize that accepting transsexuals into the feminist community is only another rather unique variation on the age-old theme of women nurturing men, providing them with a safe haven, and finally giving them our best energies.

The question arises: are women who accept transsexuals as lesbian-feminists expressing gratitude on some level to those men who are finally willing to join women and pay for their male privilege with their balls? Gratitude is a quality exhibited by all oppressed groups when they think that some in the class of oppressors have finally relinquished their benefits to join them. But, of course, it is doubtful that transsexuals actually give up their male privilege. As one woman put it: "A man who decides to call himself a woman is not giving up his privilege. He is simply using it in a more insidious way."[23] Furthermore, a man who decides to call himself a lesbian-feminist is getting a lot. The transsexually constructed lesbian-feminist is the man who indeed gets to be "the man" in an exclusive women's club to which he would have otherwise no access.

Women who think that these men are giving up male privilege seem to be naive about the sophisticated ways in which it is possible for men to co-opt women's energy, time, space, and sexuality. Transsexually constructed lesbian-feminists may be the first men to realize that "if you can't fight them, join them." In a short story entitled "The Women's Restaurant," by T. C. Boyle, which appeared recently in *Penthouse*, this point is well made.

The story begins by setting the scene in and around Grace & Rubie's Restaurant and is written from the point of view of the voyeuristic narrator. "It is a women's restaurant. Men are not permitted. . . . What goes on there, precisely, no man knows. I am a man. I am burning to find out."[24] The narrator then proceeds to caricature Grace and Rubie as butch and femme, as well as to relate his several attempts to gain entrance. After two unsuccessful endeavors, he goes to a department store, buys a pink polyester pantsuit, a bra, pantyhose, and cosmetics with which he makes himself up to pass as a woman. He gains entrance and is able to experience what he has been missing.

Here I was, embosomed in the very nave, the very omphalos of furtive femininity—a prize patron of the women's restaurant, a member, privy to its innermost secrets. . . . There they were—women—chewing, drinking, digesting, chatting, giggling, crossing, and uncrossing their legs. Shoes off, feet up. Smoking cigarettes, flashing silverware, tapping time to the music. Women among women. I bathed in their soft chatter, birdsong, the laughter like falling coils of hair. I lit a cigarette and grinned. No more fairybook-hero thoughts of rescuing Rubie—oh no, this was paradise.[25]

Having drunk six tequila sunrises and a carafe of dinner wine, the male intruder/narrator finds it necessary to relieve himself, but forgets to sit down when he urinates in the rest room, at which point he is discovered by Grace. The story ends with his savoring of the triumph of temporary infiltration and a plan for permanent invasion.

I have penetrated the women's restaurant, yes, but in actuality it was little more than a rape. . . . I am not satisfied. The obsession grows in me, pregnant, swelling, insatiable with the first taste of fulfillment. Before I am through, I will drink it to satiety. I have plans. . . . The next time I walk through those curtained doors at Grace & Rubie's there will be no dissimulation. . . . There are surgeons who can assure it.[26]

That this story appeared in *Penthouse* is no surprise. It is obvious that its editors thought it would be of interest to their readers, whether budding or closet transsexuals. In spite of the ludicrous details and caricatures, one can see that the narrator was primarily attracted to the woman-centeredness of the restaurant. "Women among women . . . this was paradise." Such an attitude is representative of the transsexually constructed lesbian-feminist who indeed gets his "paradise," because there *were* surgeons who could "assure it." Ironically, the would-be transsexual narrator of the story says that the next time he walks through the doors, "there will be no dissimulation." Transsexualism, however, is dissimulation. As I have shown previously, to not acknowledge the fact that one is a transsexual in a women's space is indeed deception. Finally, "penetrating" the women's restaurant was "little more than a rape." Little more than a rape, indeed! What "little more" is there to such an act, unless it is the total rape of our feminist identities, minds, and convictions? The transsexually constructed lesbian-feminist, having castrated himself, turns his whole body and behavior into a phallus that can rape in many ways, all the time. In this sense, he performs *total* rape, while also functioning *totally* against women's will to lesbian-feminism.

We have seen three reasons why lesbian-feminists are seduced into accepting transsexuals: liberalism, gratitude, and naiveté. There is yet another reason—one that can be perhaps best described as the *last remnants of male identification.* This is a complex phenomenon, which has various ingredients.

On the one hand, there is fear of the label "man-hater." Are women who are so accepting of the transsexually constructed lesbian-feminist trying to prove to themselves that a lesbian-feminist (she who has been called the ultimate man-hater) is really not a man-hater after all? As Adrienne Rich has pointed out, one way of avoiding that feared label, and of allowing one's self to accept men, is to accept those men who have given up the supposed ultimate possession of manhood in a patriarchal society by self-castration.[27]

On the other hand, there is a second component to this "last remnant of male identification"—i.e., *attraction to masculine presence*. As Pat Hynes has suggested, there is an *apparent* similarity between a strong woman-identified self and a transsexual who fashions himself in a lesbian image. Because there is an *apparent* similarity, some lesbian-feminists may allow themselves to express the residues of their (buried) attraction to men or to masculine presence, while pretending to themselves that transsexually constructed lesbian-feminists are really women. This allows women to do two things: to express that attraction, yet also to decide themselves.

SELF-DEFINITION

One of the most constraining questions that transsexuals, and, in particular, transsexually constructed lesbian-feminists, pose is the question of self-definition—who is a woman, who is a lesbian-feminist? But, of course, *they* pose the question on their terms, and *we* are faced with answering it. Men have always made such questions of major concern, and this question, in true phallic fashion, is thrust upon us. How many women students writing on such a feeble feminist topic as "Should Women Be Truck Drivers, Engineers, Steam Shovel Operators?" and the like, have had their male professor scribble in the margins: "But what are the real differences between men and women?" Men, of course, have defined the supposed differences that have kept women out of such jobs and professions, and feminists have spent much energy demonstrating how these differences, if indeed they do exist, are primarily the result of socialization. Yet there are differences, and some feminists have come to realize that those differences are important whether they spring from socialization, from biology, or from the total history of existing as a woman in a patriarchal society. The point is, however, that the origin of these differences is probably not the important question, and we shall perhaps never know the total answer to it. Yet we are forced back into trying to answer it again and again.*

Transsexuals, and transsexually constructed lesbian-feminists, drag us back to answering such old questions by asking them in a new way. And thus feminists debate and divide because we keep focusing on patriarchal questions of who is a woman and who is a lesbian-feminist. It is important for us to realize that these may well be non-questions and that the only answer we can give to them is that we know who *we* are. We know that we are women who are born with female chromosomes and anatomy, and that whether or not we were socialized to be so-called normal women, patriarchy has treated and will treat us like women. Transsexuals have not had this same history. No man can have the history of being born and located in this culture as a woman. He can have the history of *wishing* to be a woman and of *acting* like a woman, but this gender experience is that of a transsexual, not of a woman. Surgery may confer the artifacts of outward and inward female organs but it cannot confer the history of being born a woman in this society.

What of persons born with ambiguous sex organs or chromosomal anomalies that place them in a biologically intersexual situation? It must be noted that practically all of them are altered shortly after birth to become anatomically male or female and are reared in accordance

---

*A parallel is the abortion issue, which can also be noted in this context. The key question, asked by men for centuries, is "when does life begin?" This question is posed in men's terms and on their turf, and is essentially unanswerable. Women torture themselves trying to answer it and thus do not assert or even develop our own questions about abortion.

with the societal gender identity and role that accompanies their bodies. Persons whose sexual ambiguity is discovered later are altered in the direction of what their gender rearing has been (masculine or feminine) up to that point. Thus those who are altered shortly after birth have the history of being practically born as male or female and those who are altered later in life have their body surgically conformed to their history. When and if they do undergo surgical change, they do not become the opposite sex after a long history of functioning and being treated differently.

Although popular literature on transsexualism implies that Nature has made mistakes with transsexuals, it is really society that has made the mistake by producing conditions that create the transsexual body/mind split. While intersexed people are born with chromosomal or hormonal anomalies, which can be linked up with certain biological malfunctions, transsexualism is not of this order. The language of "Nature makes mistakes" only serves to confuse and distort the issue, taking the focus off the social system, which is actively oppressive. It succeeds in blaming an amorphous "Nature" that is made to seem oppressive and is conveniently amenable to direct control/manipulation by the instruments of hormones and surgery.

In speaking of the importance of history for self-definition, two questions must be asked. Should a person want to change his/her personal and social history and if so, *how* should one change that history in the most honest and integral way? In answer to the first question, anyone who has lived in a patriarchal society has to change personal and social history in order to be a self. History cannot be allowed to determine the boundaries, life, and location of the self. We should be change agents of our own history. Women who are feminists obviously wish to change parts of their history as women in this society; some men who are honestly dealing with feminist questions wish to change their history as men; and transsexuals wish to change their history of *wanting* to be women. In stressing the importance of female history for female self-definition, I am not advocating a static view of such history.

What is more important, however, is *how* one changes personal history in the most honest and integral way, if one wants to break down sex-role oppression. Should nontranssexual men who wish to fight sexism take on the identity of women and/or lesbian-feminists while keeping their male anatomy intact? Why should castrated men take on these identities and self-definitions and be applauded for doing so? To what extent would concerned blacks accept whites who had undergone medicalized changes in skin color and, in the process, claimed that they had not only a black body but a black soul?

Can a transsexual assume the self-definition of lesbian-feminist just because he wants to, or does this particular self-definition proceed from certain conditions endemic to female biology and history? Women take on the self-definition of feminist and/or lesbian because that defini-tion truly proceeds from not only the chromosomal fact of being born XX, but also from the whole history of what being born with those chromosomes means in this society. Transsexuals would be more honest if they dealt with their specific form of gender agony that inclines them to want a transsexual operation. This gender agony proceeds from the chromosomal fact of being born XY and *wishing* that one were born XX, and from the particular life history that produced such distress. The place to deal with that problem, however, is not the women's community. The place to confront and solve it is among transsexuals them-selves.

One should be able to make choices about who one wants to be. But should one be able to make *any* choice? Should a white person attempt to become black, for ex-ample? The question is a moral one, which asks basically about the rightness of the choice, not the possibility of it. Should persons be able to make choices that disguise cer-tain facets of our existence from others who have a right

to know—choices that feed off others' energies, and reinforce oppression?

Jill Johnston has commented that, "many women are
dedicated to working for the 'reconstructed man.'"[28] This
usually means women gently or strongly prodding their
significant men into androgynous behavior and action.
Women who accept transsexually constructed lesbian-
feminists say that these men are truly "reconstructed"
in the most basic sense that women could hope for—i.e.,
they have paid with their balls to fight against sexism. Ultimately, however, the "reconstructed man" becomes the
"reconstructed woman" who obviously considers himself
equal to and a peer of genetic women in terms of his
"womanhood." One transsexual openly expressed that he
felt male-to-constructed-female transsexuals *surpassed*
genetic women.

Genetic women cannot possess the very special courage, brilliance,
sensitivity and compassion—and overview—that derives from the
transsexual experience. Free from the chains of menstruation and
child-bearing, transsexual women are obviously far superior to
Gennys in many ways.

Genetic women are becoming quite obsolete, which is obvious,
and the future belongs to transsexual women. We know this, and
perhaps some of you suspect it. All you have left is your "ability"
to bear children, and in a world which will groan to feed 6 billion
by the year 2000, that's a negative asset.[29]

Ultimately, women must ask if transsexually constructed lesbian-feminists are our peers. Are they equal to
us? Questions of equality often center on proportional
equality, such as "equal pay for equal work," or "equal
rights to health care." I do not mean equal in this sense.
Rather I use equality to mean: "like in quality, nature, or
status" and "capable of meeting the requirements of a situation or a task." In these senses transsexuals are not equal
to women and are not our peers. They are neither equal
in "quality, nature of status" nor are they "capable of
meeting the requirements of the situation" of women who
have spent their whole lives as women.

Jill Johnston has written of lesbian-feminism: "The essence of the new political definition is peer grouping. Women and men are not peers and many people seriously doubt whether we ever were or if we ever could be."[30] Transsexuals are not our peers, by virtue of their history.

It is perhaps our mistrust of the man as the biological aggressor which keeps bringing us back to the political necessity of power by peer grouping. Although we are still virtually powerless it is only by constantly adhering to this difficult principle of the power inherent in natural peers (men after all have demonstrated the success of this principle very well) that women will eventually achieve an autonomous existence.[31]

The transsexual does not display the usual phallic aggression. Instead he violates women's bodies by taking on the artifactual female organs for himself. The transsexually constructed lesbian-feminist becomes a psychological and social aggressor as well.

Transsexually constructed lesbian-feminists challenge women's preserves of autonomous existence. Their existence within the women's community basically attests to the ethic that women should not live without men—or without the "reconstructed man." How feminists assess and meet this challenge will affect the future of our genuine movement, self-definition, and power of be-ing.

In the final analysis, transsexually constructed lesbian-feminists are in the same tradition as the man-made, made-up "lesbians" of the *Playboy* centerfolds. Every so often, *Playboy* and similar magazines feature a "Sappho Pictorial."[32] Recently, male photographers have entered the book market by portraying pseudolesbians in all sorts of positions, clothing, and contexts that could only be fantasized by a male mind.[33] In short, the manner in which women are depicted in these photographs mimics the poses of men pawing women. Men produce "lesbian" love the way they want it to be and according to their own canons of what they think it should be.

Transsexually constructed lesbian-feminists are in this tradition of pseudolesbian propaganda. Both the *Playboy* pseudolesbian and the transsexual pseudolesbian spread the "correct" (read male-defined) image of the lesbian, which in turn filters into public consciousness through the mass media as truth. By thus mutilating the true self-definition of the lesbian, men mold her image/reality according to their own. As Lisa Buck has commented, transsexualism is truly "their word made flesh!"[34]

Transsexually constructed lesbian-feminists attempt to function as image-makers of the lesbian-feminist—not only for the public-at-large, but also for the women's community. Their masquerade of the lesbian filters into women's consciousness through the feminist media as "the real thing." The ultimate tragedy of such a parody is that the reality and self-definition of lesbian-feminist becomes mutilated in women themselves. Lesbian-feminists who accept transsexually constructed lesbian-feminists as other selves are mutilating their own reality.

The various "breeds" of women that medical science can create are endless. There are the women who are hormonally hooked on continuous doses of estrogen-replacement therapy. ERT supposedly will secure for them a new life of "eternal femininity."[35] There are the hysterectomized women, purified of their "potentially lethal" organs for "prophylactic" purposes.[36] Finally, there is the "she-male"—the male-to-constructed-female transsexual. And the offshoot of this "breed" is the transsexually constructed lesbian-feminist.

What all of these events point to is the particularly instrumental role that medicine has played in the control of deviant or potentially deviant women. "The Transsexual Empire" is ultimately a medical empire, based on a patriarchal medical model. This medical model has provided a "sacred canopy" of legitimations for transsexual treatment and surgery. In the name of therapy, it has medicalized moral and social questions of sex-role oppression, thereby erasing their deepest meaning.

CHAPTER V

Therapy

as a Way of Life:

Medical Values

versus Social Change

THE medical model is at the heart of the transsexual empire. It serves as the "new theology" for the therapeutic and medical priests. From time to time there are "in-house" debates about certain elements of the model, but on the whole, it functions at an established and consistent level of orthodoxy. (I use the term *medical model* to mean an ideology that stresses: freedom from physical or mental pain or disease; the location of physical or mental problems within the individual or interpersonal context; an approach to human conflicts from a diagnostic and disease perspective to be solved by specialized technical and professional experts.)

This approach has a profound influence on the study and treatment of transsexualism. For example, if one's basic approach to the problem of transsexualism is from a psychological and medical basis, then many moral issues, as well as sociopolitical, economic, and environmental problems, are transformed into technical problems. This means also that critical awareness, choice, and responsibility are not perceived as "curative" but are replaced by technical "cures."

Ultimately, one must ask if the transsexual problem is really amenable to surgery and thus to a medical model. Is the biomedical imperative that has functioned in other areas, such as genetic technology and psychosurgery, reducible to presuppositions about the nature of women and men? If, as argued in Chapter III, transsexualism is of sociopolitical origins, can it be understood and treated by a medical model?

THE MEDICAL MODEL AS THEORETICAL AND ETHICAL CONSTRUCT

Since the nineteenth century, especially, problems of alienation have been individualized. With the advent of Freudian psychoanalysis, which was later incorporated into medical psychiatry, "health" values began to take the place of ethical values of choice, freedom, and understanding.

With the transformation of the religious perspective on man into the scientific, and in particular into the psychiatric, which became fully articulated during the nineteenth century, there occurred a radical shift in emphasis away from viewing man as a responsible agent acting in and on the world and toward viewing him as a a responsive organism being acted upon by biological and social "forces." In this process, the imagery and vocabulary of morality were replaced by biological fantasy and psychiatric metaphor.[1]

The medical model has gradually yet consistently treated problems of social alienation in the therapy of closed rooms, and more recently in the small group counseling sessions of family clinics and community mental health centers. Ernest Becker has contended that initially, "the psychoanalytic cure began its work by focusing on the individual; now, it is broadening out to the study and 'therapy' of the family."[2] I have noted in assessing the theories of Robert Stoller that much of his work involves not only individual, but family therapy, as well.

By thus treating the problem of transsexualism, the medical-psychiatric professionals have consistently used a medical model as remedy. Failing in their attempts to counsel preoperative transsexuals to "adjust" to the normative gender identity and role of their anatomical sex, transsexual clinics and therapists (after extensive evaluations, of course) succeed in "adjusting" transsexuals to the normative gender identity and role of their desired and opposite anatomical sex. Armed with the medical model, and operating on the basis of the narrow "health" values it generates, therapists speculate about the causes of transsexualism and make therapeutic diagnoses within the same framework that generated the problem to begin with (that is, within a role-defined society and its definitions of masculinity and femininity).

The goal in this "triumph of the therapeutic" is supposedly good "health," but good "health" achieved at the expense of critical awareness and exploration of the oppressiveness of the roles themselves. This goal of good "health" is particularly ironic in light of the fact that the word *health* originally meant "whole."[3] As defined by the medical model, "health" values come to mean partial solutions, which go against total integrity of the body, the individual concerned, and society in general.

The proponents of the medical model, who have extolled the professional goal of therapy, have given themselves the mandate to manipulate in the interests of reduced suffering for the transsexual. And in so doing, they have forced transsexuals back into a social system whose basic sexist norms and values remain unquestioned. Many persons express the urgency of their desire to be transsexed in terms of "normalizing" their self-perceived masculine or feminine psyche in a male or female body. The abhorrence of homosexuality, expressed by many transsexuals, and their unwillingness to be identified as such, indicate their desire to "normalize" their sexual relationships as heterosexual by acquiring the appropriate genitalia. Many express also their desire to be married, have (adopted) children, and function as part of a society where these roles and functions are both normal and normative. Thus the transsexual is generally no advocate of social criticism and change.

The medical model itself promotes this so-called normalization and in so doing limits the quest for self-transcendence. The kinds of "health" values it generates do not encourage the transsexual to recognize that such "health" may be *unhealthy* in the long run. "Health values are all of a piece again with our philosophy of adjustment, spurious individualism, and unashamed and thoughtless self-seeking."[4] Such notions of "health" make true individualism and autonomy unachievable, rendering the individual passive, acquiescent, and medically manipulatable. They deprive the individual of the possibility of transcendent activity and center him/her on false goods (gods). As Phillip Rieff has said,

By this time men have gone too far beyond the old deception of good and evil to specialize at last, wittingly, in techniques that are to be called . . . ."therapeutic," with nothing at stake beyond a manipulatable sense of well-being.[5]

The present counseling and treatment of transsexuals, based on the medical model I have described, give the transsexual no real moral options. Failing to analyze our society's definitions of masculinity and femininity, such therapy offers little encouragement and advice to help the transsexual live beyond both these containers of personhood.

Consider the possibility of counseling that encouraged the transsexual to break both stereotypes. Here, the transsexual would be encouraged to become the agent of her or his own energies and to strive for more varied modes of being and becoming. In a very real sense, at this point, the transsexual would become a social critic. All of us are in some way constricted by sex-role socialization. One way of viewing transsexuals is that they are uniquely constricted by the rigidified definitions of masculinity and femininity. The general cultural constrictions, from which we all suffer, become body-laden with them. However, deprived of an alternative framework in which to view the problem, the transsexual is unable to express the problem clearly. The gender identity clinics have a vested interest in suppressing criticism, and may collude with the transsexual to solve the problem in an ultimately uncritical way. Given a different mode of therapy where "consciousness-raising" is the primary *modus operandi*, the transsexual might not find it as necessary to resort to sex-conversion surgery.*

A society that encourages identity and role conformity based on biological sex will naturally turn to sex-conversion surgery rather than accept what it sees as a threatened obliteration of these roles. Until the problems that psychiatry has claimed for itself are broadened into a general criticism of patriarchal society, transsexualism will not be understood as a medical manipulation of social and individual action and meanings. Meanwhile, the medical model and its empire continue to domesticate the revolutionary potential of transsexuals. The potential stance of the transsexual as outsider to the conventional roles of masculinity and femininity is short-circuited. Health values and goals hide the possibility from transsexuals themselves of being "history-bearing individuals" who, instead of conforming to sex roles, are in a unique position to turn their gender agony into an effective protest against the very social structures and roles that spawned the dilemma to begin with. Rieff has pointed out that therapies and, by extension, I would say the medical model in general, consist "chiefly in participation mystiques severely limiting deviant initiatives."[6] Individuals are trained through what Rieff calls "ritual action" to express fixed wants. "The limitation of possibilities [is] the very design of salvation."[7]

---

*There is no simple definition of "counsciousness-raising," which will be discussed in the Appendix. Briefly, and in this context, it can be defined as a mode of counseling that places so-called personal problems within the larger arena of a patriarchal society. At the heart of such a process is the recognition that "the personal is political."

Thus *be-ing* is reduced to *well-being* (therapy), and ethical choices are reduced to health values.

THE DE-ETHICIZING OF PROBLEMS AND BEHAVIOR

One of the major effects of the medical model has been the de-ethicizing of problems and behavior. De-ethicization occurs when problems that have moral implications are defined as if they had none, or are redefined or reclassified, for example, as "therapeutic considerations," or "health issues," or "psychiatric management" problems. The "triumph of the therapeutic" has made transsexualism the "territorial imperative" of the psychologist, psychiatrist, and/or mental-health worker.

Thomas Szasz has noted that the conquest of human existence by the mental-health professions started with the identification and classification of so-called mental illnesses, and has culminated in our day with the claim that "all of life is a 'psychiatric problem' for behavioral science to 'solve.'"[8] Szasz has attempted to show that persons, by seeking relief from the burden of what are actually moral responsibilities, mystify and "technicize" their "problems in living." In turn, this hunger for help and health is fed by a behavioral technology ready and willing to free such persons of their moral burdens. Indeed, Szasz contends that the "mandate" of the contemporary psychiatrist is precisely "to obscure," and moreover "to deny" the ethical dilemmas of life, and to transform these into medical and technical problems susceptible to their solutions.[9] In this same way, transsexualism has been categorized as a medical and technical problem that is only resolvable by medical and technical specialties.

Mystification is at work throughout the transsexual odyssey. It operates in a variety of areas: in the claim that one is, for example, a man trapped in a woman's body; in the obscuring of the social components of the problem; in the hidden political dimensions of therapy; in the various individualized explanations; and in the very language

of transsexualism itself. As demonstrated earlier, it is biologically impossible to change chromosomal sex, and thus
the transsexual is not *really* transsexed. As Dr. Georges
Burou, a French physician who specializes in male-to-
constructed-female transsexualism phrases it: "I don't
change men into women. I transform male genitals into
genitals that have a female aspect. All the rest is in the
patient's mind."[10] Or as Jan Morris inadvertently stated:
"I wear the body of a woman."[11]

De-ethicization, of course, is defended in the name of
scientific knowledge and neutrality. However, neutrality
is a myth and the politics of diagnosis and therapy remain.
So too do the philosophical-ethical dimensions of the psychological craft. Under the guise of science, psychological
explanations often include value judgments. For example,
when John Money and Patricia Tucker assert: "Once a sex
distinction has worked or been pressured into the nuclear
core of your gender schema, to dislodge it is to threaten
you as an individual with destruction,"[12] they are using
popularized pseudoscientific language where the "oughts"
have been deleted, yet where they permeate the sentence.
Thus the reader translates: "Once a sex distinction has
worked or been pressured into the nuclear core of your
gender schema, one *should not* dislodge it, else the individual is threatened with destruction." One might also ask
here, destruction by whom? by what? Once more, the
agent is deleted.

The process of the de-ethicization of behavior by psychology and psychiatry has particular relevance for discussions of transsexualism and the consequences which
follow. By attributing transsexualism to biological or psychological causes, scientists, as stated previously, are conveying that there are only two choices: (1) adjustment to
one's body-role; or (2) surgery and counseling to transform
one's body and role. In effect, both of these choices are
biomedical—choice number one adds up to biology-is-
destiny, and choice number two states that, this failing,
hormonal and possibly surgical treatment (contingent
upon one's "passing," of course) are indicated. Either way,

the transsexual cannot really make an ethical choice because there are no *choices* to make. The only "choices"
represented are those that bio-medicine dictates in this
culture. The wider range of choices and the discovery of
meanings that would be available to one who could live
beyond sex roles, but in one's native body, are not made
available. Such reductionism and restricted counseling
fetishize the transsexual issue.

THERAPEUTIC FETISHIZATION

In discussing the various theories of transsexualism, I
often noted that both biological and psychological theories
reduced the issue of transsexualism to individual or interpersonal causes. Another way of viewing this, and thus understanding the reductionism more clearly, is to consider
these theories as fetishizations of the social. Not only the
theories, but the whole gamut of psychologizing, restrict
the issue to a very superficial area.

Ernest Becker, in *The Structure of Evil*, discusses the
function of fetishization. He views it as an attempt, in
some manageable way, to come to grips with a portion of
reality which is substituted for the whole. Fetishization,
for example, is one explanation why law-enforcement offi-
cials in our society are so obsessed with issues of traffic
violations, marijuana, and the like, but cannot cope with
the much more serious problems of rape and murder. As
Becker contends, the lesser problems, and the attention
they receive, are social fetishizations of the problem of
morality in modern times.[13] In the case of transsexualism,
it would be an overwhelming burden to attack the problem
of sex-role socialization on an individual, never mind social, level. Therefore, it is easier, applying a fetishized
logic, to confront the problem within patriarchal identity
and role limits, thereby making use of a ready-made system of knowledge and therapy that treats the problem individually on a *post-hoc* basis.

Moreover, the fetish object is precisely the one that

presents itself to our eyes in the most striking and compelling way. Obviously in the case of transsexualism, that which is most directly and immediately expressed (from the perspective of the transsexual, especially) is the feeling/knowledge that one is a woman "trapped" in the body of a man. Subsequent behavior and dress reinforce this "felt" identity and role. Evaluating whether or not a transsexual can "pass successfully" in the role of his or her desired sex monopolizes the attention and energies of those professionals in the gender identity clinics who should be evaluating the culturally prescribed roles themselves. In this same context, the reality of transsexualism is explained by the supposed effectiveness of sex-conversion surgery as the ultimate cure. These are all examples of what Becker calls "fetishizing the field," or "creating a locus of meaning in a very narrow sense, in order to be able to have some reality that calls upon one's adaptive energies."[14]

Transsexuals and transsexual "experts" focus on the genitalia of the opposite sex—the desired breasts and vagina, or the construction of an artificial phallus. These artifacts come to incarnate the essence of femaleness or maleness which the transsexual so urgently desires. The medical literature on transsexualism is filled with photographs, plates, and anatomical drawings of sexual organs that have been constructed "onto" the postoperative transsexual, in such a way as to highlight the "natural look" that the knife has wrought. Interestingly, these photographs seldom show the whole person. With a zoom lens effect, they center upon the breasts or phallus. Thus the photographs themselves illustrate the fetishizing of transsexualism. The medical-surgical solution begins to assert control in the narrow area of the chemical and surgical specialties. Attention becomes focused upon constructing the vagina, for example, in as aesthetic a way as possible.

What Becker amplified in his discussion of fetishism, Seymour Halleck discusses under the heading of "the politics of symptoms." Halleck points out that treatment which focuses on symptoms rather than on broad social or existential issues is very likely to be efficient. In the case of transsexualism, we see that 90 percent of transsexuals report satisfaction postoperatively.[15] However, as Halleck explains, this kind of satisfaction is achieved at the expense of exploring the social meaning of the symptoms.

By the instrumentality of hormones and surgery, the symptom is certainly removed but so is the indirect evidence provided by the symptom that something is amiss on a deeper level. Therefore, after medical intervention, transsexuals may have less power to cope with the forces of oppression than before they started treatment, since at this point, they fit into a role-defined world almost completely. Any critical awareness is thus diffused. Since the result of hormonal and surgical treatment is that the transsexual becomes an agreeable participant in a society which encourages sexism, primarily by sex-role oppression, then the moral and political implications of that treatment must be questioned. In this sense, transsexual surgery is a "social tranquilizer." For the sake of "health" and "wellbeing," the status quo of patriarchy is strengthened.

THE POLITICS OF TRANSSEXUAL THERAPY

Value freedom and political neutrality have long been advocated in psychiatry and the professions in general. But Seymour Halleck, in 1971, asserted what is by now a commonplace—that any kind of psychiatric or counseling intervention will have an impact upon the distribution of power in society. Psychiatric neutrality, in this perspective, is a fiction. Implicit in Halleck's position, of course, is the assertion that the psychiatrist or counselor is a social engineer, because any counselor has some preconceived ideas of what is good for people, whether these be implicit or explicit. Such values are transmitted to the person seeking help. Whatever route the counselor goes, she/he will either encourage the person to accept or to change the existing distribution of power.

As Halleck further points out, there is a strange tendency among counseling professionals to assume that any counseling intervention that is not explicitly political or that does not change the status quo is neutral. Whereas any professional activity that is explicitly change-oriented is designated as "political." Szasz formulates this same idea in a somewhat different way, emphasizing the social and ethical dimensions of a counselor's therapeutic stance.

Difficulties in human relations can be analyzed, interpreted, and given meaning only within specific social and ethical contexts. Accordingly, the psychiatrist's socio-ethical orientations will influence his ideas on what is wrong with the patient, on what deserves comment or interpretation, in what directions change might be desirable, and so forth.[16]

In our society, political power is based on sex. Kate Millett stated this most effectively back in 1970 in her work aptly titled *Sexual Politics*. By politics, she does not mean the word in the narrow sense but is referring to "power-structured relationships, arrangements whereby one group of persons is controlled by another."[17] The title, *Sexual Politics*, implies that the sex into which one is born and all that goes with biological maleness or femaleness create a category with political implications. The personal is recognized as political, and personal interaction between women and men is thereby seen to be political.

What goes largely unexamined, often even unacknowledged (yet is institutionalized nonetheless) in our social order, is the birthright priority whereby males rule females. Through this system a most ingenious form of "interior colonization" has been achieved. It is one which tends to be sturdier than any form of segregation and more rigorous than class stratification, more uniform, certainly more enduring. However its present appearance may be, sexual dominion obtains nevertheless as perhaps the most pervasive ideology of our culture and provides its most fundamental concept of power.[18]

Whereas any therapy affects the distribution of power in society, the relationship between transsexualism and sexual politics is a unique one. The encouragement that is given to transsexuals in therapy to conform to society's roles of masculinity and femininity supports the very bulwark of sexual politics—that is, sex-role socialization.

Furthermore, such therapy is not only political but morally manipulative. Therapy not only affects the distribution of power, but also brings about the alteration of values. What we have here is a very sophisticated form of behavior control and modification, on both the individual and the social level.

TRANSSEXUALISM AS BEHAVIOR CONTROL AND MODIFICATION

Transsexualism, as a proclaimed form of therapeutic surgery for nonphysical disorders, is located on a historical continuum of similar medical ventures, all of which legitimate(d) bodily intervention for purposes of improving behavior. In the nineteenth century, clitoridectomy for girls and women, and to a lesser extent, circumcision for boys were accepted methods of treatment for masturbation and other so-called sexual disorders.[19] In the 1930s, Egas Moniz, a Portuguese physician, received the Nobel Prize for his "ground-breaking work" on lobotomies. Moniz operated on state mental hospital inmates, using lobotomy for everything from depression to aggression. The new terminology for brain surgery of this nature today is psychosurgery, which its proponents have attempted to disassociate from the cruder procedures of Moniz and others by pointing to its more "refined" surgical techniques. But call it lobotomy or psychosurgery, surgeons continue to intrude upon human brains on the basis of tenuous localization theories that supposedly pinpoint the area of the brain where the "undesirable" behavior can be found and excised.[20] Finally, transsexual surgery is justified on the basis of adjusting a person's body to his/her mind.

What each of these surgical ventures has in common is

that they derive their therapeutic legitimacy from a medical model which locates behavioral problems within certain affected organs. Surgery then alters, intrudes, removes and, in the case of transsexualism, adds organs. In each venture, a surgical fetishizing takes place, reducing the social components of the problem to the most tangible and manageable forms.

Further, what each of these surgical ventures has in common is the modification and control of behavior. Clitoridectomies modify sexual behavior or fantasied sexual behavior; psychosurgery modifies the gamut of behavior from hyperactivity in preteen children to so-called manic depression in dissatisfied housewives; transsexual surgery modifies everything that comes under the heading of masculine and feminine in a patriarchal society—thus practically everything.

In the case of transsexualism, behavior modification is both a prerequisite for and an effect of the surgery. Prior to the operation, gender identity clinics and professionals require that transsexuals alter their behavior to conform to the prescribed gender role the person desiring transsexual surgery wants. In this context, it can also be pointed out that sex-role conditioning itself is a form of behavior control (i.e., the control that a patriarchal society exercises over its members). Yet, with a good number of people, this form of social control has been unsuccessful. This has happened with the transsexual, who has not been adequately conditioned into the role/identity that accompanies his or her body. Instead of seeing this unsuccessful conditioning and gender dissatisfaction as a "signal of transcendence," however, the transsexual seeks out (with the help of the transsexual technicians) another mode of behavior modification, which is transsexual treatment and surgery. This latter form of behavior modification and control then reinforces, for the transsexual, in several hormonal and surgical strokes, the behavior that it took years of sex-role conditioning to impose upon persons who belong to the sex that the transsexual desires. Thus we have a multiplication of modes of behavior modification:

1. Sex-role conditioning that accompanies a male or female body and, which, in the case of the transsexual, fails.
2. Sex-role reconditioning which accompanies and is a prerequisite for the body that the transsexual seeks and which the transsexual technicians (psychological and surgical) encourage and reinforce.
3. Transsexual treatment and surgery which solidify the presurgical conditioning.

Reinforcement is a key word for behaviorists. One of the central claims of B. F. Skinner is that the immediacy of reinforcement is what shapes successive behavior in all "learning animals." Skinner differs from classical conditioning theorists (e.g., Pavlov) in saying that behavior is shaped by what *follows* it rather than by what *precedes* it. In the past, most psychologists of this persuasion had assumed that new attitudes were necessary to develop new behavior. Skinner turned this around and said that new attitudes follow or accompany changed behavior.[21]

In the case of the male-to-constructed-female transsexual, however, feminine behavior is shaped by the *promise* of what is to follow—that is, a changed body. Encouraged by the gender identity clinics to prove transsexual status by their ability to pass as feminine, transsexuals seek hormone treatments and ultimately sex-conversion surgery as positive reinforcement of further stereotypical behavior. Thus transsexual counseling and clinics are very good examples of Skinner's "operant conditioning" philosophy: the controller, using a series of carefully planned schedules of positive and/or negative reinforcements (shortening or lengthening the "passing" time) brings about desired responses (stereotypical behavior) from the transsexual.

However, the most significant point in Skinner's philosophy is that the controller will exert hardly any control, because the controlled will control themselves voluntarily. Coercion, in the traditional sense, will not have to be employed. Skinner creates a utopia where people "will" to live. (Somewhat contradictorily, however, freedom is a "mentalistic concept" in the Skinnerian schema.) It is clear that voluntarism is a very deceptive construct in a behaviorist framework.

In like manner, the concept of voluntarism is deceptively highlighted in the transsexual literature. Sex-conversion surgery is not forced upon transsexuals. The transsexual researchers and clinicians emphasize that persons who desire to change sex seek such treatment eagerly. Like the benevolent behaviorism in Skinner, transsexual surgery is presented as something thousands request, many of whom are turned away.

To use another example: Many oppressed people use heroin to make life tolerable in intolerable conditions. Heroin usage is a highly effective yet dangerous treatment for dissatisfaction and despair. Recently, for example, black leaders have drawn attention to heroin as a pacifier of black people. As Jesse Jackson has phrased it: "We have come from the southern rope to the northern dope." In a strict sense, one cannot say that the drug is forced upon its users. Indeed they seek it eagerly. But in the long run, the willing use of the drug strengthens the position of the oppressors and the oppressed. The contentment and euphoria produced by the drug diffuses the militancy, or potential militancy, of the user. Thus heroin is a tool of behavior control and modification.

Transsexual surgery, in much the same way, produces satisfaction and relief for the transsexual. In contrast to more overt, coercive forms of behavior control and modification, such as involuntary commitment in prisons or mental institutions, or "informed consent" obtained while in these same institutions, transsexualism appears to be blissfully and freely chosen. Yet just as commentators have asked how a truly *"informed* consent" can be obtained in a coercive context, such as a prison or mental institution, I would pose the question: how can transsexuals truly give "informed consent" and freely choose to convert to the opposite sex anatomy and role when the coercive power of sex-role socialization is filtered through all institutions in a patriarchal society? Not that such socialization is deterministic, but rather that it deeply conditions one's choices as well as one's *motivation* to choose. In a traditional sense, no one forced the transsexual to change sex. No one forced the transsexual to start hormone therapy. No one forced the transsexual into opposite-sex roles and behavior. But in a society where masculinity and femininity accompany a male or female body, the options are limited, if one does not have a context of support to transcend these roles. When the transsexual experts maintain that they use transsexual procedures only with people who ask for them, and who prove that they can "pass," they obscure the social reality. Given patriarchy's prescription that one must be either masculine or feminine, free choice is conditioned.

What is significant here is that either way—by outright coercion or by employing an individual's "voluntarism" against herself or himself—the coercive impact is the same. As Willard Gaylin has noted in a different context: "Its [society's] coercive impact, incidentally, is just as great whether it was designed to produce the effect, or whether the effect was an accidental historic and developmental spin-off."[22]

We are at a point in the history of behavior control and modification where we must be very aware of its more subtle forms. Most people recognize the manipulation of human behavior and emotions at its most extreme—when that manipulation is organized, or when physical agents are used. Many people, however, would not perceive transsexual surgery as a form of behavior control and modification, even though physical instrumentation is used, because the concept of voluntarism has taken hold, and the coercion of a role-defined environment is not recognized as an influential factor. Furthermore: "It may be that the general population resists the idea of seeing emotional coercion in the same terms as physical coercion because it threatens basic beliefs about man's autonomy, because one likes to think of himself as a logical individual under the control of intellect rather than emotion."[23] But, of course, social controllers have been well-known for convincing the individual that she/he is in control.

Thus it is important, in the transsexual context, to examine the whole issue of control. Who is controlling whom? Presently, the controllers are the gender identity clinics and the transsexual experts who staff them. It is not far-fetched to conceive of a "gender identity business," as such institutions proliferate, functioning as centers of social control. We now have violence control centers, such as Vacaville, which, in the words of its main organizer, has been designed to focus on the "pathologically violent individual" and is aimed at "altering undesirable behavior."[24]

As the gender identity clinics expand and the tolerance for transsexual surgery grows, it is not inconceivable that such clinics could become sex-role control centers, for deviant, nonfeminine females and nonmasculine males, as well as for transsexuals. Such gender identity centers are already being used for the treatment of designated child transsexuals. The use of behavior modification and control is presently very widespread. It is fast becoming a tool of American law enforcement, and funding for it from state and government sources has been documented.[25] Furthermore, we can safely predict, on the basis of past and present CIA and FBI activities, that if gender identity facilities became government controlled, some gender modification activities would be reported while others would be repressed from public view; only those offering a therapeutic rationale would be revealed. Moreover, such controllers and centers for control (such as Johns Hopkins and U.C.L.A.) would continue to have a very specific philosophy about what women and men should be, how they should act, and what functions they should perform in society. In fact, gender identity clinic research and treatment has already been funded by grants from the National Institute of Mental Health and other government-affiliated funding sources. All this is happening, and will continue to happen, of course, in the name of science and therapy, and with the denial that any social engineering is taking place. Here we have institutional sexism at its most functional capacity.

A dystopian perspective, some will say, but such perspectives have a way of highlighting present and future reality by daring to predict what most persons do not, or choose not to, perceive. The point is that sex roles already do not have to be "forced" upon people; most quickly give "informed consent." But feminism has been fast chipping away at the institutions of sex-role conditioning in this society. Threatened commentators from a patriarchal perspective have been quick to call feminism "sexual suicide."[26] Just as Drs. Vernon Mark, William Sweet, and Frank Ervin suggested in the *Journal of the American Medical Association* that psychotechnology could be used for the repression of violence in the Detroit ghetto rebellion of 1967,[27] it is not inconceivable that Drs. X, Y, and Z could propose sexual technology for the repression of sex-role deviancy. It has been done before (e.g., clitoridectomies) and it can be done again. It would all be part and parcel of present "voluntaristic" therapies for the repression of deviancy. Individuals undergo psychosurgery giving "informed consent"; parents, on advice of school administrators and physicians, sign "informed consent" papers to have Ritalin administered to their children in public-school centers; women "consentingly" undergo unnecessary hysterectomies for prophylactic reasons such as the vague "threat" of uterine cancer (imagine a prophylactic penectomy!)

The potential for the benevolent control of sex-role behavior is enormous. It is my contention that it has already begun in the gender identity clinics. But control here has entered with a whimper, not with a bang. And conformity is being enforced in the name of therapy, at the individual's request, and with the effect of 90 percent "satisfied customers." If behaviorist philosophers such as B. F. Skinner are right, and behaviorist technicians such as José Delgado remains active, then future social controllers can replace control-through-torture with control-through-pleasure. What is becoming possible with Delgado's electronic brain stimulation (ESB) is also becoming possible with transsexual surgery. The following two observations are not all that different. From Delgado:

Electrodes were implanted in her right temporal lobe and upon stimulation of a contact located in the superior part about thirty millimeters below the surface, the patient reported a pleasant tingling sensation in the left side of her body "from my face down to the bottom of my legs." She started giggling and making funny comments, stating that she enjoyed the sensation "very much." Repetition of these stimulations made the patient more communicative and flirtatious, and she ended by openly expressing her desire to marry the therapist. . . . The second patient expressed her fondness for the therapist (who was new to her), kissed his hands, and talked about her immense gratitude for what was being done for her.[28]

And in the case of transsexuals:

Typical comments after the operation included feelings of deep satisfaction at having achieved, as they felt, a true female status, despite admission that they were in fact only castrated, feminized males. They reported an absence of self-consciousness and a feeling of being at ease and of having ultimately achieved a happy state with more peace of mind. Increased feelings of femininity occurred along with the development of a sense of identity with all women. They began to think of themselves as women rather than as disabled males. The fear of detection and of being suspected disappeared despite the fact that several were not entirely credible as females. Several described a sense of release and a change of mental attitude; they felt that it was now impossible to prove that they were not women. Most expressed a level of satisfaction in their new castrated status far superior to anything they had experienced as men. Acceptance as women by other women and by the world at large was their ultimate satisfaction. The possession of a female vulva was of secondary importance to this.[29]

In both examples, we see expressions of sweet, intense, and protracted satisfaction or, as one commentator has called it, "total body orgasm." Humans have been known to withstand even the most intense torture. It is doubtful,

however, that we could withstand the most intense pleasure.* As William Irwin Thompson has noted:

If the momentary "total orgasm" experienced when a drug addict
injects Methedrine is sufficient to alter the personality, then it is
obvious that a total body orgasm protracted over a period of hours
or days would be sufficient to alter a person's perception of time,
his perception of his own life history, and the self-image and character structure derived from these. From the point of view of the behavioral scientist, this would be pleasant work in what could be ami-
able surroundings.[30]

The transsexual counselors' and technicians' apparent
purpose, of course, is neither to control nor to create
massage parlors of pleasure, but to provide therapeutic
relief for those persons who feel themselves burdened with
"the wrong mind in the wrong body." However, the final
irony, as Thompson has stated, is that "at the end of
humanism, it is the human body that has become the
battleground."[31] I would add further than the real final
irony is that at the nemesis of patriarchal civilization, all
the silicone breasts and artificial vaginas cannot put *man*
back together again!

TRANSSEXUALISM AS MEDICAL EXPERIMENTATION

Therapy has historically covered a multitude of medical
sins. The welfare of the individual or the welfare of society

---

*Adrienne Rich has suggested in contrast to this interpretation, that
what really happens is that control works through the controller's
power to *cut off* pleasure at any point, rather than through his
power to confer pleasure. She also points out that there is a "social
situation of pleasure" to which persons are conditioned. For example, a woman who is socialized to identify orgasmic pleasure with
being handled and controlled by a man will more easily be stimu-
lated to pleasure by electrode brain implants than a woman whose
"social situation of pleasure" does not include such handling and
control. What Rich is saying is that, for such women, ESB would
not be pleasurable in any sense they could identify as free human
beings.

has often provided a camouflage for the worst forms of experimentation. We have seen how therapy relates to behavior control and modification. What also becomes obvious is that therapeutic goals can mask experimentation.

First of all, the nature of transsexual surgery is experimental on physical grounds alone. There is a substantial amount of evidence that transsexual hormone therapy and surgery cause cancer.[32] Transsexual treatment is far from established as a safe medical procedure and as such is still experimental. Secondly, transsexuals are "volunteering" for surgery that they hope will relieve their sex role "dis-ease" of gender dissatisfaction and dysphoria. But there is no evidence to prove that transsexual surgery "cures" what is basically a problem of transcendence. In other words, sex-conversion surgery cannot bestow upon the transsexual the sense of self that she/he lacks. Furthermore, there is evidence, at least in some postoperative cases, that transsexuals themselves have come to realize this, but too late.[33] Third, and most importantly, we have yet to see the total "fall-out" effect of transsexualism in enforcing the further institutionalization of sex roles. Until this is obvious, transsexual surgery is still experimental in terms of what effects it will have upon an already rigidly gender-defined society. And if it is true that the female-to-constructed-male transsexual is merely a token who provides the "illusion of the inclusion" of women into the transsexual context,* then one hypothesis that is being tested in the transsexual "laboratories" is whether or not it is possible for men to diminish the number of women and/or to create a new "breed" of females. Again, I would emphasize that this is not a mere feminist flight of fantasy. Scientists have already stated their "scientific" interest in diminishing the numbers of women.

Take, for example, the words of the well-known biologist John Postgate in his ringing defense of sex-selection technology. Postgate defends what he calls a "male child" pill by offering it as a proposed panacea for world popula-

*See Chapter I.

tion problems. In words that, upon first reading, appear to be satire, we quickly come to realize that Postgate is deadly serious (deadly to women, that is).

Imagine what would happen if a male child pill became freely available throughout the world through the World Health Organization. Even in developed countries there is surprising prejudice among ordinary people in favour of having male children; among most African, Asian, Central and South American peoples, this prejudice amounts to almost an obsession. Countless millions of people would leap at the opportunity to breed male: no compulsion or even propaganda would be needed to encourage its use, only evidence of success by example. . . . I hope, incidentally, that it is obvious why I specified a "man child" pill; one selecting for females would not work. [34]

As far as the leftover women would be concerned, Postgate has thought of everything.

All sorts of taboos would be expected and it is probable that a form of *purdah* would become necessary. Women's right to work, even to travel alone freely, would probably be forgotten transiently. Polyandry might well become accepted in some societies; some might treat their women as queen ants, others as rewards for the most outstanding (or most determined) males. . . . Whether the world would come to resemble a giant boy's public school or a huge male prison is difficult to predict. [35]

Finally, the social results and economic consequences of all this, Postgate predicts, would be "self-regulating."

Some of the ethical issues that have been discussed in the biomedical literature on human experimentation take a different turn when applied to transsexuals. [36] *One* issue that recurs in the literature on human experimentation again and again is that of weighing the integrity of an individual experimentee's rights against the benefits that may accrue to society. This issue has often been discussed in the context of an individual who risks her/his health in an experiment designed to acquire knowledge about a specific disease thereby benefiting society, but not necessarily directly benefiting the individual concerned. However, there is a reversal of these priorities in the transsexual situation, which focuses on the alleged benefits that accrue to the individual. In this instance, it is the ill effects that accrue to society that must be questioned. Transsexual surgery is professedly done to promote the individual transsexual's right of synchronizing body and mind. Yet what society "gains" is a role conformist person who reinforces sex roles.

Pleasure and Pain: Medical Theodicies. A *second* issue that has been discussed in the wider medical context of human experimentation is whether medicine is obliged to alleviate all suffering, that is, whether it should make the world "disease-free." In the case of transsexualism, there are many ethical objections to alleviating individual gender suffering at the expense of reinforcing, qualitatively and quantitatively, sex-role conformity. Ivan Illich's words are applicable: "Medical civilization teaches that suffering is unnecessary, because pain can be technically eliminated. . . . The subject is better understood when the social situation in which pain occurs is included in the explanation of pain."[37] However, my main point has been to show that the social situation has not been "included in the explanation of pain." Instead transsexual technicians and therapists and, by extension, transsexuals, engage in smothering the intrinsic question mark that gender "dis-ease" produces about the society in which it arises.

Medical theodicies, however, unlike many religious ones, are not passive but proclaimedly curative. One's reward is not in the next life but in this life. The ethic is reversed; do not suffer now but seek ye another body! The activity of this medical theodicy involves several steps. First of all, the transsexual therapists relate the anomic experiences of the gender-dissatisfied individual to a condition "known" as transsexualism. Once named and institutionalized in gender identity clinics, the "condition" of transsexualism explains *why* one would have the wrong mind in the wrong body. Secondly, like all theodicies, the medical theodicy is undergirded by an attitude of the surrender of self to the ordering power of the transsexual therapists and technicians. The medical order confronts transsexuals with a meaningful reality that comprehends them and all their experiences. It bestows sense on all their experiences that once seemed so unfathomable. It enables someone like Jan Morris to order, in chronological fashion, the steps in his transsexual odyssey from the age of three when he first "realized he was a woman" as he sat under his mother's piano listening to Sibelius, to his conquest of Mt. Everest and last fling with masculinity. As Peter Berger has noted:

The individual who adequately internalizes these meanings at the same time transcends himself. His birth, the various stages of his biography . . . may now be interpreted by him in a manner that transcends the unique place of these phenomena in his experience.[38]

More importantly, the denial and surrender of the self is facilitated by the transsexual order. "This is the attitude of masochism, that is, the attitude in which the individual reduces himself to an inert and thinglike object *vis-à-vis* his fellowmen. . . . In this attitude, pain itself, physical or mental, serves to ratify the denial of self to the point where it may actually be subjectively pleasurable."[39]

What has been scarcely noted in many commentaries on transsexualism is the immense amount of physical pain that the surgery entails. Generally, this fact is totally minimized. Most postoperative transsexuals interviewed seldom commented on the amount of physical pain connected with their surgery. Are we to suppose no pain is involved? Anyone who has the slightest degree of medical knowledge knows that penectomies, mastectomies, hysterectomies, vaginoplasties, mammoplasties, and the like cannot be painless for those who undergo them. There is also the pain of anxiety about possible consequences of surgery— such as cancer or faulty healing. It seems that the silence regarding physical pain, on the part of the transsexual, can be explained only by an attitude of masochism, where one of the key elements of the transsexual order is indeed the denial not only of self but of physical pain to the point "where it may actually be subjectively pleasurable," or at least subjectively negligible. At least one medical team has recognized this, although in muted and partial form. Categorizing primary clinical types who request sex reassignment, they label one type as masochist (or sadomasochist).

The masochists find that sexual arousal is facilitated by the experience of pain prior to sexual activity: they look upon the surgical excision of the genitalia (albeit unconsciously) as a form of masochistic adventure with the surgeon.[40]

Ernest Becker has stated that masochism is another word for "poverty of behavior," as is sadism.

The sado-masochist is someone who has trouble believing in the validity and sanctity of people's insides—their spirit, personality, or self. These insides could be his own or others'; if they are his own he tends to be masochistic, if they are others' he tends to be called a sadist.[41]

Transsexuals, as masochists, have great difficulty in believing in the validity and sanctity of their own insides. They are attempting to gain a sense of self not only through the acquisition of a new body, but through the pain involved in this process. Physical pain is a constant reminder to transsexuals that they are finally coming alive.

In the transsexual's quest for what may be regarded as a deeper self, pain provides the illusion of profound change. Pain is necessary to confirm what is regarded by the transsexual as more than a superficial change. This, in one way, explains why transsexuals do not settle for cross-dressing. Transvestism, for them, is too superficial and does not provide the bite or the painful experience of true conversion. Transsexuals, in their experience of pain, feel they have thus reached the essence of female or male existence.

There is also the element of sadism which is, of course, the other side of the masochistic coin.

The esthetics of the sadist is thus partly due to the deficiencies of his own self: in order for reality to be convincing, in order for him to feel his maximum powers, he wants the world to be peopled with

concrete manipulatable objects, with objects that do not have any
elusive insides. This is the reason that he expends all his effort on
manipulating the flesh: either he cannot deal with the insides of
others or he will not recognize these insides as valid.[42]

The transsexual therapist—in adjusting the transsexual
mind and behavior to the stereotype of the desired sex—
and the medical specialists—in adjusting the transsexual
body to the desired body-type of the opposite sex—are
dealing with transsexuals as manipulatable objects and reducing them to the world of appearances. "Here we can
understand the inter-changeability of the sadistic and
masochistic postures. These are terms which describe one
and the same thing: weakness and felt limitation in oneself; sharp duality of spirit and matter in people."[43] The
sadist, as well as the masochist, cannot relate to the infinite possibilities of the spirit and confines these spiritual
possibilities to the world of matter. Thus the potentiality
for infinite be-ing is reduced to static being, where it can
be rendered safe and deprived of its power to transform
the gender-defined self and the gender-defined society.

It is in this way that religious theodicies have restricted
not only the selfhood but the social protest capacity of
their believers. In so doing, of course, they have also directly legitimated the institutional order in question. As
Berger has noted, "the theodicy constitutes an essentially
sado-masochistic collusion, on the level of meaning, between oppressors and victims."[44] On both sides, the result
is one of "world-maintenance," and in the transsexual
context, the maintenance of the particular institutional
order of patriarchal society.

A not-so-incidental by-product of this particular medical
theodicy is the enlargement of medical knowledge about
manipulating organs of the body which specifically function to define biological sex. This, of course, works to the
ultimate benefit of the sadistic side of the theodicy, enabling medical research and technology to acquire a specialized body of scientific knowledge on the manipulation
of human sexuality that probably could not be acquired
by any other accepted medical procedure. At least two re-

searchers have admitted this, although the admissions, of course, are mixed with therapeutic qualifications. Richard Green has stated:

To a considerable degree, the medical profession itself is responsible for the limited extent of knowledge which currently exists about transsexualism and sex reassignment. While the current availability of gonadal hormones and the refinement of surgical techniques have made it possible to partly realize the fantasies and aspirations of the transsexual and have brought about an increasing demand for sex reassignment, *medicine, by closing the door to these patients for study and treatment, has cast away a population from whom considerable information about gender identity and human sexuality could have been obtained.* Particularly in the United States, until very recently, sex reassignment has been nearly unobtainable. Thus transsexuals sought treatment elsewhere. Consequently, neither preoperative screening nor postoperative evaluations were made. Rejection of the transsexual's request, rather than preventing him from obtaining surgery, resulted in the highly motivated, affluent patient still being able to obtain his reassignment, but, in the process, *being virtually lost to scientific study.*[45] (Italics mine.)

In a similar manner, Milton Edgerton has stated:

The current availability of reputable physician teams who offer sincere efforts to understand and treat the transsexual patient may represent the greatest progress that medicine has made over the past decade in dealing with human gender disorders. . . . *Certainly it offers doctors an unrivaled opportunity to study and understand the dynamics of gender as it relates to human function and self-imagery.* Plastic surgeons are beginning to realize that it is more important to correct the patient's "sense of deformity" or self-image than to correct his external or objective deformity.[46] (Italics mine.)

Thus transsexualism is made to appear as an "acceptable" medical venture in which scientific opportunism is admitted but only as linked to therapeutic and humanitarian goals.

A *third* issue to consider is just how informed consent can be attained, especially in the face of so many unknown hazards about the experiment. First of all, a truly informed consent would highlight, for the transsexual, the whole issue of sex roles and gender definitions themselves. It would reveal to him how moving from one stereotype to its opposite does not even minimally alter the social basis of sex-role conformity in this culture and how the transsexual, in undertaking surgery, is reinforcing this conformity. These are what might be called the social hazards of the transsexual experiment. My survey of the literature and first-hand interviews with transsexuals and transsexual clinicians thus far have revealed that these social hazards, or even their possibility, are not explored.

Furthermore, it has generally been recognized that the withholding or distortion of *any* relevant knowledge that bears upon the experiment constitutes a violation of informed consent. It is questionable whether even the physical hazards of transsexual treatment and surgery are explained to the would-be transsexual.

Finally, the issue of informed consent enters again in the context of the ethics of experimentation. Discussions on medical experimentation have focused on the question of whether a truly informed consent can ever be obtained from a "captive population."[47] As I have shown, transsexuals are just such a captive population within a patriarchal society. Otto Guttentag has written:

It is generally agreed in our culture, experimental subjects must be volunteers. What is meant by the word is, first, that the experimental subjects who agree to volunteer are judged by society as *free in the psychological sense*, as experiencing themselves ultimately as *centers of autonomy*, whatever the contingencies; and second, that they are *free in the sociological sense*, that is, not dependent *upon the experimenter* to satisfy their spiritual or physical needs.[48] (Italics mine.)

First of all, how are would-be transsexuals free "in the psychological sense"? How can they be ultimately "centers of autonomy" if their motivation to choose differently is held captive by a patriarchal society, so that even what they finally do choose (i.e., transsexual surgery) binds them even more firmly to that society? Secondly, how are transsexuals free in the "sociological sense" when indeed they do depend upon the experimenters to "satisfy" their "spiritual needs" (the conviction and fulfillment of, for example, finally becoming a woman) and "physical needs" (e.g., acquiring the hormones and body of a woman)?

Learning from the Nazi Experience. Much of the literature on medical experimentation has focused on the various captive populations of prisoners and mental patients, but the most notorious example of unethical medical experimentation on a captive population is the Nazi concentration camps. The example of the Nazi camps has often been cited in ethical arguments that attempt to sensationalize and disparage opposing views. Furthermore, ethicists especially have used these experiments to throw sand in people's eyes about such issues as abortion and euthanasia, and to create ethical arguments based on a kind of domino theory. In mentioning the Nazi experiments, it is not my purpose to directly compare transsexual surgery to what went on in the camps but rather to demonstrate that much of what did go on there can be of value in surveying the ethics of transsexualism.

The specter of unethical medical experimentation loomed large after the publicity that was given to the Nazi concentration camps during World War Two. In fact, one of the first comprehensive codes of medical ethics, specifically dealing with the ethics of experimentation, emerged from the Nuremberg trials in the wake of the famous "Doctors Trial" or, as it is sometimes called, the "Trial of the Twenty-Three."[49] The Nazi medical experiments read like a series of horror stories. The experiments were quite varied. High-altitude tests were done on prisoners to observe the point at which they stopped breathing. Inmates of the camps were subjected to freezing experiments to observe the changes that take place in a person during this kind of slow death, and also to determine the point of no return. Experiments in bone-grafting and injections with lethal viruses were commonplace. The

much-publicized sterilization experiments were carried out
on a massive scale at several camps, primarily by radiation
and surgical means, for the purpose of seeing how many
sterilizations could be performed in the least amount of
time and most "economically" (thus anaesthesia was not
used). However, the point of all this background is not
merely to recite a list of atrocities, but to highlight several points that apply to the situation of transsexualism.

As Thomas Szasz has noted: "The activities of the Nazi
physicians . . . were, unfortunately, not the aberrations of
a holy healing profession imposed upon it by the terrors of
a totalitarian regime, but, on the contrary, were the characteristic, albeit exaggerated, expressions of the medical
profession's traditional functions as instruments of social
control."[50] Historically, many physicians aided the Inqui-
sition, actively supported the military efforts of all na-
tions, and today serve as an "extralegal police force" to
control deviance, especially in the realm of psychiatry,
which wields vast political powers. Today especially, it
is no longer the alliance of church and state that should be
feared, that is, *theocracy*, but rather the alliance between
medicine and the state, that is, *pharmacracy*.[51] It is medicine that presently functions as the new secular religion,
with the continuous aid of sustained government support.
Not so incidentally, some transsexual research has been
funded by federal grants.

The Nazi doctors undertook many of their experiments
in the name of science but for the purpose of supposedly
gaining racial knowledge (e.g., how did skull measurements
differ between Aryans and non-Aryans?). The doctors who
treat transsexuals undertake many of their experiments in
the name of therapy but for purposes of gaining sexual
knowledge (e.g., is it possible to construct a functional
vagina in a male body?). What we are witnessing in the
transsexual context is a science at the service of a patriarchal ideology of sex-role conformity in the same way that
breeding for blond hair and blue eyes became a so-called
science at the service of Nordic racial conformity.

This leads into the second point to be learned from the Nazi experience—the questionableness of detached scientific fixation and so-called objective knowledge. It must be remembered that such fixation and "objectivity" led to one of the most profound inhumanities that the world has ever witnessed. It is this kind of fixation, accompanied by a cult of objective truth, which helps to explain why the Nazi doctors did what they did. "A profound inhumanity had long been presaged. This is the alchemy of the modern age, the transmogrification of subject into object, of man into a thing against which the destructive urge may wreak its fury without havoc."[52] One must remember that many of the Nazi physicians whose experiments were the most brutal refused to recognize in the end that they had done wrong. Dr. Karl Brandt, for example, during his trial at Nuremberg, offered his living body for medical experiments like those he had conducted.[53] Before Brandt met his death at the side of the gallows, he made a final speech, which included these words: "It is no shame to stand on this scaffold. I served my Fatherland as others before me."[54]

It is this kind of scientific fixation, among other things, that impels doctors to pursue transsexual surgery when there are so many more pressing concerns: when our maternal morbidity and infant mortality statistics are outrageously high; when there are still no adequate or foolproof means of birth control; and when breast cancer ranks as one of the greatest killers of women. In other words, transsexual surgery is unnecessary surgery, performed in part because of the "objective" knowledge that it offers to researchers and technicians on a subject that is not knowable from other sources; it diverts time, attention, energy, and research money away from other medical areas that are more pressing and need attention; it provides a "marketplace," so to speak, for the surgical talents of doctors; and it fattens doctors' wallets. Transsexual surgery is not cheap. Prices range from $3000 to $12,000. As stated previously, it is significant also that both govern-

ment and private medical insurance plans cover the cost
of surgery in some cases. This has always been a financial
incentive for doctors in performing surgery.

Unnecessary surgery is spiraling, especially during the
last quarter of a century. A House of Representatives subcommittee reported in July of 1975: "If the scalpels of
American surgeons remain as active as they are today,
nearly half the women in the country will undergo hysterectomies by the time they're 70, and one of every three
men will have hernia surgery."[55] The same committee
reported that at least one third of these operations was unnecessary and concluded that money was a basic factor in
their performance. "The business of surgery has boomed in
the last decade to become a $25 billion pursuit involving
more than 18 million operations a year."[56] It is not inconceivable that transsexual surgery (and various modifications of it), although it is being done on a minimal level
presently, could also skyrocket to high numbers, and that
the medical labeling of a condition "known" as transsexualism will increase the number of people with excep-
tional medical consumer status.

The third point to be learned from the Nazi experiments concerns the information that accrued to medical
science because of them. This is not a factor to which
most commentators refer. William Shirer, author of *The
Rise and Fall of the Third Reich*, claims that, "in the use
of concentration camp inmates and prisoners of war as
human guinea pigs, very little, if any, benefit to science
was achieved."[57] However, there is other evidence that
explicitly states that certain medical experiments that
went on in the camps were later taken up and used by
science, although the origins of such research were generally hidden from publication. Guttentag remarks that
"contrary to general belief, some of the experiments that
those men performed were scientifically valuable and are
quoted in Western literature."[58] One example of this is
the low temperature and freezing experiments.

While a medical procedure or experiment should not

be determined by its origin, nevertheless its origin is instructive. Applying this to the transsexual context, it is significant that the first physician on record to perform sex-conversion surgery was a German by the name of F. Z. Abraham, who reported the first case in 1931. Furthermore, Benjamin relates that the Institute of Sexual Science in Berlin did much work on transvestism (and probably transsexualism before it was named such) under the leadership of Dr. Magnus Hirschfeld. Benjamin states that it had a "famous and rich museum, clinic, and lecture hall." In 1933, he says, it was destroyed by the Nazis because, "The Institute's confidential files were said to have contained too many data on prominent Nazis, former patients of Hirschfeld, to allow the constant threat of discovery to persist."[59] Benjamin visited Hirschfeld and his Institute many times during the 1920s.

We also know that at least one transsexual operation was done in the camps. Joseph Wechsberg in his editing of *The Murderers Among Us: The Simon Wiesenthal Memoirs* recounts Wiesenthal's recollection of a victim of the camp's experimental surgery.

I met another boy whom the scientists of Auschwitz, after several operations, had successfully turned into a woman. He was then thirteen years old. After the war, a complicated operation was performed on him in a West German clinic. The doctors restored the man's physical masculinity, but they couldn't give back his emotional equilibrium.[60]

By this comparison, I do not mean to exploit the very real difference between a conditioned "voluntary" medical procedure performed on adult transsexuals and the deliberate sadism performed on unwilling bodies and minds in the camps. However, it is important to understand that some transsexual research and technology may well have been initiated and developed in the camps and that, in the past, as well as now, surgery was not performed for the present professed goal of therapy, but to accumulate medical knowledge.

At this point, it is the task of this book to suggest

different, and what I regard as more adequate, answers to the questions that transsexualism raises. In Chapter VI, I place transsexualism in a more philosophical context by discussing an ethic of *integrity*. It is my hope that this discussion will not be regarded as abstract, or as distracting, but that it will form the basis for viewing the deeper and more mythic aspects of the transsexual phenomenon.

CHAPTER VI

Toward

the Development

of an Ethic

of Integrity

THOSE who advocate transsexualism emphasize certain values. Primarily, the transsexual empire promotes *integration*. In this chapter, I propose an ethic of *integrity*. There is a crucial distinction between integration and integrity.

Briefly, *integration* means putting together a combination of parts in order to achieve completeness or wholeness. In contrast, the word *integrity* means an original wholeness from which no part can be taken away. It is my contention that, in a deep philosophical sense, transsexual therapy and treatment have encouraged integration solutions rather than helping individuals to realize an integrity of be-ing.

In its emphasis on integration, much of the recent psychological, medical, and medical-ethical literature on transsexualism, and the solutions they propose, resemble theories of androgyny. In many ways, contemporary transsexual treatment is a modern version of medieval, androgynous alchemy where stereotypical femininity is integrated with a male genotype to produce a transsexually constructed woman. As alchemy treated the qualitative as quantitative in its attempts to isolate vital forces of the universe within its laboratories of matter, transsexual treatment does the same by reducing the quest for the vital forces of selfhood to the artifacts of hormones and surgical appendages. Transsexualism is comparable to the theme of androgyny that represents biological hermaphroditism, because ultimately the transsexual becomes a surgically constructed androgyne, and thus a synthetic hybrid. Furthermore, the transsexual also becomes a sex-stereotyped hermaphrodite, often unwittingly displaying his former masculine gestures, behavior, and style while attempting to conform to his new feminine role.

The first drafts of this chapter were entitled "An Ethic of Androgyny." But as I examined the androgynous tradition and its uses in recent literature, problems of etymology, history, and philosophy arose that were not evident at first glance. These necessitated the choice of a different ethical vision, which I have called *integrity*. The word *integrity* means an original unity from which no part can be taken away—thus an original wholeness of personhood not divided by sex-role definitions. Androgyny, in contrast, connotes integration—putting together the parts of masculinity and femininity in order to complete that which is supposedly incomplete. This gives a clue to the reality of the transsexual process, which can be viewed as adding the desired body and role parts to the "native-born" self, while discarding other parts, yet never going beyond the parts themselves to a more intrinsic unity of personhood. Thus, what I call an ethic of integrity is an attempt to discuss an original unity before the Fall of sex-role stereotyping. Until those contemplating transsexual surgery come to realize that such a step does nothing to promote this integrity on both a personal and social level, they will continue to settle for many of the false and partial modes of androgynous integration.

THE ANDROGYNOUS TRADITION

The androgynous tradition in theology and philosophy represents many varied but also many similar themes.* First of all, and most often, androgyny symbolizes primal personhood or original humanity, in its bisexual or asexual condition. Maleness and femaleness were perceived as divisions resulting from the Fall and not originally intended to be part of primordial personhood. Thus, for example, Adam in the Garden of Eden is represented as originally combining and/or transcending maleness and femaleness. Such androgynous notions are present in the rabbinic commentaries on Genesis, in the Gnostics, in the Jewish Cabala, and in John Scotus Erigena. In this same context, androgyny became a salvation or reunification theme, bringing divided personhood, maleness and femaleness, back into its original and divinely intended unity of either biological bisexuality (i.e., biological hermaphroditism where maleness and femaleness are incorporated) or asexuality (i.e., beyond biological combinations of maleness and femaleness). In some descriptions, this original unified condition approximates an angelic state of personhood beyond biological sex differences and limitations.

In this sense, androgyny represents a partial recognition of an integrity that goes beyond male and female bodies. Many writers see Jesus as the unique bearer of androgynous humanity. This conception of Jesus, implicit in some of the Gnostic literature, is developed by Erigena in his portrayal of the Resurrected Jesus, and reaches its apex in Jacob Boehme. Other writers see the very nature of God as an androgynous unity, sometimes referred to as the Divine Androgyne, and sometimes portrayed as both male

*For an extensive and specific delineation of the androgynous tradition in theology and philosophy, from its prepatriarchal origins, through Plato, the Midrashim, the Gnostics, and others, up through nineteenth-century French philosophy and social theory, see: Janice G. Raymond, "Transsexualism: An Etiological and Ethical Analysis" (Unpublished Ph.D. dissertation, Boston College, 1977).

and female in its manifestations. This conception of God is most evident in the Cabala and in Jacob Boehme.

However, there is very often an undercurrent of male mothering in connection with androgyny. Although the primal Adam is written about as androgynous or hermaphroditic, one is still left with the impression that the original human was more male than female. This undercurrent is conveyed in the language of the Cabala: "[Eve] existed in Adam, in potentiality from the first." The language here is most important, for if anything, biologically speaking, it was Adam who was contained in Eve from the beginning. Other statements imply that it was Eve (woman) who separated from man, giving the impression that the female part of the original androgyne was more fragmented and less perfect than the male, so that even though the primal person was supposedly androgynous, this creature was composed of one distinctly more perfect part and one distinctly less perfect part. Thus the male portion of androgyny remains steady and constant, while the female is the wayward, unsteady half. In the Gnostics, moreover, the female must make herself male before a salvific androgyny can be reached.

As a result of this original division of the sexes, androgyny came to symbolize also completeness by reunification in love and sexual expression. In most authors, heterosexual love was seen to be an androgynous theme, uniting that which was originally separated (female and male) in the life and act of love. This heterosexual love was perceived as the bringing together of external complements. But in other authors, especially Plato, homosexual love also functioned as a form of androgyny needing no female half to complete itself, but finding the "female" within the self through loving another who was like the self.

Further, the theme of androgyny is often meant to symbolize the overcoming of all dichotomies. Here, the integration of female and male represents the overcoming of other dualisms, such as spirit and matter. However, this explanation of androgyny implies that male-female symbols are only representative of larger issues. Such an explanation still begs the question and does not adequately explain why these particular sexual symbols were chosen, and why female-male is seen as the archetypal dualism in which other dualisms participate. It fails to look at the concrete and specific symbol of the division between female and male.

Androgyny is often used to imply misogyny; that is, its attainment requires the denigration of women. Misogyny takes many forms. In the Gnostics, the female must first make herself male before becoming androgynous, but no comparable process was necessary for the man. The male, it seems, had a direct route to androgyny but the female, by virtue of her inferior starting point of femaleness, had to pass through the supposed higher level of maleness before she could reach the highest level—androgyny. In Plato, androgyny is mixed with misogyny to support male homosexuality which is regarded as the superior form of love. Intimacy can only occur between two equals—that is, between two men. Plato implies that an equal relationship is not possible between a woman and a man. John Scotus Erigena, who uses androgyny as a reunification theme, also maintains that, in the Fall, mind (man) was led astray by sentience or corporeality (woman). Therefore the man must rule woman, since soul must rule sense, as it will do in the restored life. Nikolai Berdyaev mingles androgyny and misogyny by reducing woman to procreation and uplifting man to creation, neither of which, he says, is complete without the other.

Androgyny often refers to the incorporation of the so-called feminine principle (sometimes called the female principle) within the male or within the dominant male ethos. This conception of androgyny is evident in Greek drama, especially in such plays as *Lysistrata* and *Oedipus*, and also in Comte and the Saint-Simonians. It should be emphasized that this is not comparable to the Gnostic injunctions which state that a woman must *make* herself male. Where men are exhorted to *incorporate* the feminine or female principle, it is clear that they do not have to make themselves female (as the females in the Gnostic literature were exhorted to do), but rather they can *assimilate* the female principle and thus get the best of both worlds while still remaining male. In no writing on androgyny is the male exhorted to *make* himself female before he can become androgynous.

Lastly, in the nineteenth century, androgyny becomes a theme of social reform. Where it had previously been applied to individual conceptions of personhood, it now becomes a way of talking about an ideal society. Beginning with Auguste Comte and up to the Saint-Simonians, androgyny comes to symbolize human progress, universal unity, and the removal of social oppression, especially that of female and class oppression.

The androgyne is a myth and like all myths is constantly reinterpreted, depending on different preoccupations and experiences. But a primary, common element in all of the various usages of androgyny is the notion of *integration* as *completion.*

INTEGRATION VERSUS INTERGITY

The word *androgyny* is formed from integrating the Greek *aner* and *gyne* (with the male classically coming first). This gives the impression that if one puts the archetypal masculine and feminine together, one will somehow arrive at an adequate whole—but a whole that is formed from two inadequate halves. The question thus becomes, how can two inadequate halves form an adequate whole? As Mary Daly has phrased it, androgyny connotes "scotch-taping John Wayne and Brigitte Bardot together."[1] Further evidence of this pseudo-organicism can be noted when perusing dictionary definitions of androgyny, where there is reference to plant or human hybrids. The latter, throughout the androgynous tradition, becomes synonymous with physical hermaphroditism.

Nor would the term *gynandry* be adequate. Although the female root of the word comes first, the primary image is still one of the sexual sphinx.

In appearance, the words *androgyne* and *androgen* are quite similar. In fact, *androgyny* is sometimes spelled *androgeny*. Thus to speak of androgynizing humanity comes dangerously close to androgenizing or "male-izing" humanity. This, of course, was one mode of androgyny that was expressed in the Gnostic tradition. However, an *androgenous* or male-ized humanity is no mere myth, nor is it simply a clever play on words, in light of some of the statements in John Money's work on sex differences.

In *Man & Woman, Boy & Girl*, "fetally androgenized females" develop not only physically male characteristics (perhaps an enlarged clitoris or excessive body hair) but also supposedly have the propensity to develop psychosocially conditioned, masculine behavior.

On a mytho-metaphorical level, the Gnostics exhorted women to attain the androgynous state of unified humanity by first making themselves male. "For every woman who makes herself male will enter the Kingdom of Heaven."[2] No comparable process of making one's self female is necessary for men to attain androgynous actualization and salvation. Once more, now in the scientific literature on sex differences, androgenizing—or making one's self male—becomes normative for androgyny.

The split-level hybrid or integration model of androgyny prevails currently. The basic notion of androgyny in Carolyn Heilbrun's *Toward a Recognition of Androgyny* is, as the book jacket acknowledges, "the realization of man in woman and woman in man." Heilbrun is in good company here. Unfortunately even the brilliant Virginia Woolf had a similar notion of androgyny in *A Room of One's Own.* She wrote:

And I went on amateurishly to sketch a plan of the soul so that in each of us two powers preside, one male one female; and in the man's brain, the man predominates over the woman and in the woman's brain the woman predominates over the man. The normal and comfortable state of being is when the two live in harmony together, spiritually cooperating. If one is a man, still the woman part of the brain must have effect; and a woman also must have intercourse with the man in her. Coleridge perhaps meant this when he said that a great mind is androgynous. . . . It is when this fusion takes place that the mind is fully fertilized and uses all its faculties.[3]

Likewise Betty Roszak has a hybrid or integration model of androgyny. In an essay entitled "The Human Continuum," which takes great pains to stress that if we even "think of ourselves as 'a woman' or 'a man' we are already participating in a fantasy of language," Roszak concludes: "Perhaps with the overcoming of women's oppression, the woman in man will be allowed to emerge."[4]

Obviously, Heilbrun, Woolf, and Roszak are each attempting to go beyond stereotyped definitions of masculinity and femininity. Yet it also ought to be obvious that if this is the desired goal, then writers cannot use the language of oppression nor incorporate oppressive definitions of the self to talk about a nonoppressive ideal of the same self. For in reality, the language and imagery of androgyny is the language of dominance and servitude combined. One would not put master and slave language or imagery together to define a free person. Therefore, any serious effort to describe an androgynous ideal must take issue with Heilbrun's assertion that "so wedded are we to the conventional definitions of 'masculine' and 'feminine' that it is impossible to write about androgyny without using these terms in their accepted, received sense."[5] Heilbrun fails to perceive here the eminent co-optability of this kind of language.

The co-optive potential of androgyny lies in its ability to integrate, assimilate, or absorb almost anything, particularly any sexual issue. Androgyny is not only a *word* that lends itself to co-optation. The *vision* it attempts to describe is equally susceptible to co-optation.

The most blatant example of this kind of co-optation appeared in a *Ramparts* article in December 1973. Here, androgyny was identified with what was called "The Third Sex." This "new androgyny" was supposedly released by technological culture. This freeing, together with "the

deep exploration of our psyches by acid and meditation,"
gave persons permission to explore "our true androgynous
natures, the *anima* and the *animus,* both of which we all
possess." Men are coming to realize their feminine side and
women are "excavating their masculine identities."[6] As
models for the "new androgyny," James Nolan, the
author, gives us "pansexual rock images" of David Bowie,
Janis Joplin, Mick Jagger, and Bette Midler. "David and
Mick and Janis and Bette: consider the possibilities."[7]

A fuller notion of "The Third Sex" emerges, "fertilized" by Women's and Gay Liberation, "both of which
began with strains of either man-hating or woman-hating,"
according to the author.

It seemed for awhile that Women's Liberation, for all the deep-
seated misanthropy it generated, was becoming with a lot of pushy
verbalizing and hard-edged power struggling, a caricature of the very
masculine traits which the women despised. Gay Liberation, with its
indigenous misogyny, had taken to playing house in the superficial
deco-parlor on narcissism and taste, a realm traditionally ruled over
by the very women the gay mentality found so ludicrous. But
perhaps these two militant liberation movements were just awkward
and adolescent phases we *all* had to pass through, pimply and self-
conscious and blatantly extreme, to arrive at a more whole type of
sexual identity: a way of seeing how the other half (of ourselves)
lives.[8]

Here we have the ultimate co-optation of the Women's
Movement—an "adolescent stage" that we have already
passed through. Androgyny becomes the great leap for-
ward, a synonym for an easily accessible human liberation
that turns out to be sexual liberation—a state of being that
men can enter as easily as women through the "cheap
grace" of the "wider" countercultural revolution. What
androgyny comes to mean here, in fact, *is* sexual revolution, phrased in the language of "The Third Sex."
Sex (fucking), not power, becomes the false foundation
of liberation.

Given the difficulties with the word and its eminent
susceptibility to being co-opted, is it worth even trying
to talk about whatever was intended by the word *andro-*

gyny. The questions were and are still real, but the term *androgyny* obscured the reality. In fact, my intention is not to integrate the feminine and the masculine but to transcend them.

The word *integrity* more adequately conveys possibilities of transcendence. First of all, it is a word/vision that avoids the pitfalls of the integration model of androgyny. There are various and subtle meanings of the word *integrity* that render it more adequate to express a meaningful vision of what many of us previously wanted *androgyny* to convey.

In comparison to *integration,* which is defined in the *Oxford English Dictionary* as "the making up or composition of a whole by adding together or combining the separate parts or elements" and in comparison to *integrate,* which means "to complete or perfect (what is imperfect) by the addition of the necessary parts," *integrity* is described in the following way: "The condition of having no part or element taken away or wanting; undivided or unbroken state . . . something undivided; an integral whole. . . . The condition of not being marred or violated; unimpaired or uncorrupted condition; original perfect state; soundness." Integration gives a certain validity to the parts themselves and to the process of putting those parts together. In contrast, integrity reverses this connotation and validates an original unity from which no part may be taken. Integrity gives us a warrant for laying claim to a wholeness that is rightfully ours to *begin with* and that centuries of patriarchal socialization to sex roles and stereotyping have eroded.

Thus an intuition of integrity, in this sense, is characteristic of the texture of be-ing (becoming) and prior to cultural definitions of masculinity and femininity. It is an original state that does not reside in a static historical past. Rather, integrity is the constant unfolding of a personal and social process that has the potentiality of generating for all of us a future vision of becoming, beyond a gender-defined society.

This original state of be-ing, this condition of integrity,

may indeed have been what the androgynous myths of the primal person were pointing toward. That is, proponents of androgyny may have dislocated what was really revelatory about the androgynous vision by speaking about it on a biological or hermaphroditic level. The real mytho-historical memory may have been that of an original psychosocial integrity where men were not masculine, nor women feminine, and where these definitions and prescribed norms of personhood did not exist.

The real Fall may not have been the division into biological sexes but the separation into oppressive sex roles and stereotypes. Such a separation has cleft humanity into two static states of being. What the myths of the Fall from androgynous humanity into maleness and femaleness may more fully tell us about is humanity's initial loss of the intuition of integrity in which human development has been channeled into a two-track system of masculinity and femininity. Thus "salvation" is not achieved by the union of the two but by transcending masculinity and femininity. Until those contemplating it come to realize that transsexualism will dislocate the basic sense of unity within themselves, which I have called the intuition of integrity, they will continue to settle for false and partial modes of androgyny.

ANDROGYNY, INTEGRITY, AND TRANSSEXUALISM

Many of the false and partial modes of androgyny give us clues to why transsexualism is a stunted attempt in the quest for integrity. First of all, it could be said that the transsexual, like the biological androgyne, is a physical hybrid. Of course transsexuals do everything possible to disguise the hybrid nature of their bodies. Constant electrolysis is used to remove the telltale remains of male beard stubble and localized hair residues. Cosmetic surgery is continuously sought to promote the aesthetic appearance of the post-operative body. In spite of all these measures, however, the chromosomes remain that of one's native-born sex, and their effects constantly remind transsexuals, in various unexpected physical ways, that they are really *not* the desired opposite sex but rather surgically constructed androgynes.

Instead of developing genuine integrity, the transsexual becomes a synthetic product. Synthetic parts, such as chemical hormones and surgical artifacts of false vaginas and breasts, produce a synthetic whole. Furthermore, the fact that transsexuals are synthetic products is one clue to their future demise. There have been some cases of cancer reported in the literature; much dissatisfaction with artificial breasts that slip, artificial vaginas that contract, and artificial penises that don't function sexually; and some reports of suicide, attempted suicide, and despondency *after* surgery has taken place.[9] This is not to say that whatever is natural is necessarily good, but rather that it is the harmony or integrity of the whole that is good.

As hormonally and surgically constructed androgynes, transsexuals are radically at odds with their internal environment or "bio-ecosystem." Initially, Rachel Carson demonstrated that chemical pesticides were disastrous to the planet. Barry Commoner followed by showing how so-called technological "advances" have debilitated our ecosystems, because everything is related to everything else. In a similar manner, evidence is beginning to prove that hormone treatment and surgery are destructive intrusions of the total "bio-ecosystems" of transsexuals. That is, one cannot expect to alter sexual organs without in some way negatively altering the rest of the body. Such debilitation may be the body's defense and retaliation for the disruptive hormonal and surgical changes.

As well as being surgical hermaphrodites, transsexuals are also sex-stereotyped hermaphrodites, in such things as gestures, behavior, and style. Many articles on transsexuals have testified that, while assuming the gender identity and role of the opposite sex, transsexuals have not entirely left their native-born gender identity and role behind. The example of Paul(a) Grossman, discussed in Chapter III, is a case in point. Earlier we noticed the same androgynous mix in Jan Morris's case. And this is precisely what it is—androgynous. Transsexuals often betray this socially constructed hermaphroditism.

Insofar as the androgynous ideal was based upon an opposition of supposed opposites, so too is transsexualism. Just as the androgynous tradition accepted the opposition of masculinity and femininity, positing them as dualisms in order to reconcile them in the androgynous ideal, so too does transsexualism accept these basic dualisms in order, however, to reject one and gravitate toward the other. With androgyny and with transsexualism, the categories of masculinity and femininity are accepted on their own ground, either to be united in an androgynous motif or, in the case of transsexuals, to be divided so that one can be accepted and the other rejected. Both androgynous and transsexual advocates fail to understand that the basic point is not to accept the dualisms for the sake of reunification or, in the transsexual's case, for the sake of conversion, but to go beyond and transcend both.

This is a central point, and this is precisely where integrity must serve as an ethic rather than androgynous integration. One cannot take two false or inadequate halves and put them together, or reject one in order to accept the other. Rather one must transcend the dualisms to begin with, by not accepting them as adequate descriptions of reality.

It is precisely in this realm that the transsexual unwittingly settles for androgyny instead of integrity. He latches on to what is perceived as the "other half" of humanity, for example, femininity, and credits it with an adequacy and integrity of its own, without asking deeper questions. Instead of realizing that femininity has only an artificial and socially constructed status, he accepts it as an adequate definition of personal and social integrity.

A genuine integrity would not support an integration of this sort, based upon the acceptance of false dualisms and a false opposition of opposites. It would not "help" transsexuals to *integrate* their gender suffering into a "meaningful" conformity where deeper questions of social and personal reality are not confronted. Instead it would genuinely help the transsexual to interpret pain and deviance, thus bringing about more genuine changes. For example, counseling based on an ethic of integrity would supply the language needed to understand transsexualism within the social context of sex-role stereotyping and conformity. In other words, it would meet the problem on its deeper ground, that is, the social, and not dislocate it to another level, that is, the medical-technical level. It would not replace gender suffering with an artificially prolonged and synthetic maintenance of the problem so that the transsexual becomes an uncritical and dependent spectator of his deeply decaying self.[10] Thus *interpretation* is a key element of an ethic of integrity, especially in the counseling situation.

The therapeutic ethic that presently governs transsexual counseling and surgery does not genuinely promote either personal or social integrity. An intrinsic element of personal integrity is autonomy. As Ivan Illich has pointed out, anyone who "becomes dependent on the management of his intimacy . . . renounces his autonomy, and his health *must* decline."[11] Transsexual surgery promotes the ethic that the problem of transsexualism *cannot* be confronted on an autonomous level but needs the intervention of the medical and surgical, as well as psychological, specialities.

Nor is social integrity enhanced by transsexual surgery. An ethic that promotes sex-role conformity is hardly contributing to the integrity of the social system. Transsexual surgery turns into an antisocial activity that promotes the worst aspects of a patriarchal society by encouraging adaptation to its sex roles. Gender identity clinics can be perceived as future centers of "sex-role control," where the potential social planners might well encourage, facilitate, and maintain sex-role conformity for nontranssexuals.

Another perspective that the androgynous tradition offers on the phenomenon of transsexualism is its built-in misogyny. In many of the writings on androgyny, the female half of the hybrid was regarded as inferior. Thus females who were striving for androgyny were first exhorted to make themselves male. However, in transsexualism, we might say that the misogyny theme is apparently inverted into a kind of philogyny (love of woman), this time by the male making himself female. But what really happens is that the biological female is no longer even necessary. Thus misogynism is escalated.

TRANSSEXUALISM AND TRANSCENDENCE

The transsexual odyssey can be viewed as a quest for transcendence, an effort to go beyond the limits of the self (symbolized by the acquisition of a new body). But from the perspective of transcendence, transsexualism's greatest weakness is its deflection of the "courage to be," and its short-circuiting of existential risk, creativity, world-building, and social healing—all of which are elements of genuine transcendence. Transsexualism achieves this deflection and short-circuiting by drawing up body boundaries to the ever-present and future quest for fuller and more authentic becoming.

There is no doubt that selfhood presupposes embodiment and that our bodies cannot be ignored in any authentic development of selfhood. However, even many persons who have been wracked with severe physical pain or deformed by natural or imposed crippling agents have been able to transcend these conditions. Our bodies *are* truly ourselves, but are *preconditionally* intrinsic to our being persons. As Mary Daly has pointed out, the spirit can always contain the body but the body cannot always contain the spirit. She notes that a radical feminist analysis will see the problem to be one of overcoming the containment of spirit by body.[12] In contrast to the transsexual who *embodies* transcendence, I suggest that we *"enspirit."* Daly explains this word further:

The process of the Self enspiriting the Self is Dis-possession. The enspiriting Self is not anti-matter, but pro-matter, freeing matter from its restricting/restricted role of vessel/container, unfreezing matter so that it can flow with spirit, fly with spirit.[13]

This is to say that who we are should not be defined by exclusive reference to our bodies. Our existence transcends, in important ways, the limitations imposed upon us by our bodies.

Transsexuals, however, move totally in the realm of the body while thinking that they are transcending the body. To use Daly's terminology, they are "possessed" by their bodies and cannot confront and transcend that possession. Transsexuals are thus saying that who they are is irrevocably determined by what body they are born with and by what body they surgically convert to. This is only a partial truth. We are, of course, our bodies, but we are not dominated by them.

We might say that the body is part of the creative ground of existence, but we are not bound by that structure in the full creative sense. Our spirit is bound to our bodies, as its creative ground, but surpasses it through freedom and choice. The body is present in all our choices, but as total persons, we have the freedom to be other than what culturally accompanies a male or female body.[14] Instead, however, transsexuals become enfettered by both the unwanted body they reject and the desired body they take on, in the sense that the former dictates that it is not possible to live without the latter.

Transsexualism is thus an inadequate "myth of transcendence." Herbert Richardson has written of three myths of transcendence: separation and return, conflict and vindication, integrity and transformation.[15] Transsexualism could be said to be representative of the first two myths, both of which Richardson perceives as inadequate. The first is the myth of *separation and return.* Transsexualism is a cyclic event—an ever-recurring *exitus* and *reditus.* The transsexual leaves masculinity only to return to femininity, which are different sides of the same coin and which ultimately reduce him to the same poverty of behavior. This sameness is attested to by the facile *interchangeability of roles.*

Furthermore, in embarking on the surgical journey, the transsexual will very often return for more and more sur-

gery of a "corrective" or "cosmetic" variety. The tendency
toward polysurgery, on the transsexual's part, and its
willing dispensation by the transsexual technicians, is one
more example of the *exitus-reditus* myth of transsexual
"transcendence." In a very real sense, the first act of surgery is permission to return for more and more transcendence by surgery. The transsexual, therefore, seeks
the illusion of transcendence at the hands of the surgeon.
Instead of becoming a more genuine self and overcoming
cyclic existence, the transsexual short-circuits transcendence by taking false leaps and by endowing his or her selfhood with artificial reality. The falseness of this lies not in
the desire for a different selfhood, nor in the uncertainty
of the quest, but rather in the fact that transcendent be-ing
(what Richardson would call integrity and transformation)
is sought where only cyclic and static being (separation
and return) can be found. Thus transsexuals are thrown
back against those same societal norms and stereotypes
that caused the problem to begin with.

The second myth of transcendence is that of *conflict
and vindication.* On an individual level, the transsexual
must struggle with a continuing opposition to his "native-
born" body. On a social level, the transsexual becomes a
living opponent of a gender-free society by virtue of his
uncritical acceptance of and comfortable conformity to
the stereotypes of masculinity and femininity. Further
conflict may result if transsexuals come to realize that
their surgery is a Band-Aid approach to their individual
gender suffering. Meyer and Hoopes have admitted:

In a thousand subtle ways, the reassignee has the bitter experience
that he is not—and never will be—a real girl but is, at best, a convincing simulated female. Such an adjustment cannot compensate for
the tragedy of having lost all chance to be male and of having, in the
final analysis, no way to be really female.[16]

The third myth of transcendence, that of *integrity and
transformation*, has been talked about in this work as an
ethic of integrity. Richardson maintains:

The kind of transcendence correlated with the myth of integrity and transformation is that of self-transcendence, expanded consciousness, spiritual rebirth, and divinization. . . . In our integrity, we can experience transcendence as our own potentiality to become more, as the demand for self-transformation.[17]

In the transsexual's mere process of integration, he can become *no more* than what the society has determined as masculine or feminine. Becoming a surgically constructed masculine or feminine person does not free one's spiritual energies for larger ventures of becoming, but circumscribes these vitalities within stereotypes and role boundaries. The transsexual has indeed set up a false ultimate concern, taking a short-cut to a perceived but illusory transcendence of the instant salvation variety. For the transsexual, the surgery is a false signal of transcendence—false because the role and identity it conveys cannot point beyond itself and the society's limits. Except in some narrowly achievable sense, transcendence and integrity cannot be won by elevating individual well-being over individual and societal be-ing and becoming.

INTEGRITY AND THE INTUITION OF BE-ING

Various philosophers, most notably Jacques Maritain, have written about the intuition of being. Integrity, at its depth, is an intuition of the power of be-ing.

The notion of being was originally developed within a society enclosed by a static world view, lacking any sense of process or change. Being was unchanging, and there was literally "nothing new under the sun." Static being is precisely what is achieved by the transsexual. In changing sex, and in being assimilated into the opposite sex roles, the transsexual settles for the static state of masculinity or femininity that a patriarchal culture has attached to a male or female body, and short-circuits the diversity of genuine be-ing and transcendence. In so doing, sex-conversion surgery measures the transsexual's transcendence by an unchanging state of masculine or feminine well-being that does not point beyond itself.[18]

Transsexual supporters appeal to standards of well-being, when they justify transsexualism. They attest to its efficacy in the life process of those individuals afflicted, pointing out that most transsexuals are happier and function better after surgery. I maintain, however, that the efficacy they attest to is one-sided and does not measure total integrity. In order to assess the total integrity of the transsexual situation, the following questions must be asked and answered:

1. Is individual gender satisfaction achieved at the price of individual role conformity and the enforcement of role stereotypes on a social level—thus at the price of encouraging a sexist society whose continued existence depends upon the perpetuation of those roles and stereotypes?
2. Does transsexual treatment and surgery repress the transsexual's capacity for social protest and restrict her or his potential as a social critic in the sexist society that caused the problem to begin with?
3. Is the well-being that the transsexual achieves through surgery dependent upon an integration of false opposites?
4. In connection with the former question, is transsexual well-being confined to the body that one is either born in or out of? Therefore, does it restrict the infinite possibilities of be-ing that cannot be contained by either the "native-born" or surgically constructed body?
5. Are transsexuals radically at odds with their "bio-ecosystems," and are there enough deleterious effects of treatment and surgery (for example, breast cancer) reported in the medical literature to question transsexual well-being on a biological level alone?
6. Could transsexual surgery really be called artificially prolonged maintenance? Transsexual existence initially depends upon the questionable notions of passing, synthetic hormone injections, surgery which often becomes polysurgery, and lifelong sustenance from exogenous sources. Thus the transsexual becomes dependent almost totally for his or her well-being on the medical profession.

Autonomy is at a minimum, and dependence is at a maximum.

7. Is transsexual surgery a male-defined, male-perpetuated, and male-legitimated mode of happiness? (The female-to-constructed-male transsexual, as I have argued, is in a most definite sense the disguise that obscures the patriarchal character of the transsexual empire.) Can one view the transsexual "solution" as the beginning of a world where men not only dominate women but become women and try to surpass the biological woman and her creative capacities on all levels?

All this is to say that the supposed satisfaction of the transsexual is a narrow mode of well-being, and a partial and short-circuited glimpse of be-ing. Integrity or true be-ing leads to the unfolding of process, and movement beyond the false opposition of opposites. Instead of restricting individuals to a static state of being or to partial modes of be-ing, integrity leads to, and resides in, transcendent Be-ing.

Dynamic and true be-ing ultimately poses the question of Be-ing Itself—or what some have called the Source or Power of Be-ing. As Mary Daly has shown, the experience of be-ing is a theological experience (in the best sense of the word theological), because it is experienced as force, power, ground, and source of Be-ing. While expanding the self into more self-realization, an intuition of Be-ing is also experienced as transcending the self. This experience is something that the static and anthropomorphic symbols for God could never capture. Such symbols may have conveyed personality and personalism, but they failed to convey the fact that transcendence is Be-ing. Be-ing is hardly an abstraction but eminently personal when it is recognized that the force or power of one's be-ing is within, while paradoxically still without, attainable yet unattainable. As Daly has further pointed out, there is an indwelling of the goal as yet unattained, but unfolding itself—"the final cause that is *movement* is in our imaginative-cerebral-emotional-active-creative be-ing."[19]

Thus it is that the realization of integrity comes back to the intuition of Be-ing, for such an ethic can only be ultimately grounded in this intuition. The quest for integrity is a major part of the intuition of Be-ing, for it pushes one beyond limits of selfhood into an ever-expanding process. When this intuition occurs, one suddenly realizes that a given entity exists and exercises its highest activity of be-ing in its own way, which is total. Furthermore, although Maritain and others spoke about this intuition of being as an intellectual experience, it is clear that it is associated with profound emotion. It may, in some cases, have the appearance of mystical grace.[20] Maritain explains that this intuition would be most likely to occur in a person who feels profoundly, who has a good sense apparatus, and who can enter into the depth of her/his existence by her/his sensitivity. Such a person will be one who is vividly alive, who suffers existential conflicts.[21]

While transsexuals suffer poignant existential conflicts, they do not enter into the depths of their own experience by getting beyond the role-bound and body-bound crisis. The pain of unnecessary surgery is mistaken for being vibrantly alive. As stated earlier, physical pain is a constant reminder to transsexuals that they are finally coming alive. The quest for integrity, transcendence, or the true, deep, becoming self—for Be-ing—is short-circuited, with pain providing the illusion of life.

One final word about the intuition of Be-ing. At times, Maritain's conception of the intuition of being is too individualized and thus loses its social impact, minimizing the issue of political power. In contrast, the intuition of integrity of which I have written takes political power very seriously, and has a definite social source and emphasis. It is aimed at destroying the power of patriarchal society, which has spawned the sex roles that have engendered the loss of the power of be-ing for all who have been afflicted by these roles. Moreover, it proceeds from a feminist, social, consciousness of be-ing. I stress this social origin, because, as Tillich has pointed out, being is partly known from nonbeing. "The question of being is produced by the 'shock of nonbeing.' "[22] Women have recognized this basic nonbeing, stunting, alienation, and loss of power, because women have felt most heavily the weight of sex-role oppression. Perhaps it will be possible for transsexuals, with their unique victimization by these same roles, to move from false and static being to the total Be-ing of integrity through a rejection of *both* roles.

"REPRESSIVE TOLERANCE" AND SENSITIVITY

It is my deepest hope that this book will not be viewed as an unsympathetic treatment of the anguish and existential plight of the transsexual. What I have tried to present is a different vision of where to *focus* sympathy and sensitivity.

Focused sensitivity should ask the *why* behind transsexual suffering and propose ways of dealing with such pain that confront the total situation, thus effecting change on the deepest levels involved. To focus sensitivity is to not allow it to become short-sighted or short-circuited. To encourage would-be transsexuals to hand over their bodies to the transsexual empire hardly seems to be an adequate or genuinely sensitive response to the questions that transsexualism raises. Those who advocate medicalized transsexualism as the answer to a desperate emergency situation of profound sex-role agony only serve, in my opinion, to prolong the emergency. They seem sensitive only to Band-Aid solutions that ultimately help to make more medicalized victims and to enhance the power of the medical empire. This kind of sensitivity is the outgrowth of "the triumph of the therapeutic" and can only mire its believers and transsexuals in the immediacy of "the personal solution" in which therapy becomes a way of life.

Any woman who has experienced the agony of sex-role oppression in a patriarchal society is hardly insensitive to the suffering that transsexuals experience. Like transsexuals, many women have felt hatred of their bodies and its

functions, and have found themselves in a psychically dis-
jointed state because they could not accept their role.
Through feminism, however, many women have come to
understand this physical and psychic fragmentation in
political/social terms—i.e., as the product of a patriarchal
society that has imposed images and definitions of female
existence. Thus feminists have become social critics and
have organized, as feminists, around issues of sexism and
sex-role oppression.

Isn't it possible for persons who desire sex-conversion
surgery, and who have also experienced sex-role oppression
and dissatisfaction with their bodies, to band together
around their own unique form of gender agony—especially
those who claim to have a deep commitment to feminism?
Many will say that this is too much to ask of transsexuals.
Yet it is no more than women have asked of ourselves—
those who have taken feminism seriously and have tried
to live unfettered by gender in a gender-defined society.

This book will, no doubt, be dismissed by many transsexuals and transsexual advocates as intolerant. Tolerance,
however, can easily become repressive, as Marcuse has
pointed out. It is often a variation on the "poverty of
liberalism," functioning as sympathy for the oppressed.
I strongly believe that one of the tasks of those who would
be truly open and sensitive to transsexualism is to take
stands that are informed, honest, and sensitive to all the
issues involved. Obviously, those who take a critical position will be subjected to accusations of dogmatism and in-
tolerance, when in fact those who are unwilling to take a
stand are exercising the *dogmatism of openness at any
cost*. This time, the cost of openness is the solidification
of the medical empire and the multiplying of medical
victims.

Those who advocate tolerance of medicalized transsexualism are expressing a false sympathy which, in both
the immediate and ultimate context, can only facilitate
and fortify the possession of women by men. Such sympathetic tolerance will only strengthen a society in which
sex roles are the norm, and where deep existential choices

become subject to medicalization. When tolerance serves mainly to protect the fabric by which a sexist society is held together, then it neutralizes values. It is important to help break the concreteness of oppression by showing its theoretical inconsistencies and by stretching minds to think about solutions that only *appear* to be sensitive and sympathetic.

Tolerance also fosters a *laissez-faire* attitude to problems—"different strokes for different folks." Social control flourishes under this ideological umbrella, whether it is called "free choices," "radical solutions," and/or "liberating boundaries." Furthermore, tolerance is essentially a passive position. Marcuse, in his essay "Repressive Tolerance," has written:

The political locus of tolerance has changed: while it is more or less quietly and constitutionally withdrawn from the opposition, it is made compulsory behavior with respect to established policies. Tolerance is turned from an active into a passive state, from practice to non-practice. . . . It is the people who tolerate the government, which, in turn tolerates opposition within the framework determined by the constituted authorities.[23]

Many feminists are opposed to transsexualism. Yet that opposition, having moved outside the limits of tolerance set up by the medical authorities, will often be decried as intolerant. What is happening here is a fundamental reversal. "Tolerance toward that which is radically evil now appears as good because it serves the cohesion of the whole on the road to affluence or more affluence."[24] It is not only tolerance in the service of medical affluence that we witness in the transsexual situation, but tolerance in the service of medical control—specifically the control of women.

It is a critical time for woman-identified women. Medicalized transsexualism represents only one more aspect of patriarchal hegemony. The best response women can make to this is to see clearly just what is at stake for us with respect to transsexualism and to assert our own power of naming who we are.

APPENDIX

Suggestions

for

Change

I HAVE argued that the issue of transsexualism is an ethical issue that has profound political and moral ramifications; transsexualism itself is a deeply moral question rather than a medical-technical answer. I contend that the problem of transsexualism would best be served by morally mandating it out of existence.

Does a moral mandate, however, necessitate that transsexualism be legally mandated out of existence? What is the relationship between law and morality, in the realm of transsexualism? While there are many who feel that morality must be built into law, I believe that the elimination of transsexualism is not best achieved by legislation prohibiting transsexual treatment and surgery but rather by legislation that limits it—and by other legislation that lessens the support given to sex-role stereotyping, which generated the problem to begin with.

THE RELATIONSHIP BETWEEN LAW AND MORALITY

Many see a very definite connection between social morality and its preservation in law.[1] They would argue that if
there were a broad social consensus about the immorality
of transsexual surgery, then the law should incarnate that
social morality. Others, of course, would argue that to
ground issues of law in the social conscience is not always
protective of individual rights and may, in fact, be destructive of those rights. They would say that the law can only
legislate against individual rights when they can be shown
to be directly harmful to another's rights.

I do not wish to argue either of these positions. Rather,
I would contend that the more that can be left out of the
law, the better. The prevention of transsexual surgery, and
the social conditions that generate it, are not achieved by
legislation forbidding surgery. In the case of transsexual
surgery, the good to be achieved, that is, the integrity of
the individual and of the society, does not seem best
served by making transsexual surgery illegal. Rather it
is more important to regulate, by legal measures, the
sexist, social conditions that generate transsexual surgery,
and also legally to limit the medical-institutional complex
that translates these sexist conditions into the realm of
transsexualism. Thus I am advocating a *limiting legislative*
presence, along with *First Cause* legislation, which, instead
of directing legal action to the consequences of a gender-
defined society (in this case, to transsexualism), directs
action to the social forces and medical institutions that
produce the transsexual empire.

Legislation dealing with First Causes would concern itself
with the network of sex-role stereotyping that produces
the schizoid state of a "female mind in a male body." The
education of children is one case in point here. Images of
sex roles continue to be reinforced, at public expense, in
school textbooks. The message is that such roles are assigned to male and female bodies in our society. Another
example of First Cause legislation is the legal mandating

of programs and funds for the promotion of nonsexist physical education in schools receiving federal money. This has been initiated, to a certain extent, with Title IX legislation, but still has not been implemented extensively. Building up women's bodies in the active way to which men have been accustomed would also build a body image and role that is quite different from the objectified, weak, and passive image that women and men now have of women. This would help to eliminate the bodily stereotype to which the transsexual wishes to convert.

These, of course, are but a few examples of First Cause legislation where it would be possible for the law to step in at the beginning of a destructive sexist process that leads ultimately to consequences such as transsexualism. Although this is not the place to delve into a lengthy listing of all the social contexts in which the law might possibly intervene to prevent the sexist supports of the transsexual phenomenon, it is my contention that it is at the beginning and not at the end of the transsexual process that legislation is imperative.

Along with First Cause legislation to stop the "procreation" of transsexualism, limiting legislation is also necessary to inhibit the massive medical-technical complex of institutions that promote and perform more treatment and more surgery. Such institutions have a built-in growth power and thus legal limits should be placed on their ability to multiply. I would favor restricting the number of hospitals and centers where transsexual surgery could be performed.

CONSCIOUSNESS-RAISING COUNSELING

Nonsexist counseling is another direction for change that should be explored. The kind of counseling to "pass" successfully as masculine or feminine that now reigns in gender identity clinics only reinforces the problem of transsexualism. It does nothing to develop critical awareness, it makes transsexuals passive spectators of their own decline, it manages transsexuals' intimacy, and ultimately it makes them dependent upon the medical-technical solution. Such counseling destroys integrity and the potential of transsexuals to deal with their problem in an autonomous, genuinely personal, and responsibly social way. The transsexual becomes a kind of acolyte to his doctor and psychiatrist, and learns to depend upon these professionals for maintenance. The baptism of "passing" behavior that is conferred upon the transsexual, plus the administration of exogenous hormones, along with constant requests for corrective polysurgery, turn him into a lifelong patient. Ivan Illich has called this cultural iatrogenesis.

Cultural iatrogenesis . . . consists in the paralysis of healthy responses to suffering, impairment, and death. It occurs when people accept health management designed on the engineering model, when they conspire in an attempt to produce, as if it were a commodity, something called "better health." This inevitably results in the managed maintenance of life on high levels of sub-lethal illness.[2]

What I advocate, instead of a counseling that issues in a medicalization of the transsexual's suffering, is a counseling based on "consciousness-raising." In the early stages of the current feminist movement, consciousness-raising groups were very common. These groups were composed of women who talked together about their problems and directions as women in a patriarchal society. Gradually, these groups came to the insight that "the personal is political," thus providing the first reconciliation between what had always been labeled the "personal" and the "political" dimensions of life. Women, who had felt for years that the dissatisfaction they had experienced *as women* was a personal problem, came to realize in concert with other women that these problems were not peculiar to them as individuals but were common to women *as a caste.* Until feminism focused attention on the debilitating social-political framework of sexism, most women had categorized their dissatisfaction as "merely personal." From these consciousness-raising groups came much of the initial political action of the women's movement.

Five elements or processes appear repeatedly, under

different names, in literature about consciousness-raising groups.

1. Self-revelation. This involves each individual talking about her attitudes and life.

2. Sharing. Experiences and attitudes revealed often weave a tapestry of similarity so that the commonality of personal experiences becomes obvious, and its political character is revealed.

3. Analysis. Recognition of the reasons and causes for the commonality of such personal experiences with an extensive analysis of the social-political, economic, and moral forces that support such experiences.

4. Abstracting. Theorizing about concrete experiences and about social forces and sources, while drawing on the insights of others for perspective.

5. Action. Concretizing analysis into appropriate tasks, goals, projects, and the like.[3]

Would it be possible for these elements of consciousness-raising to be transplanted into a one-to-one counseling situation where they could be used to explore the social origins of the transsexual problem and the consequences of the medical-technical solution? Counseling of this nature would raise the kinds of questions that I advocated previously, such as: is individual gender suffering relieved at the price of role conformity and the perpetuation of role stereotypes on a social level? In "changing sex," does the transsexual encourage a sexist society whose continued existence depends upon the perpetuation of these roles and stereotypes? Does transsexual treatment repress the transsexual's capacity for social protest and criticism? Does it act as a social tranquilizer? These and similar questions are seldom raised in transsexual therapy at present.

However, aside from this one-to-one form of counseling, the model of consciousness-raising emphasizes the group process itself. As women have analyzed their own problems *as women* in consciousness-raising groups, it is extremely important that transsexuals, as persons wishing to change sex, take their particular manifestation of gender oppression into their own hands. Transsexuals are *not* women. They are *deviant males*, and their particular manifestation of gender deviancy needs its own unique context of peer support.

Peer support has been one of the crucial aspects of consciousness-raising in feminist groups. Given the support of other women, it became possible for many to break the bonds of so-called "core" gender identity. In the same way, peer support could be extremely insightful for transsexuals. It could help surface the deeper issues that lie behind the problem of *why* one finds one's self with, for example, a "female mind in a male body." It could then assist in exploring whether indeed this is the proper label for the transsexual's unique form of sex-role oppression.

Such counseling and group interaction would be far more honest than the present forms of therapy that promote passing. I am not so naive as to think that they will make transsexualism disappear overnight, but they would at least pose the existence of a real alternative to be explored and tried. Given peer encouragement to transcend cultural definitions of both masculinity and femininity, *without* changing one's body, persons considering transsexualism might not find it as necessary to resort to sex-conversion surgery.

DEMYSTIFYING AND DISMANTLING THE MEDICAL-TECHNICAL HEGEMONY

People concerned about sex-role oppression must work to take the transsexual problem out of the hands of the transsexual professionals and the gender identity clinics. One way of doing this is through the legal measures suggested previously; another way is through public education.

Up to this point, the transsexual and the transsexual professionals have been the sources of information for the general public. The mere existence of the postoperative transsexual, moreover, and the mere availability of transsexual counseling and surgery, permit people to restrict their thinking about sex-role dissatisfaction to these medical/surgical boundaries. In addition, the transsexual professional becomes a force in the community at large, defining his constituency, and generating a clientele of persons with this unique medical consumer status.

One way in which education about transsexualism has reached the general public is through the media. Articles on transsexualism, especially in the aftermath of public exposure of famous transsexual personages such as Jan Morris or Renee Richards, appear in the weekly news magazines. Several times a year, transsexuals and transsexual professionals appear on various television talk shows. Thus the transsexual empire has become "media-ized."

However, I would suggest that different perspectives on the issue of transsexualism need to receive more attention and publicity. We have seen enough of those transsexuals and professionals in the media who are in favor of transsexual surgery as the solution to so-called gender dissatisfaction and dysphoria. We need to hear more from those men and women who, at one time, thought they might be transsexuals but decided differently—persons who successfully overcame their gender identity crises without resorting to the medical-technical solution. We need to hear more also from professionals such as endocrinologist Charles Ihlenfeld who, after helping one hundred or more persons to "change their sex," left the field. Ihlenfeld decided that "we are trying to treat superficially something that is much deeper."[4] And finally we need to hear more from persons, such as feminists and homosexual men, who have experienced sex-role oppression but ultimately did not become transsexuals.

In the final analysis, however, it is important to remember that transsexualism is merely one of the *most obvious* forms of gender dissatisfaction and sex-role playing in a patriarchal society. It is one of the most obvious because, in the transsexual situation, we have the stereotypes on stage, so to speak, for all to see and examine in an alien body. What can be overlooked, however, is that these same stereotypes, behaviors, and gender dissatisfactions are lived out every day in "native" bodies. The issues that transsexualism can highlight should by no means be confined to the transsexual context. Rather they should be confronted in the "normal" society that spawned the problem of transsexualism to begin with.

NOTES

PREFACE, PAGES xiii–xxvii

1. For an extensive introduction to the techniques and philosophy of subliminal seduction, see Wilson Bryan Key, *Subliminal Seduction* (New York: Signet Books, 1973). Key's latest work, *Media Sexploitation* (Englewood Cliffs, N.J.: Prentice-Hall, 1976), gives examples of subliminal ads that use transsexual themes. Key illustrates and explains an advertisement for Jantzen beachwear in which two persons, supposedly male and female, were wearing swimsuits. If the reader observed closely, however, the male had the female trunks on and vice versa. "In short, she is wearing his and he is wearing hers." Why? "The art director has utilized a subliminal sex-role reversal strategy. This dissonant idea of men wearing women's clothes, highly taboo in our culture, will not be perceived consciously. But it will be instantly perceived at the unconscious level" (p. 4). And later it might possibly be associated with the "need" to buy a Jantzen bathing suit.

2. See Mary Daly, *Gyn/Ecology: The Metaethics of Radical Feminism* (Boston: Beacon Press, 1978), especially the Introduction, pp. 1–9, for an extensive discussion of *the background* and *the foreground*. Daly developed these concepts from a conversation with Denise Connors.

3. What becomes clear to anyone researching transsexual and gender literature, history, and activities is that there is a *Trinity* of men

who dominate the field. John Money could be said to function as God the Father whose Son is Richard Green, a former student of Money's at Johns Hopkins. Money and Green together produced the first interdisciplinary volume on the subject of sex conversion, *Transsexualism and Sex Reassignment*. Green is also the editor in chief of the *Archives of Sexual Behavior*, to which Money is a frequent contributor. Formerly, Green was the Director of the Gender Identity Research Treatment Program at U.C.L.A. where Robert Stoller is a professor of psychiatry and where he has taught for the last twenty-five years. Stoller, although another "father" to Green, can be said to more adequately parallel the third person of the classical Christian Trinity—the Spirit. Stoller's writings seem more imbued with the personal nuances of the individual case study—i.e., with the living and "breathing" moments of the "gender-disturbed or -disatisfied" individual—and less concerned with "hard data." Richard Green's acknowledgments in his book *Sexual Identity Conflict* express eloquently this male bonding Trinitarian relationship.

4. See John Money and Florence Schwartz, "Public Opinion and Social Issues in Transsexualism: A Case Study in Medical Sociology," in Richard Green and John Money, eds., *Transsexualism and Sex Reassignment* (Baltimore: Johns Hopkins Press, 1969), pp. 253-66.

5. I thank Emily Culpepper for this expression, which neatly illustrates my contention that, while transsexuals are *masculine* or *feminine*, they are not fundamentally male or female. As I demonstrate later, transsexuals undergo superficial, stereotypical, and artifactual changes that reinforce socially constructed roles and identities. Therefore, the words *feminine* and *masculine* are appropriate, but the words *he* and *she* are not. Thus also, transsexuals do not change from male to female but from male to *constructed* female.

6. Angela Douglas, Letter, *Sister*, August–September 1977, p. 7.

7. David M. Rorvik, "The Gender Enforcers," *Rolling Stone*, October 9, 1975, pp. 53, 67. In general Rorvik's article is a very astute analysis of the gender identity "mills." Thus it is all the more ironic to read that Rorvik arranged an experiment in cloning a human being which, according to him, has been successful, and is documented in his book, *In His Image: The Cloning of a Man* (New York: Lippincott, 1978). Rorvik seemingly, if his experiment is not a hoax, is not able to see that sexism in the gender identity clinics is inextricably related to the impulses that propel men to clone so-called "motherless" children.

8. Author's conversation with Mary Daly, Boston, Mass., February 1978.

9. G. J. Barker-Benfield has noted that in 1845, the year of the Seneca Falls convention, Dr. Charles Meigs told his students of gynecology that in studying the female organs they would under-

stand a woman's whole being. See G. J. Barker-Benfield, *Horrors of the Half-Known Life* (New York: Harper & Row, 1976), p. 83. In the years immediately following the Women's Rights Convention, J. Marion Sims "fathered" the science of modern gynecology. Initially, he surgically experimented on black women in his backyard "hospital." One woman underwent thirty operations. He later founded the Woman's Hospital in New York (1855) and went on to pioneer both clitoridectomy and female castration in the 1870s.

10. Author's conversation with Mary Daly, Boston, Mass., April 1978.

11. Robert Stoller, "Parental Influences in Male Transsexualism," in Green and Money, *Transsexualism and Sex Reassignment*, p. 166.

12. Information on when medicine began to turn its attention to women who wanted to become (constructed) men is difficult to obtain. I have contacted Johns Hopkins several times for data on the first female-to-constructed-male transsexual operation performed both at Johns Hopkins and in the U.S. No one in either the Office of Psychohormonal Research or the Sex Behavior Consultation Unit had this information.

13. See Mario Martino with harriet, *Emergence: A Transsexual Autobiography* (New York: Crown Publishers, 1977).

14. J. Hoenig *et al*, "Epidemiological Aspects of Transsexualism," *Psychiatria Clinica*, 6 (1973): 65–80.

15. Martino. *Emergence*, p. 236.

16. Barker-Benfield, *Horrors*, pp. 120–32.

17. *Ibid.*, p. 122.

18. *Ibid.*, p. 126.

19. Harry Benjamin, *The Transsexual Phenomenon* (New York: Julian Press, 1966), p. 28.

20. John Money, "Sex Reassignment," *International Journal of Psychiatry*, 9 (1970–71): 249.

21. What has also escaped notice is that transvestism and transsexualism both involve consistent role-playing. Homosexuality of the "butch-femme" variety is again most certainly role-playing. However, some homosexuals and many lesbians see role-playing as an essential aberration, one that betrays an essentially heterosexist consciousness. As many feminists have noted, this is one of the key differences between male homosexuals and lesbians who are feminists. Many male homosexuals treat their male partners as men treat women—as sexual objects. Thus the male partner becomes a female substitute and is put in a woman's role. Male homosexuality has also not been located in a political context equivalent to lesbian-feminism. However, role-playing is intrinsic to transvestism and transsexualism. With homosexuals, it *may* occur.

22. Author's conversation with Mary Daly, Wellfleet, Mass., July 1976.

23. "Children from Transsexual or Lesbian Home Are Hetero-sexual," *Clinical Psychiatry News*, 6 (1978): 1, 36.

INTRODUCTION, PAGES 1-18

1. Harry Benjamin, *The Transsexual Phenomenon* (New York: Julian Press, 1966), p. 26.

2. D. H. Russell, "The Sex-Conversion Controversy," *The New England Journal of Medicine*, 279 (September 1968):535.

3. Milton T. Edgerton, Norman J. Knorr, and James R. Callison, "The Surgical Treatment of Transsexual Patients," *Plastic and Reconstructive Surgery*, 45 (January 1970): 38.

4. *Ibid.*, p. 42.

5. The various definitions of *sex* can be found in John Money, "Sex Reassignment as Related to Hermaphroditism and Trans-sexualism," in Richard Green and John Money, eds., *Transsexualism and Sex Reassignment* (Baltimore: Johns Hopkins University Press, 1969), pp. 91-93.

6. Robert Stoller, *Sex and Gender* (New York: Science House, 1968), pp. viii, ix.

7. Ira Pauly, "Adult Manifestations of Female Transsexualism," in Green and Money, *Transsexualism*, p. 44.

8. John Money and Anke A. Ehrhardt, *Man & Woman, Boy & Girl* (Baltimore: Johns Hopkins University Press, 1972), p. 4.

9. Quoted in *Time*, January 21, 1974, p. 64.

10. Jon K. Meyer and John E. Hoopes, "The Gender Dysphoria Syndromes," *Plastic and Reconstructive Surgery*, 54 (October 1974): 447.

11. *Idem.*

12. See Daniel Callahan, *Abortion: Law, Choice & Morality* (New York: Macmillan, 1970).

13. See R. A. Stebbins, "The Unstructured Research Interview as Incipient Interpersonal Relationship," *Social and Sociological Research*, 56 (January 1972): 164-79.
The goal of such unstructured techniques as explained by R. A. Stebbins is to provide some sort of conscious data for research purposes. Dean and Whyte have listed the kinds of subjective data that are elicited in such interviews as: (a) current emotional states; (b) opinions on a subject; (c) attitudes toward some object; (d) values or the underlying principles that organize opinions, attitudes, and subsequent behavior; (e) hypothetical reactions to certain circumstances; (f) actual reactions in specified situations. In interviewing both pre- and postoperative transsexuals, I was most interested in obtaining information with respect to (d) values or the underlying principles that organize opinions, attitudes, and subsequent behavior, especially as it influenced the transsexual's background of sex-role conditioning and his/her subsequent desire to be transsexed.

The various questions I asked transsexuals should help to make the preceding categories more specific. Aside from the commonly asked questions about family, class, educational, religious, and geographical background, I asked each transsexual the following questions: (a) Were they satisfied with the surgery? Did they ever look back and wish they had done differently? Is their gender dissatisfaction relieved? (b) What is their opinion about feminism? What do they think about homosexuality? (c) What clothes do they like to wear? What jobs interest them? (d) Why did they want to become women (or men)? What do they expect from life? What did they feel lacking before surgery? Would they like to see what are called masculine and feminine qualities and characteristics disappear? How do they relate to women and men? (e) I asked transsexuals to react to the hypothetical situation of a role free society in which people were able to be themselves. Would they then feel it necessary to change sex? I also asked the transsexuals I interviewed how they would react to a hypothetical meeting with a feminist who told them that they were reinforcing sex-role stereotypes by changing sex. (f) In some cases, where I felt I could express my own opinion, I admitted I was the feminist who felt much ambiguity about the rightness of transsexualism because it reinforced sex-role stereotypes.

14. Mary Daly, *Beyond God the Father* (Boston: Beacon Press, 1973), especially pp. 179-98.

I: "EVERYTHING YOU ALWAYS WANTED TO KNOW ABOUT TRANSSEXUALISM," PAGES 19-42

1. D. O. Cauldwell, "Psychopathia Transsexualis," *Sexology,* XVI (1949): 274-80.

2. Christine Jorgensen, *A Personal Autobiography* (New York: Bantam Books, 1968). Jorgensen's autobiography was subsequently made into a movie.

3. Neils Hoyer, *Man Into Woman: An Authentic Record of a Change of Sex* (New York: Dutton, 1933). Harry Benjamin in his introduction to Money and Green's *Transsexualism and Sex Reassignment* cites this as being the first popularized account of transsexualism.

4. F. Z. Abraham, "Genitalumwandlung an zwei maennlichen Transvestiten," *Sexualwiss,* 18 (1931): 223-26.

5. Harry Benjamin first became interested in sex conversion (which he later named transsexualism) when sex researcher Alfred Kinsey referred him to a case that he, Kinsey, could not understand. Kinsey was preparing a second volume on sexual behavior and discovered in the taking of his case histories a young boy whose great ambition was to become a girl. Benjamin subsequently began seeing other cases of a similar nature, began referring candidates abroad

for surgery before the operation could be performed legally in the United States, and published the first systematic and professional account of transsexualism in a volume entitled *The Transsexual Phenomenon* (New York: Julian Press, 1966).

6. Author's interview with Zelda Suplee, New York City, May 1974. The Erickson Foundation, which was in operation until 1977 and is now defunct, was probably the group most familiar with the world and national situation on transsexualism. The Janus Information Center in Galveston, Texas, is attempting to continue the referral and public-information services supplied previously by the Erickson Foundation. In the planning stages at this point, however, is the Harry Benjamin International Academy for Gender Dysphoria, which, if established, will attempt to set standards of referral and surgery, and collect vital statistics on transsexualism worldwide.

7. Paul Walker and John Money in their review of Donald R. Lauband and Patrick Gaudy, eds., *Proceedings of the 2nd Interdisciplinary Symposium on Gender Dysphoria Syndrome*, that appeared in *Archives of Sexual Behavior*, 4 (1975): 311.

8. Cited in the *Erickson Educational Foundation Newsletter*, 8 (Spring 1975): 1.

9. Ira B. Pauly, "Male Psychosexual Inversion: Transsexualism," *Archives General Psychiatry*, XIII (August 1965): 172.

10. Author's interviews with John Money, Baltimore, Maryland, February 1974, and Canon Clinton Jones, Hartford, Connecticut, March 1975.

11. Anke Ehrhardt, Commentary on Norman Block and Arthur Tessler, "Transsexualism and Surgical Procedures," *Surgery, Gynecology, and Obstetrics*, 132 (March 1971): 527.

12. Quoted in Benjamin, *The Transsexual Phenomenon*, p. 148.

13. Ira B. Pauly, "Adult Manifestations of Female Transsexualism," in Richard Green and John Money eds, *Transsexualism and Sex Reassignment* (Baltimore: Johns Hopkins Press, 1969), p. 60. The Kinsey hypothesis that Pauly refers to can be found in A. C. Kinsey, et al., *Sexual Behavior in the Human Female* (Philadelphia: W. B. Saunders, 1953).

14. Judith Long Laws, "The Psychology of Tokenism: An Analysis," *Sex Roles*, I (1975), 51.

15. *Idem.*

16. Mary Daly, *Gyn/Ecology: The Metaethics of Radical Feminism* (Boston: Beacon Press, 1978), p. 57.

17. The case of Rosalyn Franklin is a primary example of a woman who made an initial and major contribution to the discovery of the structure of DNA, yet was not part of the group that received the Nobel Prize for this discovery. See Anne Sayre, *Rosalyn Franklin and the DNA* (New York: W. W. Norton, 1975). An even more famous example of the male scientific erasure of a woman's discovery is the case of Helen Taussig who discovered the method for saving

the lives of "blue babies." Alfred Blalock took the credit for this discovery, and it has since been named the Blalock method.

18. Karen Horney, *Feminine Psychology* (New York: W. W. Norton, 1967).

19. Ralph Greenson, quoted in Charles J. McFadden, *Medical Ethics* (Philadelphia: F. A. Davis, 1967), p. 282.

20. Barbara Seaman, *Free and Female* (New York: Fawcett-Crest, 1972).

21. Barbara Ehrenreich and Deirdre English, *Witches, Midwives, and Nurses: A History of Women Healers* (New York: Feminist Press, 1972); and *Complaints and Disorders: The Sexual Politics of Sickness* (New York: Feminist Press, 1973).

22. Christian Hamburger, "Endocrine Treatment of Male and Female Transsexualism," in Green and Money, *Transsexualism*, p. 291. Hamburger, the surgeon who transsexed Christine Jorgensen, is credited with being the first to develop surgical specialties for the medical treatment of transsexualism.

23. Harry Benjamin and Charles L. Ihlenfeld, "Transsexualism," *American Journal of Nursing*, 73 (March 1973): 460.

24. Hamburger, "Endocrine Treatment," p. 297.

25. C. Hamburger, G. K. Sturrup, and E. Dahl-Iversen, "Transvestism," *Journal of the American Medical Association*, 152 (1953): 391.

26. Norman L. Block and Arthur N. Tessler, "Transsexualism and Surgical Procedures," *Surgery, Gynecology and Obstetrics*, 132 (March 1971): 523.

27. Benjamin and Ihlenfeld, "Transsexualism," p. 461.

28. W. S. C. Symmers, "Carcinoma of the Breast in Transsexual Individuals After Surgical and Hormonal Interference with the Primary and Secondary Sex Characteristics," *British Medical Journal*, 2 (1968): 83.

29. Leo Wollman, "Office Management of the Postoperative Male Transsexual," in Green and Money, *Transsexualism*, p. 332. Obviously, Wollman's medical jargon of "running risks" obscures the fact that it is the medical empire that initiates and promotes such risks.

30. See Harry Ziel and William Finkle, "Increased Risk of Endometrial Carcinoma Among Users of Conjugated Estrogens," and Donald Smith et al., "Association of Exogenous Estrogen and Endometrial Carcinoma," *New England Journal of Medicine*, 293 (December 4, 1975): 1167–70; 1164–66. Both of these articles confirm the connection between estrogenic therapy and cancer of the endometrium and the breast, a connection that has been suspected for many years and previously demonstrated by many health feminists. This evidence written up in the *New England Journal of Medicine* confirms that "conservative" doses of estrogen therapy given to the "normal female" may be cancer-inducing. In fact, Smith *et al.*

found: "Our data also indicate that the exogenous estrogen-related risk is highest for women classified as normal—i.e., those with none of the 'classic' predisposing signs" (p. 1166).

31. Benjamin and Ihlenfeld, "Transsexualism," p. 461.

32. Creighton G. Bellinger and Dicran Goulian, "Secondary Surgery in Transsexuals," *Plastic and Reconstructive Surgery*, 51 (June 1973): 630.

33. Milton T. Edgerton, Norman J. Knorr, and James R. Callison, "The Surgical Treatment of Transsexual Patients: Limitations and Indications," *Plastic and Reconstructive Surgery*, 45 (January 1970): 43–44.

34. Quoted in Bellinger and Goulian, "Secondary Surgery in Transsexuals," p. 628.

35. J. Hoenig et al., "Surgical Treatment for Transsexuals," *Acta Psychiatra Scandinavia*, 47 (1971): 106–36.

36. John E. Hoopes, "Operative Treatment of the Female Transsexual," in Green and Money, *Transsexualism*, p. 337.

37. *Ibid.*, p. 341. Hoopes also lists the various attempts at phallus construction (p. 343). Each attempt has aimed at constructing a functionally sexual phallus. Rigidity has been achieved in various ways. Autogenous rib cartilage grafts have proven most satisfactory (Bogoras, 1936; Franklin, 1944; Bergman, Howard, and Barnes, 1948; Gelb, Malament, and Lo Verme, 1959). This method is is certainly an interesting variation on the theme of "Adam's rib," this time Eve's rib providing the necessary material for Adam's phallus. However, given the fact that Adam is genetically still Eve, such surgery is actually a pseudoversion of the androgynous person.

Acrylic implants have been utilized by several investigators (Goodwin and Scott, 1952; Morales, O'Connor, and Hotchkiss, 1956; Loeffler and Sayegh, 1960) and have been found to be unsatisfactory. Morales *et al.* used implanted steel mesh. Munawar implanted a periosteal tibial bone graft. Farina and Freire (1954) observed that rigid implants are unnecessary due to the fact that ibrosis with the abdominal tube pedicle flap provided sufficient rigidity. Millard (1966) described a patient who enjoyed satisfactory sexual intercourse with the aid of a "stiffener" inserted into the "skin urethra[sic]. " Finally, there is the most recent method, explained in the text, of a stiffener inserted into an envelope of the skin of the constructed phallus, which presses against the embedded clitoris during intercourse, thus enabling orgasm.

38. Benjamin, *The Transsexual Phenomenon*, p. 150.

39. Hoopes, "Operative Treatment," p. 341.

40. All the preceding information concerning legal statutes was summarized in Robert Veit Sherwin, "Legal Aspects of Male Transsexualism," in Green and Money, *Transsexualism*, pp. 417–20.

41. *Ibid.*, p. 420.

42. *Idem.*

43. John Money and Florence Schwartz, "Public Opinion and Social Issues in Transsexualism: A Case Study in Medical Sociology," in Green and Money, *Transsexualism*, p. 260.

44. Sherwin, "Legal Aspects," pp. 420–21.

45. Cited in Money and Schwartz, "Public Opinion," pp. 258–59.

46. *Ibid.*, p. 257.

47. Donald W. Hastings, "Inauguration of a Research Project on Transsexualism in a University Medical Center," in Green and Money, *Transsexualism*, p. 251.

48. Money and Schwartz, "Public Opinion," p. 258.

49. Robert Sherwin, "The Legal Problem in Transvestism," *American Journal of Psychotherapy*, III (April 1954): 243–44.

II. ARE TRANSSEXUALS BORN OR MADE— OR BOTH?, PAGES 43-68

1. Quoted in Richard Green, "Mythological, Historical, and Cross-Cultural Aspects of Transsexualism," in Richard Green and John Money, eds., *Transsexualism and Sex Reassignment* (Baltimore: Johns Hopkins University Press, 1969), p. 14.

2. *Organicism* signifies "integration" here.

3. Among other writings at this point, see John Money, "Developmental Differentiation of Femininity and Masculinity Compared," in *The Potential of Women*, eds. Seymour M. Farber and Roger H. L. Wilson (New York: McGraw-Hill, 1963), p. 51.

4. John Money and Anke Ehrhardt, *Man & Woman, Boy & Girl* (Baltimore: Johns Hopkins University Press, 1972), p. 1.

5. *Ibid.*, pp. 3–4.

6. *Idem.*

7. *Idem.*

8. *Ibid.*, p. 9.

9. *Ibid.*, p. 2.

10. *Ibid.*, p. 21.

11. *Ibid.*, p. 60.

12. *Ibid.*, pp. 63–64.

13. *Ibid.*, p. 71.

14. *Ibid.*, p. 103.

15. *Ibid.*, p. 10.

16. John Money and John G. Brennan, "Sexual Dimorphism in the Psychology of Female Transsexuals," in Green and Money, *Transsexualism*, pp. 149–50.

17. Money and Ehrhardt, *Man & Woman*, p. 161.

18. Money and Brennan, "Sexual Dimorphism," p. 150.

19. Ann Oakley, *Sex, Gender, & Society* (New York: Harper Colophon Books, 1972), p. 113.

20. *Ibid.*, p. 77.

21. Elizabeth Adkins, "Genes, Hormones, and Gender" (paper presented at the 144th National Meeting of the American Associa-

tion for the Advancement of Science, Washington, D.C., February 14, 1978), p. 21.

22. *Ibid.*, p. 19.

23. *Idem.*

24. Oakley, *Sex, Gender, & Society*, p. 127.

25. Adkins, "Genes, Hormones, and Gender," p. 13.

26. See J. W. Mason, "Psychologic Stress and Endocrine Function," in E. J. Sacher, ed., *Topics in Psychoendocrinology* (New York: Grune & Stratton, 1975).

27. Martin Duberman, "The Case of the Gay Sergeant," the *New York Times Magazine*, November 9, 1975, p. 67.

28. Thomas Aquinas, *Summa Theologiae*, I, 92, I, ad. I.

29. Estelle Ramey, "Sex Hormones and Executive Ability," *Annals of the New York Academy of Sciences*, 208 (March 15, 1973): 238.

30. Warren Gadpaille, "Research into the Physiology of Maleness and Femaleness," *Archives of General Psychiatry*, 26 (March 1972): 195.

31. Author's conversation with Eileen van Tassell, Amherst, Mass., July 1978.

32. Robert Stoller, "The 'Bedrock' of Masculinity and Femininity," *Archives of General Psychiatry*, 26 (March 1972): 209.

33. John Money and Patricia Tucker, *Sexual Signatures: On Being a Man or a Woman* (Boston: Little, Brown, 1975), pp. 15-16.

34. In speaking about "appropriate" versus "inappropriate" utterances, Julia Stanley has written: "An appropriate utterance is one that is fully meaningful . . . and open to question." In order for an utterance to be open to question, the words must have referential value with respect to the context. (See Julia Stanley, "The Stylistics of Belief," in Daniel J. Dieterich, ed., *Teaching About Doublespeak* [Urbana, Ill.: National Council of Teachers of English, 1976], p. 177.) The words on page 59 quoted from *Sexual Signatures* are totally separated from Money's "overriding effects of androgen" statements in *Man & Woman, Boy & Girl*. The reader is left wondering how, if androgen is the activating hormone, there can be an effectual content to the "Eve base view."

35. Money and Ehrhardt, *Man & Woman*, p. 103.

36. Money and Tucker, *Sexual Signatures*, pp. 88-89.

37. *Ibid.*, p. 89.

38. Money and Ehrhardt, *Man & Woman*, p. 13.

39. Money and Tucker, *Sexual Signatures*, pp. 86-87.

40. *Ibid.*, p. 119.

41. *Ibid.*, p. 230.

42. Peter Berger and Thomas Luckmann, *The Social Construction of Reality* (New York: Doubleday, 1966), p. 156.

43. *Ibid.*, p. 157.

44. "Biological Imperatives," *Time*, January 8, 1973, p. 34.

45. Money and Tucker, *Sexual Signatures*, p. 230.

46. *Ibid.*, p. 231.

47. *Ibid.*, p. 193.

48. *Ibid.*, p. 231.

49. *Ibid.*, p. 233.

50. Money and Ehrhardt, *Man & Woman*, p. 186.

III. "MOTHER'S FEMINIZED PHALLUS" OR FATHER'S
CASTRATED FEMME?, PAGES 69-98

1. Robert Stoller, *The Transsexual Experiment* (London: Hogarth Press, 1975), pp. 38–55.

2. Robert Stoller, "Parental Influences in Male Transsexualism," in Richard Green and John Money, eds., *Transsexualism and Sex Reassignment* (Baltimore: Johns Hopkins University Press, 1969), p. 166.

3. Stoller, *The Transsexual Experiment*, pp. 223–244.

4. Harry Benjamin and Charles L. Ihlenfeld, "Transsexualism," *American Journal of Nursing*, 73 (March 1973): 458.

5. John Money and Patricia Tucker, *Sexual Signatures: On Being a Man or a Woman* (Boston: Little, Brown, 1975), p. 91.

6. Richard Green, *Sexual Identity Conflict in Children and Adults* (New York: Basic Books, 1974), p. 303.

7. *Ibid.*, p. 302.

8. *Idem.*

9. Another issue that could be raised in this context is the insignificance of biological fatherhood. If, as the psychologists assert, fathers have only a passive influence on transsexual development, then is this an unintended commentary on the inconsequentiality of paternal ability to affect. "Blaming the mother," although it is a negative influence, is still an influence. Furthermore, mothers have been "credited" with such negative ability to affect in many areas of child development. As Mary Daly has asked, does it then become the self-appointed task of the medical and therapeutic fathers to take over a faded and ineffectual biological fatherhood? Is their construction of a transsexual empire an unwitting admission that the biological father is impotent and must be stabilized by technological paternity?

10. N. Lukianovicz, "Survey of Various Aspects of Transvestism in the Light of Our Present Knowledge," *Journal of Nervous and Mental Disorders*, 128 (1959): 36.

11. Lionel Ovesey and Ethel Person, "Gender Identity and Sexual Psychopathology in Men: A Psychodynamic Analysis of Homosexuality, Transsexualism, and Transvestism," *Journal of the American Academy of Psychoanalysis*, 1 (1973): 54.

12. *Ibid.*, p. 65.

13. Henry Guze, "Psychosocial Adjustment of Transsexuals: An Evaluation and Theoretical Formulation," in Green and Money, *Transsexualism*, p. 179.

14. *Idem.*

15. Interview with Allen Raysdon, *Daily Local News*, West Chester, Pa., Oct. 7, 1974, p. 2.

16. Judy Klemesrud, "A Transsexual and Her Family: An Attempt at Life as Usual," *New York Times*, Oct. 23, 1973.

17. William Cockerham, "Prisoner Requests Sex-Change Surgery," Hartford *Courant*, May 5, 1974.

18. Tommi Avicolli, "Crossing Sexual Borders," *Gay Community News*, May 3, 1975, p. 12. For the correlation between transsexualism and prostitution, see also: Thomas Kando, *Sex Change: The Achievement of Gender Identity among Feminized Transsexuals* (Springfield, Ill.: Charles C. Thomas, 1973), pp. 46–59; J. Hoenig, J. C. Kenna, and A. Yond, "Surgical Treatment for Transsexuals," *Acta Psychiatra Scandinavia*, 47 (May 1974): 106–36. Hoenig *et al.* give statistics of transsexuals who turn to prostitution. They also relate an example of a prosperous businessman who, after changing sex, couldn't find work as a woman; Harry Benjamin, *The Transsexual Phenomenon* (New York: Julian Press, 1966). He reports that prostitution is fairly common among transsexuals.

19. Kando, *Sex Change*, p. 8. Since a large section of the text is devoted to Kando's study, the remaining page references quoted will be placed in parentheses in the text.

20. John Money and John G. Brennan, "Sexual Dimorphism in the Psychology of Male Transsexuals," in Green and Money, *Transsexualism*, p. 139.

21. Peter Berger, *The Sacred Canopy* (New York: Doubleday, 1967), p. 85.

22. *Idem.*

23. George Gilder, in *Sexual Suicide*, expressed this same reasoning, but from quite a different perspective. In attacking the women's movement for its impatience with man's constant need to prove his masculinity, Gilder accuses feminists of misunderstanding a basic point about masculinity: "Unlike femininity, relaxed masculinity is at bottom empty, a limp nullity. While the female body is full of internal possibility, the male is internally barren (from the Old French *bar*, meaning man). Manhood at the most basic level can be validated and expressed only in action. For a man's body is full only of undefined energies. And all these energies need the guidance of culture. He is therefore deeply dependent on the structure of the society to define his role" (p. 18).

24. Money and Tucker, *Sexual Signatures*, p. 206.

25. *Ibid.*, p. 192. This is a change in Money's thinking. When I interviewed him at Johns Hopkins in February 1974, he stated that

he perceived no relation between transsexualism and sex-role stereotyping.

26. Diane Dumanoski, "Transsexuals: Anatomy Need Not be Destiny," The Boston *Phoenix*, November 25, 1975.

27. Robin Morgan, "Lesbianism and Feminism: Synonyms or Contradictions?" *The Second Wave*, 2, no. 4 (1973): 18.

28. Kando, *Sex Change*, pp. 113-14.

29. Kando, *Sex Change*, p. 114. Many transsexuals reject the terms *sex conversion surgery* and *transsexual surgery*. They speak instead of *corrective surgery*.

30. Jan Morris, *Conundrum* (New York: Signet, 1974), pp. 89, 90, 91.

31. *New York Times Magazine*, March 17, 1974, p. 94.

32. *Idem.*

33. Morris, *Conundrum*, p. 177.

34. Susan Brownmiller, *Against Our Will: Men, Women, and Rape* (New York: Simon & Schuster, 1975), pp. 257-68.

35. Ernest Becker, *The Structure of Evil* (New York: George Braziller, 1968), p. 185.

36. See Avicolli, "Crossing Sexual Borders."

37. Norman Knorr, Sanford Wolf, and Eugene Meyer, "Psychiatric Evaluation of Male Transsexuals for Surgery," in Green and Money, *Transsexualism*, p. 278.

38. Harry Benjamin, *The Transsexual Phenomenon* (New York: Julian Press, 1966), p. 110.

39. Norman Block and Arthur Tessler, "Transsexualism and Surgical Procedures," *Surgery, Gynecology, and Obstetrics*, 132 (March 1971): 522.

40. Jon K. Meyer and John E. Hoopes, "The Gender Dysphoria Syndromes: A Position Statement on So-Called 'Transsexualism,'" *Plastic and Reconstructive Surgery*, 54 (October 1974): 447.

41. Quoted in Benjamin, *The Transsexual Phenomenon*, p. 109.

42. Erickson Educational Foundation, "Counseling the Transsexual: Five Conversations with Professionals in Transsexual Therapy," pp. 9-10.

43. *Ibid.*, p. 14.

44. *Idem.*

45. Joyce Strait, "The Transsexual Patient After Surgery," *American Journal of Nursing*, 73 (March 1973): p. 462.

46. George A. Rekers and James W. Varni, "Self-Monitoring and Self-Reinforcement Processes in a Pre-Transsexual Boy," *Behaviour Research and Therapy*, 15 (1977): 177. Rekers presently heads a treatment and research program at U.C.L.A. on childhood "gender problems" supported by U.S. Public Health Service Research Grants and grants from NIMH. Formerly, Richard Green was the director of this program. See also George A. Rekers, O. Ivar Lovaas, and Benson Low, "The Behavior Treatment of a 'Transsexual' Preadoles-

200   The Transsexual Empire

cent Boy," *Journal of Abnormal Child Psychology*, 2 (June 1974): 99–116. For an insightful critique of the work of the Child Gender Program at U.C.L.A., see David M. Rorvik, "The Gender Enforcers," *Rolling Stone*, October 9, 1975, pp. 53, 67, 86–88. Rorvik cites organized opposition to the gender program from the "Coalition Against the Dehumanization to Children." This group claimed to have intercepted a personal memo from Rekers which sought help in locating more prepubertal males with so-called gender identity problems for "diagnostic study."

47. Richard Green, Lawrence E. Newman, and Robert J. Stoller, "Treatment of Boyhood 'Transsexualism,'" *Archives General Psychiatry*, 26 (March 1972): 213.

48. Nowhere in this report do the authors define masculinity or femininity. It is assumed that there is a commonly agreed upon, though invisible, consensus. A major question that could be asked about this article is how it squares with Money's contention that gender identity is fixed by eighteen months. If this is so, then it seems that no amount of treatment, even of boyhood transsexual tendencies, would alter core gender identity.

49. Green, Newman, and Stoller, "Boyhood 'Transsexualism,'" p. 214.

50. Meyer and Hoopes, p. 445.

51. Ernest Barker, *The Political Thought of Plato and Aristotle* (New York: Dover Publications, 1959), p. 398.

52. Green, Newman, and Stoller, p. 216.

53. Meyer and Hoopes, p. 445.

54. Julia Stanley, in "The Stylistics of Appropriateness: A Redefinition" (paper presented at the Conference on College Composition and Communication, New Orleans, Louisiana, April 1973), offers an incisive linguistic commentary on such words: "The adjectives *appropriate* and *inappropriate* belong to the general class of PSYCHOLOGICAL PREDICATES. Specifically, these adjectives are *judgment verbals*. Such predicates . . . 'designate psychological states, processes, or attributes.' But as with other psychological predicates, like *seem* and *appear*, these predicates can imply that the underlying presuppositions are not subjective at all, but are based on some universal consensus regarding behavior. The usage of appropriate and inappropriate covertly suggest that the judgment is attributable to more than just the individual speaker."

55. Green, Newman, and Stoller, p. 217.

56. *Idem.* Rorvik, in "The Gender Enforcers," responds to this kind of argument. "The Researchers' stance is thus a 'liberal' one . . . one nods approvingly as the researchers pay liberal lip service to the idea that *society* should change in order to accommodate greater expression of effeminacy among males. But then, they sigh, society will not do this; so it's up to them to make the gender male misfit

fit into society, for his own good . . . It all seems terribly logical, until one reflects: How will society ever change if accommodating psychotechnologists keep changing *us* to conform to society?" (p. 53).

57. Max Stackhouse, *Ethics and the Urban Ethos* (Boston: Beacon Press, 1972), p. 28. Stackhouse has stated: "The personalist position does not fulfill its own intention; it does not deal with the whole person or the new shapes of personality. . . . The isolation and absolutization of the concept of the person extracted from the actual social matrix is a fundamental distortion of what it means to be a self and what it takes to promote authentic self and small group relations."

IV. SAPPHO BY SURGERY: THE TRANSSEXUALLY CONSTRUCTED LESBIAN-FEMINIST, PAGES 99-119

1. In June/July of 1977, twenty-two feminist musicians, sound technicians, radio women, producers, and managers sent an open letter to Olivia Records via *Sister*, a West Coast feminist newspaper. The letter focused on the employment of Sandy Stone, a male-to-constructed-female transsexual, as Olivia's recording engineer and sound technician. The signers protested Stone's presence at Olivia and the fact that Olivia did not inform women that Stone was a postoperative transsexual. They criticized Stone's participation in women-only events and accused him of taking work away from the "few competent women sound technicians in the Bay Area . . . whose opportunities are extremely limited." They noted that Stone's male privilege gave him access to his skills, and that he has never had to suffer the oppression that women face every day. The letter concluded by stating that "it is not our intention to discredit or trash Olivia," and requested that they publish a statement in response.

In the same issue of *Sister*, Olivia replied that: 1. Surgery alone does not make a transsexual a woman. "This too-publicized step is merely the confirmation of a process that has already gone to near completion by that time." 2. Aside from a few well-publicized transsexuals, a person does not gain privilege by becoming a transsexual. Because Stone gave up his male identity and lives as a "woman" and a "lesbian," he is faced with the same kinds of oppression that "other" women and lesbians face, along with the added ostracism that results from being a transsexual. 3. A person's history is important but most significant is what that person's actions are now. 4. Day-to-day interaction with Sandy Stone has convinced the Olivia women that Sandy is a "woman we can relate to with comfort and trust." 5. Olivia did not indicate Stone's transsexual status, because they were afraid he would be "objectified." "We see transsexualism as a state of transition, and we feel that to continue to define a person primarily by that condition is to stigmatize her at the expense of her growth process as a woman." 6. Stone has trained women in technical skills and will build Olivia's recording studio where many women will apprentice. He is also writing a how-to book for women explaining the recording process. Thus Stone does not take employment away from women but provides it and may be "perhaps even the Goddess-sent engineering wizard we had so long sought."

2. Author's conversation with Pat Hynes, Cambridge, Mass., January 1978.

3. Author's conversation with Mary Daly, Boston, Mass., February 1978.

4. Rosemary Anderson, Letter entitled "Transsexual Feminism?" *Sister*, August–September 1977, p. 7.

5. Recently, questions have been raised by transsexuals who claim to be lesbian-feminists and by some professionals in gender identity clinics about clinic requirements of "passing" and about the stereotypical behavior of transsexuals. "We urge professionals *not* to assume or expect that all transsexuals will be heterosexually oriented or politically conservative and not to judge (for example) lesbianism in a male-to-female transsexual as invalid while accepting it in a genetic woman. Biological women and male-to-female transsexuals present a similarly vast range of sexual orientation and life-style choices; different choices are valid for different people. . . . Positively, we recommend a setting where the client is not forced to avow rigid self-definitions, but is permitted and even encouraged to find her/his own answers to the difficult and complex questions of sexuality and identity that confront us all." Deborah Heller Feinbloom *et al.*, "Lesbian/Feminist Orientation Among Male-to-Female Transsexuals," *Journal of Homosexuality*, 2 (Fall 1976): 70–71.

There are several criticisms that can be made of such a stance. First, nonstereotypical behavior is encouraged as one choice among "different choices [that] are valid for different people." Thus there is no commitment to eradicating stereotypical behavior but only to encouraging alternative behavior ("different strokes for different folks"). And thus there is no commitment to ultimately phasing out gender identity control over *various* styles of behavior. The authors' conclusions coincide with John Money's recommendations in *Sexual Signatures* for "flexible" stereotypes.

Second, the unanswered question is why are such transsexuals and transsexual professionals still advocating surgery. Transsexual surgery would not be necessary if rigid self-definitions had not produced the phenomenon of a "female mind in a male body." This self-definition would make no sense in a society that did not accept that split. Therefore, to support behavior and orientation that is not stereotypical, yet to continue advocating transsexualism is contradictory.

Such recommendations only make the issue of "passing" and stereotypical behavior more invisible. These authors *appear* to get beyond the stereotypes, but they are actually supporting "passing" behavior on a deeper level. In effect, they are now advocating that men "pass" as lesbian-feminists, thus making a "role" out of lesbian-feminism that can be taken on by anyone. Ultimately, this brings lesbian-feminism within the confines of the gender identity clinics, where it can be observed, studied, *and controlled*—first in transsexuals, and then perhaps in lesbian-feminists. With the acceptance of transsexuals as lesbian-feminists by the gender identity clinics, the "passing" requirements only become modified. The transsexual "passes" what are the current (seemingly avant-garde) requirements of the gender identity clinics. In order to become transsexed, however, his "passing" behavior must still be "baptized" as legitimately female.

It is significant that these recommendations are coming from male-to-constructed-female transsexuals. Here is a clear admission that lesbian-feminism is perceived as important and that more is at stake in transsexual surgery than obtaining the body and the traditional role of a woman. There is a recognition here that female power/energy/creativity is at the heart of the matter. Why are there no female-to-constructed-male transsexuals, for example, who are seeking to "pass" as homosexual men?

6. Author's conversation with Mary Daly, Boston, Mass., February 1978.

7. Robert Spencer, "The Cultural Aspects of Eunuchism," *CIBA Symposia*, 8 (1946): 407.

8. *Ibid.*, p. 408.

9. *Ibid.*, p. 413.

10. Another parallel is that some royal eunuchs also wore women's clothing, and their physical characteristics, especially as represented on Assyrian monuments, resembled those of women. Eunuch priests of goddess temples were said to wear women's garb and perform women's tasks. See John L. McKenzie, "Eunuch," *Dictionary of the Bible* (Milwaukee: The Bruce Publishing Company, 1965), 252.

11. Simone de Beauvoir, *The Second Sex* (New York: Bantam Books, 1953), p. 174.

12. See Mary Daly, *Gyn/Ecology: The Metaethics of Radical Feminism* (Boston: Beacon Press, 1978), pp. 66–67.

13. Philip Slater, *The Glory of Hera: Greek Mythology and the Greek Family* (Boston: Beacon Press, 1968), p. 211.

14. Jane Harrison, *Mythology* (New York: Harcourt, Brace and World, 1963), p. 97.

15. See comments in Chapter I about transsexual desire for female creativity as represented in female biology.

16. Radicalesbians, "The Woman Identified Woman," in Anne Koedt, Ellen Levine, and Anita Rapone, eds., *Radical Feminism* (New York: Quadrangle/New York Times Book Co., 1973), p. 241.

17. Norman O. Brown, *Love's Body* (New York: Random House, 1966), p. 116.

18. Daly, *Gyn/Ecology*, pp. 67–68.

19. Elizabeth Rose, Letter to the Editors, *Chrysalis*, 5 (1978): 6.

20. *Idem.*

21. Daly, *Gyn/Ecology*, p. 67.

22. *Ibid.*

23. Judy Antonelli, "Open Letter to Olivia," *Sister*, August–September 1977), p. 6.

24. T. C. Boyle, "The Women's Restaurant," *Penthouse*, May 1977, p. 112.

25. *Ibid.*, p. 132.

26. *Ibid.*, p. 133.

27. Conversation with Adrienne Rich, Montague, Mass., May 1977.

28. Jill Johnston, *Lesbian Nation: The Feminist Solution* (New York: Simon & Schuster, 1973), p. 180.

29. Angela Douglas, Letter, *Sister*, August–September 1977, p. 7.

30. Johnston, *Lesbian Nation*, p. 278.

31. *Ibid.*, p. 279.

32. See, for example, photographer J. Frederick Smith's "portfolio of stunning portraits inspired by ancient Greek poems on loving women," in *Playboy*, October 1975, pp. 126–35.

33. One photographer who is particularly obsessed with "capturing" women in pseudolesbian poses is David Hamilton. He is the creator of the following books of photography:

Dreams of a Young Girl, text by Alain Robbe-Grillet (New York: William Morrow and Co., 1971).

Sisters, text by Alain Robbe-Grillet (New York: William Morrow and Co., 1973). This book has an outrageous pictorial section entitled "Charms of the Harem."

Hamilton's Movies—Bilitis (Zug, Switzerland: Swan Productions AG, 1977).

34. Lisa Buck (Unpublished notes on transsexualism, October 1977), p. 3.

35. An example of this literature is Robert Wilson's *Feminine Forever* (New York: M. Evans, 1966). This book sold 100,000 copies in its first year, as well as being excerpted in *Look* and *Vogue*.

36. See Deborah Larned, "The Greening of the Womb," *New Times*, December 12, 1974, pp. 35–39.

V. THERAPY AS A WAY OF LIFE:
MEDICAL VALUES VERSUS SOCIAL CHANGE, PAGES 120-153

1. Thomas Szasz, *Ceremonial Chemistry* (New York: Doubleday, 1975), p. 149.
2. Ernest Becker, *The Structure of Evil* (New York: George Braziller, 1968), p. 297.
3. See the *Oxford English Dictionary* listing for the word *health*, which traces the word from its Old English spelling originally meaning "whole."
4. Becker, *The Structure of Evil*, p. 298.
5. Philip Rieff, *The Triumph of the Therapeutic* (New York: Harper and Row, 1966), p. 13.
6. *Ibid.*, p. 15.
7. *Idem.*
8. Thomas Szasz, *Ideology and Insanity* (New York: Doubleday, 1970), p. 3.
9. *Ibid.*, p. 11.
10. Quoted in *Time*, January 21, 1974, p. 64.
11. Jan Morris, *Conundrum* (New York: New American Library, 1974), p. 177.
12. John Money and Patricia Tucker, *Sexual Signatures: On Being a Man or a Woman* (Boston: Little, Brown, 1975), pp. 230-31.
13. Becker, *The Structure of Evil*, p. 282.
14. *Ibid.*, p. 182.
15. Percentages vary slightly but most authors doing postoperative follow-up report that "the majority" or "most of" the transsexuals they surveyed are satisfied, both with the results of the surgery and their own state of being after the operation. Harry Benjamin reported on thirty-one male transsexuals and concluded that the results of such operations were "excellent" in sixteen cases, "satisfactory" in eleven cases, "doubtful" in four. See Harry Benjamin, "Nature and Management of Transsexualism with a Report on 31 Operated Cases," *Western Journal of Surgery, Obstetrics and Gynecology*, 72 (1964): 105-11.

Benjamin in 1966 published findings on a larger number of postoperative transsexuals (fifty-one). "Assessment of postoperative adjustment was made and was considered 'good' if the total life situation was successful, and with good integration into the world of women and acceptance by society and by the patient's family—seventeen cases (thirty-three percent). If the result lacked one of these features, including the ability to experience orgasm, the result was considered "satisfactory"—twenty-seven cases (fifty-three percent). Where appearance and sexual function were unsatisfactory, despite relief from unhappiness in the male role, the result of the operation was designated 'doubtful'—five cases (ten percent). Only

206   The Transsexual Empire

one patient was regarded as having an unsatisfactory result (a patient Dr. Benjamin did not endorse)." See Benjamin, *The Transsexual Phenomenon* (New York: Julian Press, 1966).

These apparently satisfactory results of transsexual surgery are not, however, endorsed by all reporters. See, for example, P. Clarkson and D. Stafford-Clark, "Role of the Plastic Surgeon and Psychiatrist in the Surgery of Appearance," *British Medical Journal* (December 17, 1960), 1768. See also M. Ostow, Letter to the Editor, *Journal of the American Medical Association*, 152 (1953): 1552–53. However, these reports are the results of a much earlier period of transsexual surgery.

John Randell in "Preoperative and Postoperative Status of Male and Female Transsexuals," in Richard Green and John Money, eds., *Transsexualism and Sex Reassignment* (Baltimore: Johns Hopkins University Press, 1969), pp. 1, 32, concluded the following after working with thirty-five postoperative transsexuals. The postoperative results in the case of six female transsexuals "were almost universally satisfactory" (p. 378). The evaluation of twenty-nine male-to-constructed-female transsexuals was:

Excellent	7	Poor	1
Good	14	Very Poor	4
Fair	3		

"The postoperative results reported above indicate that the majority of males and females undergoing operation for sex reassignment are subjectively improved both in their adjustment to their environment and in their own feelings of well-being and satisfaction in their gender role" (379).

However, as Henry Guze notes, "While a frequent response is elation at being closer to one's imaged self, there are noteworthy exceptions." See Henry Guze, "Psychosocial Adjustment of Transsexuals: An Evaluation and Theoretical Formulation," in Green and Money, *Transsexualism*, pp. 171–200. ". . . both subtle and gross expressions of psychological disorder have been observed in some nine patients." These included dreams of death, inexplicable phobias, concern about physical appearance, dreams of previous masculine selves, guilt, remorse, and depression. Two patients felt angry and hopeless that they could not return to their previous masculine state. In Randell's study, there were four cases in which the postoperative adjustment was worse than before the operation (p. 373). "There the result can be designated 'very poor.'" The behavior included suicide, suicidal impulse, moral depravity, and a wish to reverse the effects of operation. Two of these men succeeded in committing suicide.

16. Szasz, *Ideology*, p. 18.

17. Kate Millett, *Sexual Politics* (New York: Doubleday, 1970), p. 23.

18. *Ibid.*, p. 25.

19. See G. J. Barker-Benfield, *The Horrors of the Half-Known Life* (New York: Harper and Row, 1976). It is estimated that clitoridectomies are still being performed on over 9 million women today, particularly in Northern Africa. See past issues of the *Women's International Network News*, especially vol. 2 (Summer 1976), ed. by Fran P. Hosken (187 Grant St., Lexington, MA 02173). See also for present evidence of clitoridectomies: Diane E. H. Russell and Nicole Van de Ven, eds., *The Proceedings of the International Tribunal on Crimes against Women* (Millbrae, CA: Les Femmes, 1976).

20. For the most extensive documentation about current psychosurgery theories, practices, and groups of people on whom such surgery is being performed, see Peter Breggin, "The Return of Lobotomy and Psychosurgery," *Congressional Record.* Proceedings and Debates of the 92nd Congress, Second Session, Feb. 24, 1972. See also Peter Breggin, "New Information in the Debate over Psychosurgery," *Congressional Record.* Proceedings and Debates of the 92nd Congress, Second Session, March 30, 1972.

21. See B. F. Skinner, *Beyond Freedom and Dignity* (New York: Alfred A. Knopf, 1971).

22. Willard Gaylin, "On the Borders of Persuasion: A Psychoanalytic Look at Coercion," *Psychiatry*, 37 (February 1974): 7.

23. *Ibid.*, p. 8.

24. Quoted in Al Huebner and Terry Kupers, "Violence Center: Psychotechnology for Repression," *Science for the People*, VI (May 1974): 17.

25. See Breggin, *Congressional Record.* He cites the fact that in 1970, William Sweet, Frank Ervin, and Vernon Mark were awarded a $500,000 grant from NIMH (National Institute of Mental Health). In 1971, Sweet et al. also received $188,000 from LEAA (Law Enforcement Assistance Administration) which was used to study the supposed biological basis of criminal behavior.

26. See George Gilder, *Sexual Suicide* (New York: Quadrangle/ New York Times Book Co., 1973).

27. Vernon Mark, William Sweet, and Frank Ervin, "Role of Brain Disease in Riots and Urban Violence," *Journal of the American Medical Association*, 201 (1967): 895.

If slum conditions alone determined and initiated riots, why are the vast majority of slum dwellers able to resist the temptations of unrestrained violence? Is there something peculiar about the slum dweller that differentiates him from his peaceful neighbor? . . . It would be of more than passing interest to find what percentage of the attempted and completed murders committed during the recent wave of riots were done without a motive . . . We need intensive research and clinical studies of the individuals committing the violence. The goal of such studies would be to pinpoint, diagnose and treat these people with low violence thresholds before they contribute to further tragedies.

208   The Transsexual Empire

28. José Delgado, *The Physical Control of the Mind: Toward a Psychocivilized Society* (New York: Harper and Row, 1960), p. 145.

29. Randell in Green and Money, *Transsexualism*, pp. 374–75.

30. William Irwin Thompson, *Evil and World Order* (New York: Harper and Row, 1976), p. 27.

31. *Ibid.*, p. 39.

32. See Kenneth L. Lehrman, "Pulmonary Embolism in a Transsexual Man Taking Diethylstilbesterol," *Journal of the American Medical Association*, 235 (February 2, 1976): 532–33. The conclusion of this study was that: "With increased acceptance of sex reassignment operations . . . and attempts to alter secondary sex characteristics, we believe that the possible association of thromboembolism and estrogen therapy should be considered as strongly in the young man as in the young woman" (p. 533). This conclusion was based on a study of a twenty-nine-year-old male-to-constructed-female transsexual with no prior history of varicosities, injuries, or prolonged inactivity.

J. Hoenig *et al.*, in their article, "The Surgical Treatment for Transsexuals" (*Acta Psychiatra Scandinavia*, 47 [May 1974]: 106–36), state that surgical treatment to increase breasts in male transsexuals should not be undertaken, especially if such treatment is followed up with estrogen therapy, since there is a risk of malignancy. They cited the study of W. Symmers, "Carcinoma of the Breast in Transsexual Individuals after Surgical and Hormonal Interference with the Primary and Secondary Sex Characteristics," *British Medical Journal*, 2 (1968): 83. Symmers reported two cases who came to autopsy with carcinoma of the breast. He suggests that the malignance was entirely due to the hormonal imbalance created by castration plus the massive doses of estrogen received. Jan Stiefel has noted the significant factor that serious and accepted research was being done on transsexuals with breast cancer resulting from exogenous estrogen therapy, long before a comparable serious and accepted study was done on native-born women.

Other studies that have investigated the correlation between male-to-constructed-female transsexualism and cancer are:

The Veteran's Administration Cooperative Urological Research Group, "Treatment and Survival of Patients with Carcinoma of the Prostate," *Surgery, Gynecology, and Obstetrics*, 124 (1967): 1011.

K. A. Hanash, *et al.*, "Relationships of Estrogen Therapy for Carcinoma of the Prostate to Atherosclerotic Cardiovascular Disease: A Clinicopathologic Study," *Journal of Urology*, 103 (1970): 467.

J. D. Bailar and D. P. Byar, "The Veteran's Administration Cooperative Urological Research Group: Estrogen Treatment for Cancer of the Prostate: Early Results with Three Doses of Diethylstilbesterol and Placebo," *Cancer*, 26 (1970): 257.

33. See Guze, "Male and Female Transsexuals," in Green and Money, *Transsexualism*, pp. 171–200. Meyer and Hoopes note that while most of their patients are emotionally and socially satisfied and stable post-operatively, "Another group of patients have done extraordinarily poorly—with inappropriate and self-destructive relationships, multiple and serious suicide attempts, drug abuse, serious physical complications, etc."

Charles L. Ihlenfeld, the endocrinologist, whose work on transsexualism has been quoted in this book and who was a prominent protégé of Harry Benjamin and co-author of several articles with him, has left the field after helping one hundred or more transsexuals change sex. He is reported to have given the reason that: "Whatever surgery did, it did not fulfill a basic yearning for something that is difficult to define. This goes along with the idea that we are trying to treat superficially something that is much deeper." Quoted in the *National Observer*, October 16, 1976, p. 14.

34. John Postgate, "Bat's Chance in Hell," *New Scientist*, April 5, 1973, pp. 14–15.

35. *Ibid.*, p. 15.

36. The literature on human experimentation is voluminous. Some primary sources for discussion of the issues of informed consent and the individual versus societal benefits are the series of articles in: Paul A. Freund, ed., *Experimentation with Human Subjects* (New York: George Braziller, 1969).

37. Ivan Illich, *Medical Nemesis, The Expropriation of Health* (London: Calder and Boyars, 1975), p. 95. I have used the British edition, because this quote does not appear in the American edition in the same way.

38. Peter Berger, *The Sacred Canopy: Elements of a Sociological Theory of Religion* (New York: Doubleday and Co., 1969), p. 54.

39. *Ibid.*, p. 55.

40. Jon K. Meyer and John H. Hoopes, "The Gender Dysphoria Syndromes: A Position Statement on So-Called Transsexualism," *Plastic and Reconstructive Surgery*, 54 (October 1977): 448.

41. Becker, *The Structure of Evil*, p. 182.

42. *Ibid.*, pp. 184–85.

43. *Ibid.*, p. 185.

44. Berger, *Sacred Canopy*, p. 59.

45. Green, "Conclusion," in Green and Money, *Transsexualism*, p. 467.

46. Milton T. Edgerton, "Transsexualism—A Surgical Problem?" *Plastic and Reconstructive Surgery*, 54 (October 1974): 448.

47. "Captive populations" generally include prisoners, mental patients, the poor, or any group in which the element of coercion conditions the choices of those groups, usually through the institutional context in which they are placed, and often in subtle ways.

48. Otto E. Guttentag, "Ethical Problems in Human Experimentation," in E. Fuller Torrey, ed., *Ethical Issues in Medicine: The Role of the Physician in Today's Society* (Boston: Little, Brown, 1968), p. 204.

49. See William L. Shirer, *The Rise and Fall of the Third Reich, A History of Nazi Germany* (New York: Simon and Schuster, 1959), especially pp. 979–91. Also see Alexander Mitscherlich and Fred Mielke, *Doctors of Infamy: The Story of the Nazi Medical Crimes* (New York: Henri Schuman, 1949).

50. Szasz, *Ceremonial Chemistry*, p. 116.

51. Szasz discusses the notion of *pharmacracy* in *Ceremonial Chemistry*, p. 128, in the following manner: "Inasmuch as we have words to describe medicine as a healing art, but have none to describe it as a method of social control or political rule, we must first give it a name. I propose that we call it *pharmacracy*, from the Greek roots *pharmakon*, for "medicine" or "drug" and *kratein*, for "to rule" or "to control. . . . As theocracy is rule by God or priests, and democracy is rule by the people or the majority, so pharmacracy is rule by medicine or physicians."

52. Alexander Mitscherlich and Fred Mielke, *Doctors of Infamy: The Story of the Nazi Medical Crimes* (New York: Henry Schuman, 1949), p. 152.

53. Brandt conducted freezing and warming experiments, as well as mass sterilization experiments with no anaesthesia.

54. Quoted in Mitscherlich and Mielke, *Doctors of Infamy*, p. 147.

55. Report of a House of Representatives subcommittee on unnecessary surgery, the Boston *Globe*, July 1975, p. 1.

56. *Idem.*

57. Shirer, *Rise and Fall*, p. 979.

58. Guttentag, "Ethical Problems," p. 200.

59. Harry Benjamin, *The Transsexual Phenomenon* (New York: Julian Press, 1966), p. 12.

60. Joseph Wechsberg, ed., *The Murderers among Us: The Simon Wiesenthal Memoirs* (New York: McGraw-Hill, 1967), p. 155.

VI. TOWARD THE DEVELOPMENT OF AN ETHIC OF INTEGRITY, PAGES 154-177

1. Mary Daly, "The Qualitative Leap Beyond Patriarchal Religion," *Quest: A Feminist Quarterly*, I (Spring 1975): 30. Daly has updated her androgyny imagery as "conveying something like John Travolta and Farrah Fawcett-Majors Scotch-taped together. . ."

2. *The Gospel of Thomas*, Logion 114, pl. 99, vs. 18-26.

3. Virginia Woolf, *A Room of One's Own* (New York: Harcourt, Brace and World, 1957), p. 102.

4. Betty Roszak, "The Human Continuum," in Betty Roszak and Theodore Roszak, *Masculine/Feminine* (New York: Harper and Row, 1969), p. 304.

5. Carolyn Heilbrun, *Toward a Recognition of Androgyny* (New York: Alfred Knopf, 1973), p. xv.

6. James Nolan, "The Third Sex," *Ramparts*, December 1973, p. 24.

7. *Idem.*

8. *Ibid.*, p. 25.

9. Refer to notes 15 and 32 for Chapter V.

10. See Ivan Illich, *Medical Nemesis* (New York: Random House, 1976). See especially Chapter 3, "The Killing of Pain," pp. 133–54.

11. *Ibid.*, p. 275.

12. Mary Daly, *Gyn/Ecology: The Metaethics of Radical Feminism* (Boston: Beacon Press, 1978), pp. 337–43.

13. *Ibid.*, p. 340.

14. Paul Tillich, *Systematic Theology*, vol. I, *Reason and Revelation, Being and God* (Chicago: University of Chicago Press, 1951), p. 267.

15. Herbert Richardson, "Three Myths of Transcendence," in Herbert W. Richardson and Donald R. Cutler, eds., *Transcendence* (Boston: Beacon Press, 1969), pp. 98–113.

16. Jon K. Meyer and John E. Hoopes, "The Gender Dysphoria Syndromes: A Position Statement on So-Called Transsexualism," *Plastic and Reconstructive Surgery*, 54 (October 1974), p. 450.

17. Richardson, "Three Myths," p. 112.

18. Because the ontological tradition generated such a static notion of being, modern ethicists have talked about its impossibility for providing a basis for ethics. They have often pointed to the need for a postmetaphysical way. Yet the split between being and becoming is not a necessary one, as Mary Daly has pointed out, and has always seemed rather artificial and imposed as compared to the experience of being and its philosophical intuition in individual lives. Thus Daly speaks about being as *be-ing.* Be-ing is the initial power of everything, not as static structure, but as the direction of a process.

How then does this notion of be-ing serve as an ethical criterion. In making be-ing an ethical norm, one must test human actions against a texture of be-ing, a texture that is not static but moving. To do this, the texture of be-ing must be more explicitly described as a moral criterion. Tillich attempted to do just this when he spelled out love, power, and justice in ontological terms. Love, power, and justice, however, obviously do not account for the whole texture of be-ing. One could also talk about faith, courage, hope, among other qualities. I have chosen to focus on *integrity* because this is essentially what is at stake in the transsexual situation. It is also dislocated or completely eclipsed by integration—an integration whose source is not in be-ing but rather in a narrow and immediate sense of well-being or static being.

The final question thus becomes how does one verify ontological ethical judgments—specifically how does one measure integrity in the transsexual situation? At this point, I would join ontology with pragmatism in asserting that the only way of testing whether or not a particular procedure, value, etc., is good, is to test its efficacy in the life process. This is a verification standard somewhat similar to William James's pragmatic yardstick. Thus one would have to examine transsexual procedures in light of how such ventures contribute to human be-ing—that is, to the self-actualization of individuals and to the world-building processes of society. Therefore, the question of verification of ontological judgments, the question of method, cannot be answered before the method is applied successfully or unsuccessfully—that is, before its efficacy in human lives and community is tested.

19. Mary Daly, *Beyond God the Father* (Boston: Beacon Press, 1973), pp. 189–90.

20. Jacques Maritain, *Sept leçons sur l'être et les premiers principes de la raison spéculative* (Paris: Pierre Tequi, 1934), p. 54.

21. *Ibid.*, p. 30.

22. Tillich, *Systematics*, I, p. 186.

23. Herbert Marcuse, "Repressive Tolerance," in Robert Paul Wolff, Barrington Moore, Jr., and Herbert Marcuse, *A Critique of Pure Tolerance* (Boston: Beacon Press, 1965), pp. 82–83.

24. *Ibid.*, p. 83.

APPENDIX: SUGGESTIONS FOR CHANGE, PAGES 178–185

1. See, for example, the Hart-Devlin debate on law and morality, which is contained in: Patrick Devlin, *The Enforcement of Morals* (London: Oxford University Press, 1965); H. L. A. Hart, *Law, Liberty, and Morality* (Stanford: Stanford University Press, 1963).

2. Ivan Illich, *Medical Nemesis* (New York: Random House, 1976), pp. 33–34.

3. See, for example, the articles on consciousness-raising in Anne Koedt, Ellen Levine, and Anita Rapone, eds., *Radical Feminism* (New York: Quadrangle/New York Times, 1973), pp. 280–85.

4. Charles Ihlenfeld was very active in doing much initial work on transsexualism with Harry Benjamin. Together they co-authored several key articles on the subject. Thus Ihlenfeld's statement— quoted in "A Doctor Tells Why He'll No Longer Treat Transsexuals," *The National Observer*, October 16, 1976, p. 14—represents a significant defection from the transsexual empire.

INDEX

Abraham, F. Z., 21, 52
Adam, 194
  the androgynous tradition and, 156-57
  mythic dimensions of trans-sexualism, 106
Adkins, Elizabeth, 54-56
Adrenogenital syndrome, 56
  Money's study of, 52, 56, 160
Against Our Will: Men, Women and Rape (Brownmiller), 90
Alienation, 81-82, 121
Anatomical or morphological sex, 7, 10
Androgen, 160
  adrenogenital syndrome and, 56
  in animal experiments, 53-55
  ill-effects of, 36
  I.Q. and, 51, 51n
  "overriding effects" of, 40, 50-53, 57, 59
  as a prenatal factor, 48-49, 58
  as treatment, 35-36
Androgeny, 160
Androgyne, Divine, 156
Androgyny, 100, 154-68
Animal experimentation, 48-49, 53-57
Apollo, 108-9
Aquinas, Thomas, 57
Aristotle, 16, 57, 96-97
Athena, 106

Bagby, Eleanor, 15
Barker, Ernest, 96
Barker-Benfield, G. J., xxiii, xv
Becker, Ernest, 90, 121, 127-28, 144

Behavior control and modification
  control-through-pleasure, 137-139
  electronic brain stimulation (ESB), 137-139
  historical (surgical) precedents for, 131
  as limiting transcendence, 132
  public funding for, 136
  reinforcement of sex-role stereotypes and, 132-137
  as a tool of American law enforcement, 136
  voluntarism and, 134-35
Being, 171, 173, 211-12
Be-ing, 17-18, 125, 145, 211-12
  integrity and the intuition of be-ing, 171-75
  integrity as the original state of be-ing, 163
Be-ing, 173-74
  political power and, 174
  as short-circuited by trans-sexualism, 174
Benjamin, Harry, 4-5, 19-22, 24, 32, 92, 152, 191, 205-6, 209
Berdyaev, Nikolai, 158
Berger, Peter, 14, 64, 81-82, 143, 145
"Blaming the mother," 42, 72-73, 75, 85, 197
  Richard Green on, 74-75
  John Money on, 73
  as psychologists' ploy, 69
  Robert Stoller on, 71
Blue Cross/Blue Shield, 24
Boehme, Jacob, 156-57
Boyle, T. C., 111

213

transsexualism as an ethical issue, 178
Eunuchs, 203
as forerunners of transsexually constructed lesbian-feminists, 105-6
as keepers of women, 105-6
Eve, 106, 157, 194
"Eve base view," 59
Exhibitionism, 83-84, 88n
"Experience deprivation," 76

Fall, the, 156, 158, 164
into masculinity and femininity, 164
Family, 43, 60-70, 77
childhood transsexualism and, 95-98
Father, 95
role in development of transsexualism, 69, 71-75, 96, 197
"Fear of discovery," 37, 138
Feinbloom, Deborah Heller, 202
Female castration, xxiii-xxv
Female-to-constructed-male transsexualism
as assimilation of potentially deviant women, xxiii, xv
hormonal and surgical treatment, 35-38
incidence of, xxi-xxii
Female-to-constructed-male transsexuals, 203
difficulty in obtaining data on, 25, 189
experience of role strain, 81-82
identification with men, xxv, 84-85
as tokens, xxi, xxiv, 27-28, 140
Feminism, 80, 85, 114-15, 177, 184
alteration of core gender identity and, 64
consciousness-raising and, 181
transsexuals' claims to be feminist, 89, 91, 99-100n
transsexuals' opinion of, 82
Femininity/feminine
use of these terms, 3

Fetish
definitions of, 30
Fetishization (*see also* Objectification)
as process of control, 31
in surgery, 132
in therapy, 127-29
as typified in transsexualism, 29-31
First Cause
legislation, 179-80
of transsexualism, 16, 70, 86, 185
Freud, Sigmund, 54, 63, 71

Gadpaille, Warren, 58
Gender, 8, 9
Gender dysphoria, 9, 11-12
Gender identity, 3, 46-50, 52-53, 60-68 (*see also* Core gender identity)
animal experiments and, 48-49, 53-57
gender role and, 9
"locking tight" of, 46, 62-65, 200
native language and, 46, 60-62
Gender identity clinics, 142, 199-200, 202-3
behavior control and modification and, 132-39
establishment of, 23
as future centers of sex-role control, 136-37, 167
as perpetuators of sex-role stereotyping, 13, 77, 91-98, 180
tokenism and, 27
Gender role, 9
Genital or gonadal sex, 7, 10
Gennys, 117
Gilder, George, 198
Gnosticism, 156-60
God, 106, 156
Green, Richard, 73-74, 146
Grossman, Paula (Paul), 78, 165
Guttentag, Otto, 147, 151
Guze, Henry, 76, 87, 206
Gynandry, 160
Gyn/Ecology: The Metaethics of Radical Feminism (Daly), 107

cross-dressing, 38, 41–42
disorderly conduct statutes, 38, 42
female impersonation, 38, 42
liability in tort, 40
mayhem statutes, 40
prostitution, 79n
Legal sex, 7, 10–11
Lesbian-feminism
as boundary-crossing, 108
as not man-made, 105–6
self-definition and, 101, 113–19
Lobotomy, 131 (*See also* Psychosurgery)
Luckmann, Thomas, 64
Lukianovicz, N., 75
Lysistrata, (Aristophanes), 158

"Male child" pill, 140–41
"Male mothering," 29, 74, 75n, 107, 157
Mammoplasty, 33, 143
Man & Woman, Boy & Girl (Money and Ehrhardt), 9, 46, 53, 59, 160
Man Into Woman: An Authentic Record of a Change of Sex (Hoyer), 21
Marcuse, Herbert, 176–77
Maritain, Jacques, 171, 174
Mark, Vernon, 137, 207
Martino, Mario (Marie), xxii
Mary, 106
Masculinity/masculine
use of these terms, 3
Masochism. *See* Sado-masochism
Mastectomy, 143
as transsexual surgery, 36–37
Medical experimentation, 139–53, 209, 210
in Nazi concentration camps, 148–52
Medical model, 1–2
as de-ethicizing, 125–27
definition of, 120
as fetishizing, 127–29
"health" values and, 121–24
as theoretical and ethical construct, 119–25
Menstruation, 35–36
Meyer, Jon, 12, 170

Millett, Kate, 130
Misogyny, 158, 167–68
Money, John, 1–2, 6, 9, 11, 15, 22–25, 28, 43–53, 56–68, 73–74, 81, 83, 126, 160, 198, 200
Moniz, Egas, 131
Morality, 121, 123, 131
the law and, 179–80
reclassified as a technical problem, 2, 125
Morgan, Robin, xxv, 85
Morris, Jan (James), 78, 83, 86–90, 126, 143, 166, 184
Mother, 95
role in development of transsexualism, 71–76, 96–97
Murderers Among Us, The: The Simon Wiesenthal Memoirs (Wechsberg), 152
Mystification, 125

Native language
gender identity and, 46, 60–62
Nature-nurture debate, 1, 44–49
Nazi medical experimentation, 148–52
New York State Code of Criminal Procedure, 38, 41
Nolan, James, 162
Nuremberg trials, 148, 150
Nurses
as models of femininity for transsexuals, 94

Oakley, Ann, 49, 53–54
Objectification, 79, 93 (*see also* Fetishization)
as typified in transsexualism, 29–30
Oedipus (Sophocles), 158
Olivia Records, 102–3, 201
Oophorectomy (ovariotomy)
as surgical procedure in female-to-constructed-male transsexuals, 36
as taming potentially deviant women, xxiii–xxiv, 36n
Operant conditioning, 133
Ovariotomy. *See* Oophorectomy
Ovesey, Lionel, 76